Artificial Intelligence: Unleashing the Future

Authored by

Madhu Bala

Computer Science and Engineering Department, Lovely Professional University, Punjab, India

&

Ritika Sharma

Computer Science and Engineering Department, Maharaja Agrasen University, Himachal Pradesh, India

Artificial Intelligence: Unleashing the Future

Authors: Madhu Bala & Ritika Sharma

ISBN (Online): 979-8-89881-051-1

ISBN (Print): 979-8-89881-052-8

ISBN (Paperback): 979-8-89881-053-5

Published by Bentham Science Publishers Pte. Ltd. Singapore, in collaboration with Eureka Conferences, USA. All Rights Reserved.

First published in 2025.

need for a court order if at any point you breach any terms of this License Agreement. In no event will any delay or failure by Bentham Science Publishers in enforcing your compliance with this License Agreement constitute a waiver of any of its rights.

3. You acknowledge that you have read this License Agreement, and agree to be bound by its terms and conditions. To the extent that any other terms and conditions presented on any website of Bentham Science Publishers conflict with, or are inconsistent with, the terms and conditions set out in this License Agreement, you acknowledge that the terms and conditions set out in this License Agreement shall prevail.

Bentham Science Publishers Pte. Ltd.
No. 9 Raffles Place
Office No. 26-01
Singapore 048619
Singapore
Email: subscriptions@benthamscience.net

BENTHAM
SCIENCE

CONTENTS

FOREWORD i

PREFACE ii

ACKNOWLEDGEMENTS iii

CHAPTER 1 THE RISE OF ARTIFICIAL INTELLIGENCE 1

  1. INTRODUCTION 1

    1.1. Historical Background 1

      1.1.1. Groundwork of AI (1943-50) 2

      1.1.2. Maturation and Birth of AI (1950-56) 3

      1.1.3. Golden Age of AI (1957-79) 3

      1.1.4. AI Winter (1979-1980) 3

      1.1.5. The Emergence Phase (1980-1993) 3

      1.1.6. Intelligent Agents Phase (1993-till Present) 3

    1.2. Key AI Technologies 4

      1.2.1. Overview of Machine Learning (ML) 5

      1.2.2. Computer Vision 8

      1.2.3. Natural Language Processing 8

      1.2.4. Robotics 9

    1.3. Supervised Machine Learning Models 10

      1.3.1. K- Nearest Neighbour(KNN) 10

      1.3.2. Naive Bayes Algorithm 11

      1.3.3. Decision Tree 13

      1.3.4. Random Forest (RF) Algorithm 14

      1.3.5. Support Vector Machine 15

    1.4. Regression 16

      1.4.1. Simple Linear Regression 16

      1.4.2. Multiple Regression 17

    1.5. Unsupervised Learning 18

      1.5.1. Clustering 19

      1.5.2. Association Rules 21

    1.6. AI's Impact on Different Sectors: Case Studies and Examples ... 22

      1.6.1. Healthcare 22

      1.6.2. Finance 23

      1.6.3. Manufacturing and Supply Chain 23

      1.6.4. Retail and Marketing 24

      1.6.5. Education 24

      1.6.6. Agriculture 25

  CONCLUSION 25

  REFERENCES 26

CHAPTER 2 INVESTIGATING THE INFLUENCE OF ARTIFICIAL INTELLIGENCE WITH DEEP LEARNING 30

  1. INTRODUCTION 30

    1.1. Artificial Intelligence and Deep Learning 32

    1.2. Delving into the realm of Artificial Intelligence and Deep Learning ... 32

    1.3. Deep Learning Vs Conventional Machine Learning 34

    1.4. Significance of Deep Learning 36

  2. FOUNDATION OF DEEP LEARNING 37

    2.1. Artificial Neural Networks (ANN) 38

2.2. Neurons 40

2.3. Role of Neurons in ANN 41

2.4. Activation Functions 42

2.5. Loss Functions 43

3. DEEP LEARNING ARCHITECTURES 43

3.1. Convolutional Neural Networks (CNNs) 44

3.1.1. CNNs Architecture 44

3.1.2. Components of CNNs 45

3.1.3. Types of CNNs 46

3.1.4. Use Cases of CNNs 48

3.2. Recurrent Neural Networks (RNNs) 49

3.2.1. RNNs Architecture 49

3.2.2. Types of RNNs 49

3.2.3. Use Cases of RNNs 50

3.3. Generative Adversarial Networks (GANs) 50

3.4. Autoencoders 51

3.5. Reinforcement Learning Networks 52

2.3.6 Transformers 52

4. DEEP LEARNING FRAMEWORKS FOR MODEL DEVELOPMENT 53

5. APPLICATIONS OF AI AND DEEP LEARNING MODELS 54

6. FUTURE TRENDS AND CHALLENGES OF AI AND DEEP LEARNING 55

CONCLUSION 56

REFERENCES 56

CHAPTER 3 SMART FIELDS: REVOLUTIONIZING AGRICULTURE WITH ARTIFICIAL INTELLIGENCE 60

1. INTRODUCTION 60

1.2. Soil Health Monitoring 62

1.3. Plant Disease Detection 64

1.3.1. Different Methods of AI Used in the Detection of Plant Diseases. 66

1.4. Sowing seeds 67

1.5. Weather Prediction 69

1.5.1. Monitoring the Weather in Real Time 70

1.5.2. Long-Term and Seasonal Forecasting 70

1.5.3. Using Predictive Analytics to Manage Risk 70

1.6. Smart Irrigation 70

1.7. Robotic Farming 72

7.1.1. Extraordinary Aspects of Robotic Farming 73

1.8. Examples of AI Applications in Agriculture 74

CONCLUSION 75

REFERENCES 76

CHAPTER 4 ENHANCING CYBERSECURITY THROUGH INTELLIGENT DEFENCE 81

1. INTRODUCTION 81

1.2. Cyber-attacks and Malware 83

1.3. AI in Cybersecurity 84

1.3.1. Detection of DoS 85

1.3.2. Phishing attack detection 85

1.3.3. Real-time network monitoring 86

1.4. Machine Learning Algorithms for the Detection of Attacks 87

1.4.1. Random Forest 87

1.4.2. Naive Bayes (NB) 87

1.4.3. Support Vector Machine(SVM) 88
1.5. Adversarial Attacks 88
1.6. Malware Detection and Mitigation 90
    1.6.1. Machine Learning and Artificial Intelligence 91
    1.6.2. Awareness and Education of Users 91
1.7. AI Tools for Cybersecurity 92
Darktrace Detect: 92
Benefits: 92
Limitations: 93
Splunk: 93
Benefits: 93
Limitations: 93
Trellix: 93
Benefits: 93
Limitations: 93
Tenable: 94
Benefits: 94
Limitations: 94
1.8. Emerging Cybersecurity Ethical Dilemmas 94
1.9. Implementation of AI Solutions in Real-World 95
CONCLUSION 96
REFERENCES 96

CHAPTER 5 THE FUTURE OF DIAGNOSIS, TREATMENT, AND CARE WITH AI-POWERED HEALTHCARE 100
  1. INTRODUCTION TO AI IN HEALTHCARE 100
    1.1. Significance of AI in Healthcare 101
  2. APPLICATION OF AI IN THE HEALTHCARE SECTOR 104
  3. AI IN DIAGNOSTICS 105
    3.1. The Importance of Accurate Diagnostics in Healthcare 106
    3.2. AI-Powered Medical Imaging: Revolutionizing Radiology and Pathology 106
    3.3. Predictive Analytics in Diagnostics: Harnessing Big Data for Early Detection 107
    3.4. AI in Genomics and Personalized Diagnostics 108
    3.5. AI-Assisted Diagnostic Decision Support Systems 109
  4. AI IN PERSONALIZED MEDICINE 109
    4.1. The Role of AI in Personalized Medicine 109
    a. AI-Driven Genomic Analysis 109
    b. AI in Cardiovascular Disease Management 110
    c. AI in Psychiatry and Mental Health 110
    d. AI in Pain Management 110
    4.2. AI in Personalized Vaccines and Immunotherapy 110
    a. AI in Cancer Immunotherapy 111
    b. AI in Infectious Disease Vaccination 111
    c. AI for Personalized Preventive Healthcare 111
    d. AI and Predictive Health Risk Assessment 111
  5. AI IN SURGERY AND ROBOTICS 111
    5.1. The Rise of Robotic-Assisted Surgery 112
    a. AI in Robotic-Assisted Surgeries: Improving Precision and Reducing Recovery Times ... 112
    b. Enhanced Surgical Precision 112
    c. Personalized Surgical Approaches 113
    d. Minimally Invasive Techniques and Faster Recovery 113

5.2. Autonomous Surgical Robots: Enhancing Surgeon Capabilities 113
a. The Evolution of Autonomous Surgical Robots 113
b. AI in Autonomous Endoscopy 113
c. Autonomous Robots in Orthopedic Surgery 114
5.3. AI-Driven Real-Time Analytics During Surgical Procedures 114
a. AI-Powered Image Recognition and Analysis 114
b. Intraoperative Decision Support 115
c. AI and Augmented Reality in Surgery 115
6. REMOTE MONITORING AND VIRTUAL HEALTH 115
7. WEARABLE DEVICES FOR CONTINUOUS PATIENT MONITORING 116
a. AI-Driven Continuous Monitoring 116
b. Early Intervention and Emergency Response 116
c. Chronic Disease Management 117
8. TELEMEDICINE PLATFORMS: REMOTE CONSULTATIONS AND PATIENT FOLLOW-UPS 117
a. AI-Powered Remote Consultations 118
b. Remote Diagnostics and AI-Assisted Image Analysis 118
c. AI-Enhanced Patient Follow-Ups 119
9. AI IN MOBILE HEALTH APPS 119
a. AI for Personalized Wellness and Fitness Tracking 119
b. The Role of Data Privacy and Security 120
i. Ensuring Data Security 120
ii. Patient Consent and Transparency 120
iii. Addressing Health Inequities 121
c. The Role of Healthcare Providers in AI Integration 121
i. Training and Education 121
ii. Collaboration Between AI Developers and Clinicians 121
10. OPTIMIZING HOSPITAL WORKFLOWS, PATIENT SCHEDULING, AND RESOURCE MANAGEMENT 122
10.1. AI in Hospital Workflows 122
10.2. AI in Patient Scheduling 122
10.3. AI in Resource Management 123
10.4. Reducing Administrative Burdens through AI-Powered Tools 123
10.4.1. AI-Powered EHR Management 124
10.4.2. Predictive Analytics for Patient Care Pathways 124
11. ETHICAL, REGULATORY, AND DATA PRIVACY CONSIDERATIONS 125
11.1. Informed Consent 125
11.2. Autonomy and Decision-Making 125
11.3. Accountability and Liability 126
11.4. Privacy Concerns with Patient Data 126
11.4.1. Ethical Consideration in Patient Data Privacy 126
11.4.2 Regulatory Challenges with AI in Healthcare 127
12. CHALLENGES AND OPPORTUNITIES IN AI INTEGRATION 128
CONCLUSION 129
REFERENCES 129

CHAPTER 6 ARTIFICIAL INTELLIGENCE IN EDUCATION: THE FUTURE OF LEARNING 131
1. INTRODUCTION 131
1.1. Importance of AI in Technology 132
1.2. Impact of AI 133

6.2 APPLICATIONS OF AI IN EDUCATION 133

3. TYPES OF TECHNOLOGIES IN EDUCATION 135

    3.1. Natural Language Processing 135

    3.2. Machine learning (ML) 136

    3.3. Robotics 137

    3.4. Predictive Analytics 137

4. PERSONALIZED LEARNING 138

5. BENEFITS OF AI IN EDUCATION 139

    5.1. Benefits to Learners 139

    5.2. Benefits to Educators 141

6. IMPLEMENTATION STRATEGIES 141

6.7 CHALLENGES WITH AI SOLUTIONS IN EDUCATION 142

8. FUTURE TRENDS AND INNOVATIONS 145

CONCLUSION 145

REFERENCES 146

SUBJECT INDEX 149

FOREWORD

The field of Artificial Intelligence (AI) is leading a revolution that is changing how we work, live, and engage with the world. What was formerly the domain of science fiction has permeated every aspect of our daily lives, impacting industries as varied as entertainment, healthcare, education, and transportation. "Artificial Intelligence: Unleashing the Future" is a compelling example of this revolutionary period, providing a forward-thinking perspective on the seemingly endless potential of AI.

This book explores the quickly changing field of artificial intelligence, following its development from theoretical underpinnings to its current function as an innovation accelerator. It tackles important issues about how AI systems learn, make choices, and help address global issues including illness prevention, cyber security, and fair resource distribution. From revolutionizing healthcare and education to powering smart cities and sustainable agriculture, the reach of AI knows no bounds.

Whether you are a student, a professional, or simply a curious mind, this book offers insights that will deepen your understanding of AI and its potential to redefine our world. Let it be your guide as you explore a future where intelligence—both human and artificial—joins forces to shape a better, more inclusive world.

Pradeepta Kumar Sarangi
Department of Computer Science and Engineering
Chitkara University, Himachal Pradesh, India

PREFACE

The human tale is one of the unrelenting inquiries and discoveries. As we approach the dawn of a new age, Artificial Intelligence (AI) presents itself as a creation unlike anything before. This book is an invitation to explore this amazing world, where robots are discovering, adjusting, and changing at a rate never seen before. AI was mostly found in science fiction for many years when it was used to create sentient robots and self-aware machines. The last several years have seen a rapid advancement in AI technology that has permanently changed the environment, even though the reality is still developing. Applications of AI are quickly encroaching on every aspect of our livese, from self-driving automobiles to facial recognition software. But these are only the beginnings; AI has far more potential. We are on the cusp of a revolution that will drastically alter the way we live, work, and engage with the world.

This book titled "Artificial Intelligence: Unleashing the Future" goes beyond being a technical guide. It serves as a bridge, guiding you from the limits of artificial intelligence to the reaches of possibilities. The fundamental ideas of deep learning, artificial neural networks, and machine learning—the three main technologies behind contemporary AI systems—will be covered in detail. Our investigation, however, extends beyond the algorithms. The evolution of AI will be examined, starting from the earliest days of digital technology and ending in the state-of-the-art research facilities that will shape the field's future.

This book is primarily concerned with recent developments in artificial intelligence (AI), how AI can be applied in many fields, and how using AI computations and models might alter these fields. AI presents fresh strategies for handling challenging issues. It is noteworthy to see that new models and theories undergo a major change due to artificial intelligence. In terms of tools and approaches, advances in instrument technology have resulted in considerable change. Consequently, it has had and will continue to have an equally significant influence on the production and manufacturing sectors through the development of industries.

The main goal of this book is to provide an introduction to the field of artificial intelligence, its systems and architectures, and how this may be used to solve real world problems. The book is mainly intended for students, and researchers of various fields who are interested in artificial intelligence. The structure of this book is organized in five different chapters. We sincerely hope that businesses and developers will find its use in the industry intriguing.

Madhu Bala
Computer Science and Engineering Department
Lovely Professional University
Punjab, India

&

Ritika Sharma
Computer Science and Engineering Department
Maharaja Agrasen University
Himachal Pradesh, India

ACKNOWLEDGEMENTS

The journey of writing this book, "Artificial Intelligence: Unleashing the Future", has been a rewarding experience, and it would not have been possible without the support of many individuals and organizations.

First and foremost, we would like to express our deepest gratitude to Maharaja Agrasen University, Himachal Pradesh, India, and Lovely Professional University, Phagwara, Punjab, India, whose unwavering support and resources were instrumental in completing this work. Their commitment to innovation and knowledge sharing has truly been inspiring.

To our family, your love, patience, and encouragement have kept us grounded throughout this journey. Special thanks to our parents for their emotional support and we always knew that you wanted the best for us.

A heartfelt thank you to our dear friends and colleagues, for your understanding and for always being there to provide thoughtful advice, feedback, and companionship during both the challenging and triumphant moments. Finally, we would like to extend my gratitude to all the readers and researchers who continue to push the boundaries of what artificial intelligence can achieve. Your curiosity and passion are what drive innovation forward.

Thank you all for being a part of this journey.

CHAPTER 1

The Rise of Artificial Intelligence

Abstract: The human brain is one of the most important organs that help us think, learn new things, and remember what we have seen. With the advancements in technologies, artificial intelligence (AI) came into the picture which is nothing but the simulation of the human brain. The current chapter will throw light on the evolution, technologies, and transformative changes of AI in various sectors. Beginning with the historical background, it traces the journey of AI from its early stages to the advanced machine learning and deep learning models in the present. This knowledge is important for those who are seeking relevant skills and stay updated in a competitive environment. It is believed that a more well-informed person can engage himself in meaningful discussions, contributing to the democratic shaping of its future. Knowing the history of AI is important to have a clear understanding that where it is now and where it may go in the future.

Keywords: Machine learning, Neurons, Neural networks, Simulation, Transformers.

1. INTRODUCTION

1.1. Historical Background

The human brain consists of 86 billion neurons interconnected by trillions of synapses. This network enables the human brain to perform and process vast amounts of tasks. It is an extremely powerful organ that has finite speed, memory, and ability to work 24x7 without any fatigue. However, these cognitive functions have certain limitations like limited working memory and susceptibility to mental health conditions. Due to this, AI is required to augment human intelligence and address these challenges. It involves the development of various algorithms and software that enable computer systems to perform tasks like problem-solving, experience-based learning, pattern recognition, *etc* that would require human intelligence. In the current scenario, AI has made significant changes in various fields [1, 2]. AI systems are useful tools in a variety of applications, from self-driving cars and virtual assistants [3] to healthcare diagnostics [4] and financial analysis, because they are built to analyse data, adapt to new information, and complete tasks autonomously. The relationship between AI and the human brain is a fascinating subject that bridges the gap between neuroscience, computer science, and cognitive psychology. By exploring how AI mimics the human brain or neural processes, it would be easier to know the potentials of human and artificial intelligence.

Artificial intelligence is a much older technology than anyone would imagine. AI started to evolve in the early 1900s when different scientists began to ask questions like: can an artificial brain be created? The history of AI can be explained in various phases (shown in Fig. **1**) which is a very interesting story to know how AI evolved from its birth to till date.

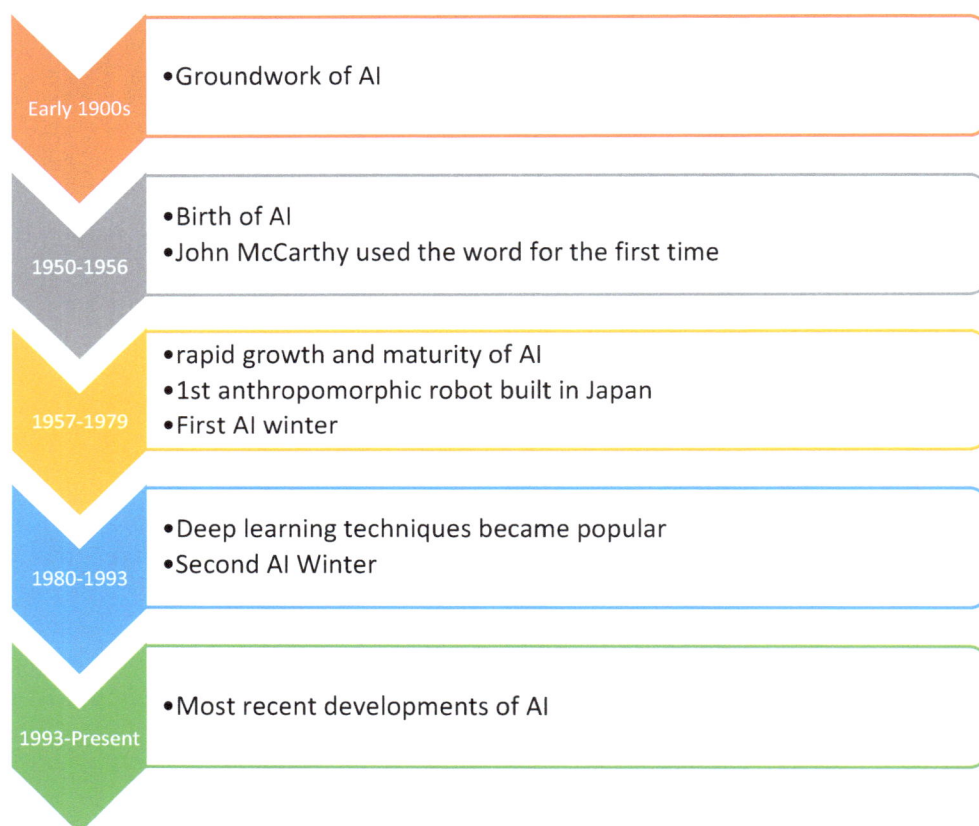

Early 1900s
- Groundwork of AI

1950-1956
- Birth of AI
- John McCarthy used the word for the first time

1957-1979
- rapid growth and maturity of AI
- 1st anthropomorphic robot built in Japan
- First AI winter

1980-1993
- Deep learning techniques became popular
- Second AI Winter

1993-Present
- Most recent developments of AI

Fig. (1). Evolution of artificial intelligence.

1.1.1. Groundwork of AI (1943-50)

In 1950, Alan Turing, an English mathematician, and computer scientist gave the concept of the "Turing test", which formed the basis for AI. John McCarthy, known as the father of AI held a workshop in 1955 at Dartmouth where he introduced the word "Artificial Intelligence" for the very first time, and from then, this word came into popular usage by the people.

1.1.2. Maturation and Birth of AI (1950-56)

AI matured during the years 1957-1979. Arthur Samuel introduced the term machine learning in 1952 during his speech that how machines can play chess better than humans whereas in 1955 Simon and Allen Newell developed the first AI-based program that was designed for the proofs of mathematical theorems. In a conference, John McCarthy introduced AI as an academic coin and also developed LISP as the first programming language for AI research in 1958.

1.1.3. Golden Age of AI (1957-79)

In 1966, a chatbot was developed that was able to converse with humans. The American Association of Artificial Intelligence (AAAI) was also founded in 1979. In the era of 1980s, the concept of deep learning came into the picture. The first neural network named 'Neocognitron' was developed by Kunihiko Fukushima in 1979. This network was designed using multiple pooling and convolutional layers to recognize visual patterns.

1.1.4. AI Winter (1979-1980)

The term AI winter was also introduced during these years. It refers to the tough time period when there was a decrease in funding for research and interest in the publicity of AI was also decreased. These years are also termed the 'first AI Winter'. In 1980, AI wastrained again with the introduction of expert systems and deep learning techniques. LISP machines were getting into use commercially and a significant downturn was observed.

1.1.5. The Emergence Phase (1980-1993)

In 1985, the Bayesian network was introduced by Judea Pearls for causal analysis of statistical methods. Further, in 1989, Yan LeCun demonstrated backpropagation at Bells Lab. It was the first practical demonstration where a convolutional neural network was combined with backpropagation to read the handwritten characters. Due to high costs and not getting efficient results, the government and other investors stopped giving funds to the researchers. The time period between 1987 to 1993 was the second AI winter.

1.1.6. Intelligent Agents Phase (1993-till Present)

A significant forward leap was found in 1993 especially in the development of intelligent computer programs. AI professionals started using AI to perform specific tasks and some of the noteworthy tasks are mentioned below:

- 1990: IBM introduced 'Deep Blue', a computer, as an expert system to play chess under regular time control. In 1997, it won a chess game against a reigning world champion where world chess champion GARY Kasparov was defeated by Deep Blue.
- 2002: AI in the form of Roomba, which was a vacuum cleaner entered our homes.
- 2006: AI gained entry into the business world and companies like Facebook, and Twitter started using AI.
- 2009: A research paper based on the implementation of GPUs for the training of neural networks was published by Rajat Raina *et al*.
- 2012: "Google Now" an Android app was launched by Google to provide information to users as a prediction.
- 2018: With two expert debaters, the IBM "Project Debater" engaged in difficult debates and did very well. Meanwhile, Google introduced a new program called 'duplex', a virtual assistant which was capable of taking appointments on calls.
- 2020: A beta test on GPT-3 was performed. It was an advanced model based on deep learning techniques that could write code, poetry, and any other kind of writing task.
- 2021: Dall-E was created by OpenAI to generate captions for images depending on users' requirements.
- 2022: Key models like OpenAI's GPT-3.5, Google's PaLM, and DeepMind's Gopher came into the picture. GPT 3.5 is a large model with billions of parameters that became prominent in terms of conversational AI.
- 2023: Multimodal capabilities and accessibility both are increased with the introduction of GPT-4 allowing text and image processing. Meta's LLaMA and Google's Gemini are other examples used for content generation, education, research, and industry-oriented solutions as well.

By the end of 2025, GPT-5 is also anticipated whereas Google is planning to launch its advanced Gemini multimodal with enhanced integration, comprehensive handling of documents, and ethical safeguards.

1.2. Key AI Technologies

The AI environment consists of many technologies as shown in Fig. (**2**) that enable the machines to learn and act like human beings. With the passage of time, these technologies are bringing tremendous changes in different fields making human life more easier and comfortable. It is a good fit for applications that involve identifying patterns and relationships in the data given as an input.

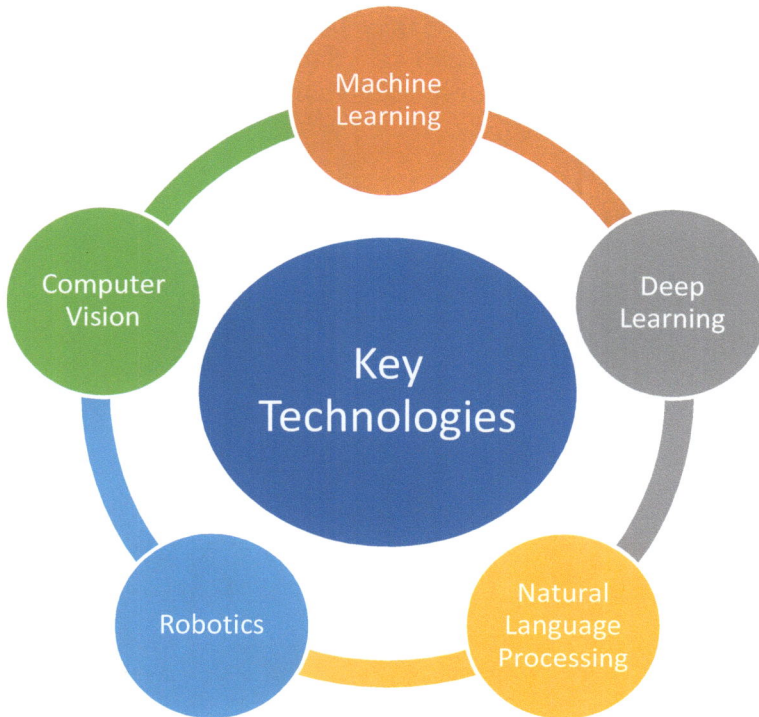

Fig. (2). Some key AI technologies.

For example, it can detect cancer in the human body with more accuracy and at a faster rate just by analysing the input images. In the manufacturing field, automatic robots [5] are established so well that hazardous tasks are performed by these robots thereby reducing the risk to human life. They are helping in increasing the overall productivity of an organization. From speech recognition to decision-making, AI is everywhere now.

All these applications involve machine learning and deep learning methods for implementation. Both these technologies are the subset of artificial intelligence and are quite different from one another. AI is an imitation of human behaviour and machine learning is helping machines to learn and predict the results. On the other hand, deep learning is a subset of machine learning that uses complex architectures to train the models such that accuracy can be enhanced [6].

1.2.1. Overview of Machine Learning (ML)

Machine learning is one of the important parts of artificial intelligence that focuses on the development of algorithms that can learn and give output in the same way as humans do. Data is given as an input to the machine to train it well and to identify patterns from it [7]. These patterns can be used by machines to make predictions. It is further divided into three categories (depicted in Fig. **3**): supervised, unsupervised, and reinforcement learning.

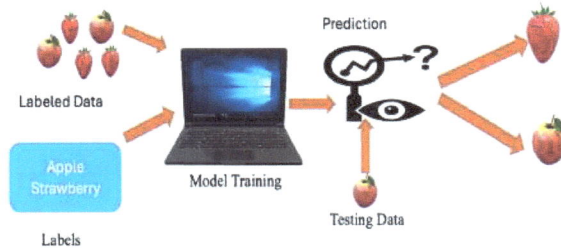

(a)

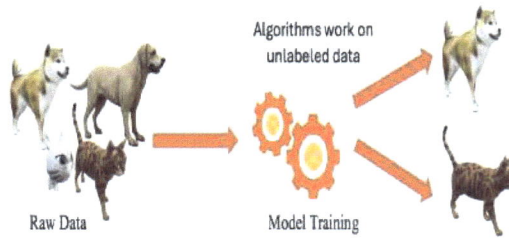

(b)

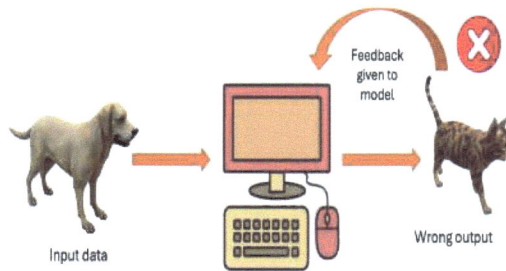

(c)

Fig. (3). Types of machine learning **a**) supervised learning in which the machine is trained with labelled data; **b**) represents unsupervised learning in which raw data is given as input and the machine will extract features itself; **c**) reinforcement learning in which the machine learns from the mistakes.

Supervised machine learning further has two categories (shown in Fig. **5**): classification and regression. Classification is the process in which a machine divides the data into different classes based on the discrete labeled data. For example, the data is classified according to whether the patient is covid positive or covid negative. SVM, KNN, and Naive Bayes are examples of supervised algorithms. It can be binary or it can be multiclass (Fig. **4**).

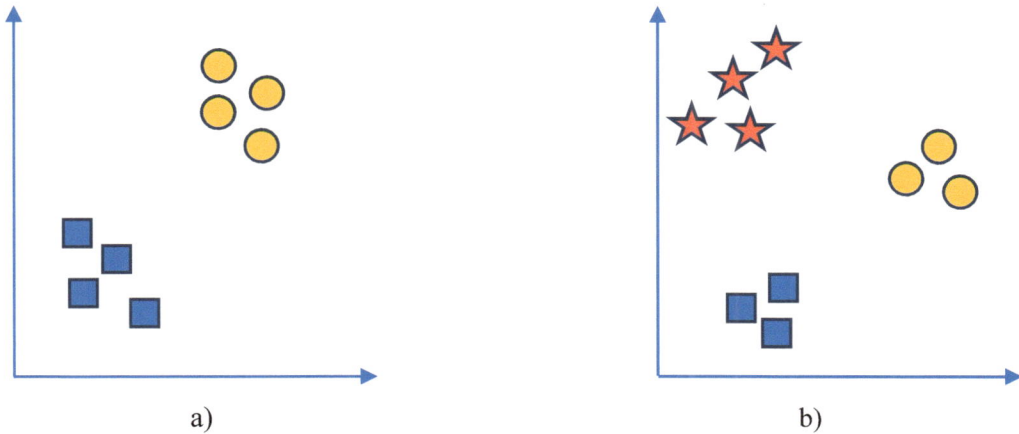

a)   b)

Fig. (4). Difference between **a**) binary classification and **b**) multiclass classification.

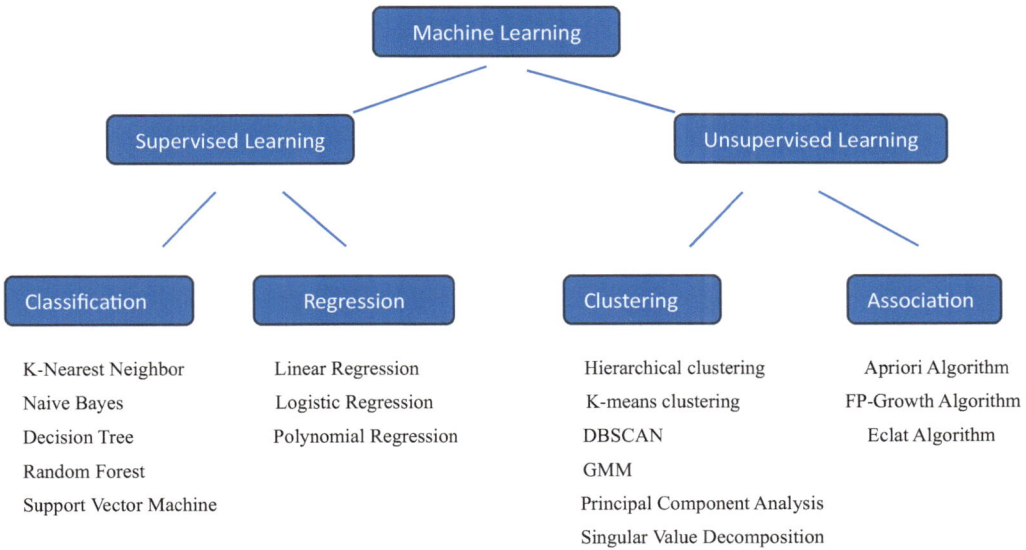

Fig. (5). Classification of machine learning.

On the other side, regression is the process of predicting continuous variables which represent numerical values; for instance, predicting the cost of an air conditioner based on its star ratings, size, wiring, *etc*.

Unsupervised algorithms such as k-means clustering, and DB-Scan work on unlabeled data to identify patterns and relationships among the variables. Consider an example, where runs and wickets taken by a player are given as input data, and based upon this, the model should be able to predict whether the player is a batsman or a bowler. Unsupervised learning has two more categories namely clustering and association. When the data is grouped into different clusters based on the similarity features, it is called clustering whereas the process of finding relationships between variables of the dataset is known as the association rule.

Reinforcement learning is the process where a machine learns from the errors produced by itself. Here, the machine keeps on learning and increasing its performance using feedback to know about the patterns; for example, computer-based games where reinforcement learning teaches the agent how to play games.

1.2.2. Computer Vision

It is a technology with the help of which machines can be trained to identify and recognize visual patterns like humans. Speech recognition, facial expression identification, and analysis of traffic data are all examples of computer vision (CV) technology [8]. It enables the machines to identify objects such as highlighting cars present in an image (shown in Fig. **6**), track movements and know about spatial relationships. Image classification is one of the important tasks of CV where the system recognizes the objects in an image. Preprocessing, feature extraction and then applying machine learning algorithms to the data are basic steps to be performed for image classification. Object detection and segmentation are other significant tasks of computer vision. Techniques like YOLO (You Look Only Once) and R-CNN offer real-time analysis of objects more effectively. In real-world applications, computer vision is becoming popularized. Self-driving cars are able to recognize traffic signals, obstacles, and other factors for safe and better navigation. In the healthcare field, the detection of various diseases and real-time surgeries from remote areas are also possible nowadays.

1.2.3. Natural Language Processing

Human language was the barrier to communicating with the machine but with the help of AI, this hurdle has also been removed. Natural language processing (NLP) [9]is one of the key technologies that enable machines to understand human language and generate responses accordingly. It is also known as computational linguistics. Different chatbots, google translators, and voice recognition systems are all applications of NLP. With the advent of transformer architectures, BERT (bidirectional encoder representations from transformers) tremendous change has been observed in NLP-based applications like language translation, summarization, sentiment analysis, *etc*. Siri and Alexa are virtual assistants that are powered by NLP models [10]. One can talk in different languages with these virtual voice assistants. In today's era, generative AI and image generation models are the results of NLP research.

Fig. (6). Object detection (cars) in a given image using computer vision.

1.2.4. Robotics

Robotics is a field that is a combination of various branches of science and engineering. Replicas of humans are robots that can perform any type of task ranging from simple to complex. It can work in factories to perform cumbersome tasks as well as in homes to carry out household activities such as cleaning. The foundation of robotics is the mechanical engineering branch that deals with the physical construction of various components to configure a robust robot. Electronics and electrical engineering deals with sensors and actuators that help the robots to deal and interact with the environment. Movement of various parts and the robot itself is handled by control systems. Computer Science and engineering deal with software installation and training robots to recognize objects and people. In the field of production, robotics plays a major role in accomplishing tasks like painting, welding, packaging, assembly, and many more.

1.3. Supervised Machine Learning Models

As already discussed, supervised algorithms [11, 12] work on labeled data that is given as input to the model. Depending upon the labels, the model is capable of categorizing the data into different classes. Some of the popular supervised machine learning algorithms are KNN, SVM, Naive Bayes, random forest, *etc.*

1.3.1. K- Nearest Neighbour(KNN)

KNN is a supervised machine learning algorithm that handles classification and regression problems. It is one of the very basic classification algorithms of machine learning that was developed in 1951 by Thomas Cover. It has applications in the areas of data mining, pattern recognition, classification problems, and many more. It is a non-parametric algorithm that can give predictions based on the similarity of the data points given in the dataset. Let T be the training dataset having n sample points. Let U be the labels and each sample point is represented by m_i and n_i. The algorithm works as follows:

Step 1: Select the value of k. Although there is no specific method to find its value, cross-validation can be used to find its optimal value for making predictions.

Step 2: When a new sample is to be classified, the distances between the new sample and the existing samples are calculated either using the Euclidean distance or Manhattan distance formula.

Assume a new sample *i.e.* X_{test} is represented by (m_1, n_1), and the existing sample point is represented by (m_2, n_2). The following equation depicts the Euclidean formula:

$$Distance = \sqrt{(m_2-m_1)^2+(n_2-n_1)^2} \qquad (1)$$

Several other metrics (depicted in Table **1**) can be used to calculate the distance between the new and existing sample points. The selection of metrics depends on the nature of the dataset used to train the model.

Step 3: The value of k will decide how many nearest sample points (whose distance will be lowest) are to be considered for making the predictions. For example, if k=1 then only one existing sample point having the least distance value will be considered for classification.

Step 4: The class with the majority voting will be identified as the target class of the new sample point.

Table 1. Metrics to calculate the distance between sample points of a given dataset.

Metrics used to Calculate Distance	Purpose
Taxicab Geometry	It is used when values are different *i.e.* for heterogeneous data types.
Euclidean Distance	Commonly used when data is quantitative.
Hamming Distance	Used for categorical variables.
Minkowski Distance	For real-valued vectors.

In Fig. (**7**), it is shown that if the value of k is set to 1, then X_{test} will be placed in the red class whereas, if the value of k=3 is taken, the majority voting goes to the blue class and hence X_{test} will be considered in blue class.

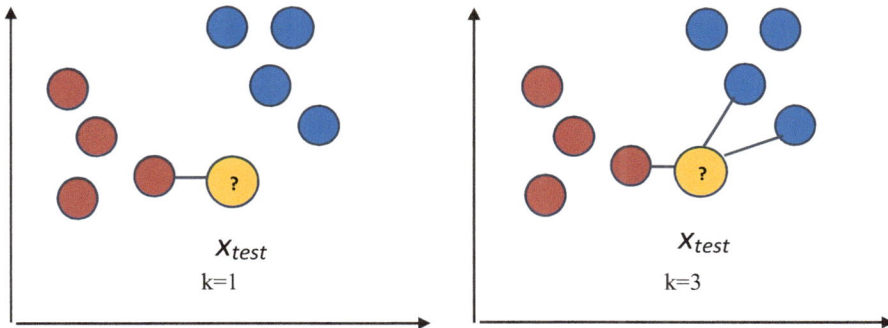

Fig. (7). How the value of K effects the classification.

Limitations of KNN

- The value of K should be chosen carefully because the lower value of K can overfit the data hence results in wrong predictions.
- This model is sensitive to noise and noisy samples degrade the performance.
- It assumes that all features of the dataset are equally important but in reality, some of the features are more important than others.

1.3.2. Naive Bayes Algorithm

The name of this algorithm consists of two words Naive and Bayes where Bayes means that the algorithm is based on Bayes theorem and the term naive means that whatever features are considered for making predictions, are independent of each other. Consider an example of 2 bags B1 and B2 consisting of red and blue coloured balls as shown in Fig. (**8**).

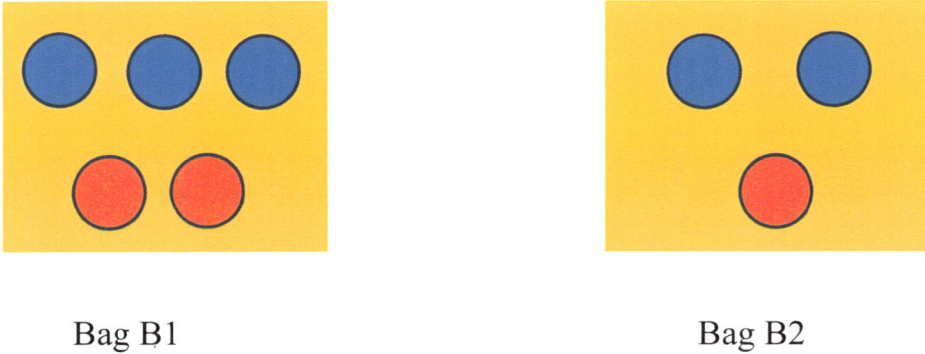

Bag B1   Bag B2

Fig. (8). The probability of finding the red-coloured ball from B1 is 2/3 and from B2 it is 1/2.

If it is asked that we have the red coloured ball, find the probability from which bag it is picked? Here comes the concept of Bayes theorem, where the result or condition is known, and its probability is to be found using equation (2).

$$P\left(\frac{P}{Q}\right) = \frac{P\left(\frac{Q}{P}\right)*P(P)}{P(Q)} \qquad (2)$$

Where P(Q) represents the ball is red and P(P) is either the ball is picked from bag B1 or B2. As per the given example, the probability value for each of the bags will be calculated and the highest probability value will be the result. In equation (2),

$$Q = (q_1, q_2, q_3 \ldots \ldots q_n)$$

$$P\left(\frac{P}{Q}\right), posterior\ probability$$

$$P\left(\frac{Q}{P}\right), likelihood\ probability$$

$$P(P), prior\ probabilty$$
$$P(Q), marginal\ probability$$

This method is applicable for discrete values, for continuous values, Gaussian Naive Bayes is used.

Limitations of NB

• The naive Bayes algorithm suffers from a zero frequency problem. It means, that if there is no categorical variable in the dataset, the model will not be able to

predict as it assigns zero probability in this case.
- It is computationally expensive when a large dataset is given for training.
- Its independence assumption of variables is another drawback that is rarely true in real-world applications.

1.3.3. Decision Tree

The decision tree is a supervised machine learning algorithm in which a tree-like structure is formed based on the training data for making predictions [13]. Though it can be used for both classification and regression problems, mostly it gives fruitful results for classification tasks.

The tree shown in Fig. **9** consists of a root node, decision nodes, and leaf nodes where leaf nodes represent the outcome. Decision nodes may have several branches and are used to make any decision.

While implementing a decision tree, it is very important to know that out of given attributes what will be the root node [14]. Attribute selection measure(ASM) is used to solve this problem. A root node can be found in two ways: either by using information gain or by using the Gini index.

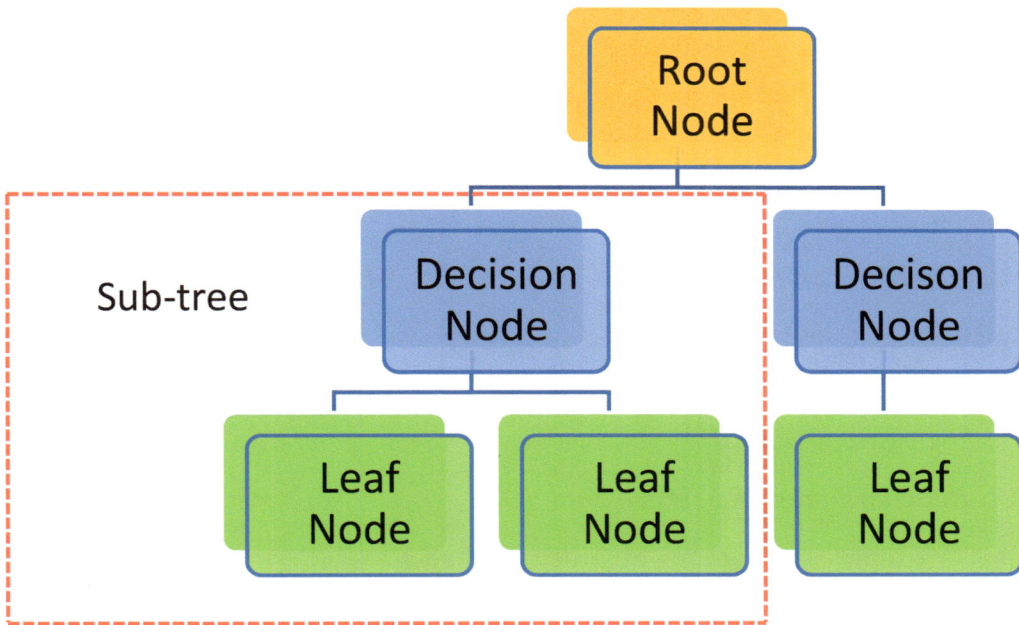

Fig. (9). Structure of decision tree.

- Information gain: It helps us to know which attribute is giving more information about the dataset. Basically, it is a measure to decide the effectiveness of an attribute for splitting the dataset into different categories. Equation 3 is used to calculate the information gain.

$$Information\ gain(IG) = Entropy(S) - [weighted\ average * Entropy\ of\ each\ feature] \quad \textbf{(3)}$$

where, Entropy(S) represents entropy of entire dataset

- Entropy: It is defined as the degree of randomness of the data. If the entropy is higher, the more impure will be the data. Entropy can be calculated using the following equation:

$$Entropy(S) = -\sum_{i=1}^{n} y_i log_2\ y_i \quad \textbf{(4)}$$

Gini index: It is another method in the decision tree that helps in deciding the best feature/attribute to split the data. The formula for finding the decision tree is:

$$Gini = 1 - \sum_{i=1}^{n} (y_i)^2 \quad \textbf{(5)}$$

y_i is the probability of an element being classified.

Implementation of decision trees requires certain algorithms such as CART, ID3, and C4.5. CART algorithms use the Gini index whereas information gain is used in ID3 and C4.5 algorithms. Once a root node is found, recursive partitioning/splitting is carried out until leaf nodes consisting of classifiers are obtained.

Limitation of decision tree

- Small changes in the values of the dataset can cause huge and major changes in the structure of the tree and give variations in the result.
- They are more prone to overfitting if their growth is not restricted.
- More sensitive to noise.

1.3.4. Random Forest (RF) Algorithm

It is also a supervised learning algorithm, which works in two phases [15]. In the first phase, a random forest is created with the number of decision trees, and in the second phase, prediction from each tree is taken, and based upon majority values, the final output is predicted. The steps of algorithms are:

Step 1: From the dataset, random sample points are selected.

Step 2: Decision trees are built corresponding to selected sample points.

Step 3: During training, the prediction result is produced by each decision tree.

Step 4: When a new sample point is to be checked, the prediction of each tree is found. The majority values will be considered for classification.

Limitations of RF

- When more trees are used for making predictions, random forests become slower.
- Interpretation of RF becomes more difficult when there are many decision trees.
- A small change in the sample data can significantly change the output of the model.
- Sensitive to hyperparameters.

1.3.5. Support Vector Machine

The main objective of SVM is to divide the data sample points into different categories by creating a decision boundary line known as a hyperplane [16, 17]. If any new sample point comes into the dataset, it can be easily placed in a particular class. The extreme points (vectors) are chosen to create the hyperplane. Consider Fig. (**10**) to choose the best hyperplane.

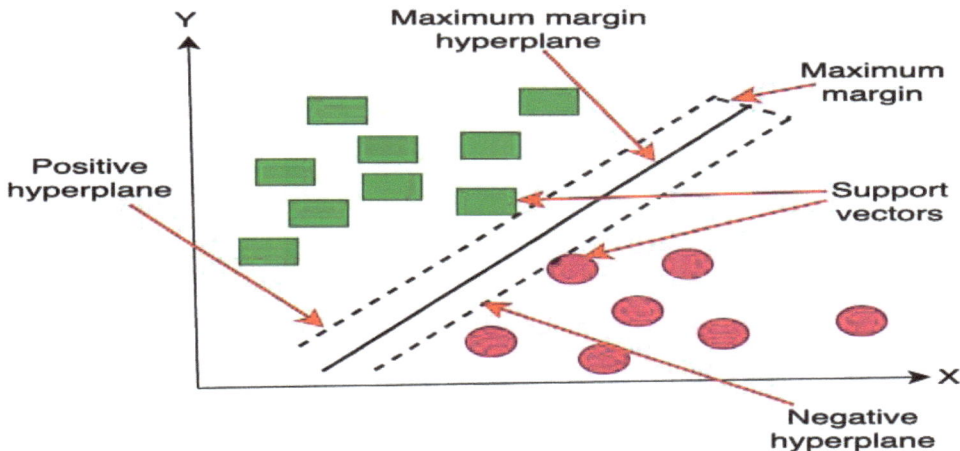

Fig. (10). Two different categories classified by boundary line.

SVM finds the nearest or closest sample points from both classes. The margin is the distance between these sample points and the hyperplane. The hyperplane with the maximum margin will be the optimal hyperplane.

Limitations of SVM

- For large datasets, training time to train the model also increases.
- Since a large number of kernels are available, it is difficult to choose the right one.
- Computationally expensive.
- Overfitting can be seen when classes overlap.

1.4. Regression

Regression can be defined as a statistical method that establishes a relationship between two types of variables that are dependent and independent variables. Dependent variables depend on other variables and change in response to other variables. An independent variable does not show any change in response to another variable. For example, consider a scenario where the marks of the student are based on the number of hours he/she spends studying. Marks are dependent and the number of hours are independent variable in this case.

Predictions are made through various regression models. There are many different forms of regression but the simplest method is linear regression. The primary objective of regression is to find the best hyperplane, which goes through the sample points and establishes a connection between them. There are several terminologies related to regression analysis:

- **Outliers:** These are the sample points which are having either very low or very high values as compared to the other sample points present in the data set.
- **Overfitting and underfitting:** Overfitting occurs when an algorithm is giving good results for training but is performing poorly on testing whereas underfitting indicates that the performance of the model on both the training and testing part is poor.

1.4.1. Simple Linear Regression

Simple linear regression is used to find the relationship between two variables, out of which, one is dependent and another is independent.

Fig. (**11**) shows the linear relationship between dependent and independent variables. For instance, if study hours are more, he will get more marks. This will result in a positive slope. Consider another example, with the passage of time, the price of the vehicle will decrease and this will result in a negative slope.

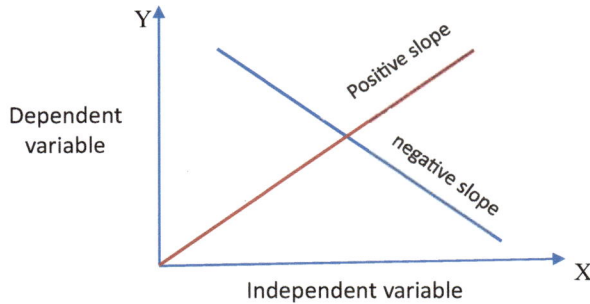

Fig. (11). Showing the relationship between dependent and independent variables.

1.4.2. Multiple Regression

Multiple regression is used when more than one independent variables are used to predict a continuous dependent variable. With two independent variables, x_1 and x_2, it can be stated as:

$$y=f(x_1,x_2) \tag{6}$$

$$y= a_0+a_1x_1+a_2x_2 \tag{7}$$

Where, a_0, a_1 and a_2 are coefficients of the multiple linear regression model.

When a relationship between a dependent variable and an independent variable follows some non-linear pattern, then it is called non-linear regression. It basically provides flexibility in modeling a wide range of functional forms.

For example, if we have data sample points, distributed in a non-linear way as presented in Fig. (**12a**), then linear regression will not work properly and will generate large errors. So, to overcome this problem, a curve should be drawn as depicted in Fig. (**12b**).

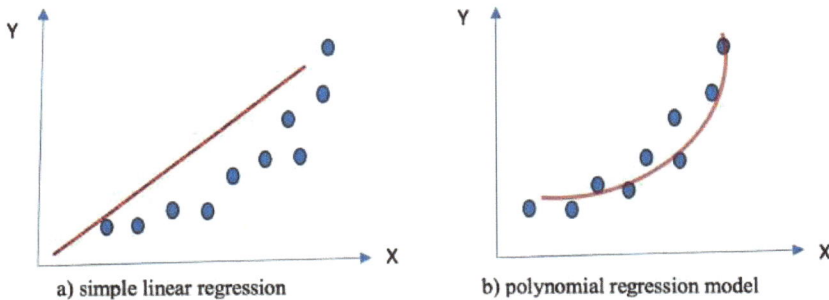

a) simple linear regression　　　　　b) polynomial regression model

Fig. (12). Simple *vs* polynomial regression model.

To decrease the errors, two methods can be used:

• Transformation, where non-linear data is converted into linear data. Consider the polynomial equation:

$$p=ae^{bx} \tag{8}$$

Apply log functions on both sides of the above equation.

$$log(p)=log(e^{bx}) \tag{9}$$

$$log(p)=log(a)+bx*log(e) \tag{10}$$

$$log(p)=log(a)+bx \tag{11}$$

Now, linear regression can be applied to equation (11)

• Polynomial regression- In this, the relationship between dependent and independent variables can be stated as nth degree polynomial in x.

Consider a polynomial of degree 2

$$p=a_0+a_1x+a_2x^2 \tag{12}$$

The coefficients a_0, a_1 and a_2 can be calculated by using the following formula:

$$a=X^{-1} B$$

$$X=\begin{bmatrix} n & \sum x_i & \sum x_i^2 \\ \sum x_i & \sum x_i^2 & \sum x_i^3 \\ \sum x_i^2 & \sum x_i^3 & \sum x_i^4 \end{bmatrix} \qquad B=\begin{bmatrix} \sum p_i \\ \sum(x_i,p_i) \\ \sum(x_i^2,p_i) \end{bmatrix}$$

p_i is the dependent variable, which can be found using above-mentioned matrices.

1.5. Unsupervised Learning

A machine learning technique that deals with labeled data and can give predictions without human intervention is called unsupervised learning [18]. The unsupervised models predict or discover the patterns from the given data on their own without receiving explicit instructions from the user. Any noisy or unstructured dataset can be given to the unsupervised models. Various unsupervised methods are explained below:

1.5.1. Clustering

Based on similar features or patterns, clustering helps in dividing the entire dataset into different groups, and where each group is known as a cluster. For instance, a fictitious patient study intended to assess a novel treatment regimen. Patients provide information about the frequency and intensity of their symptoms each week during the research. Researchers can create groupings of patients who respond to treatment similarly by using clustering analysis. A potential partition of the simulated data into three clusters is shown in Fig. (**13**).

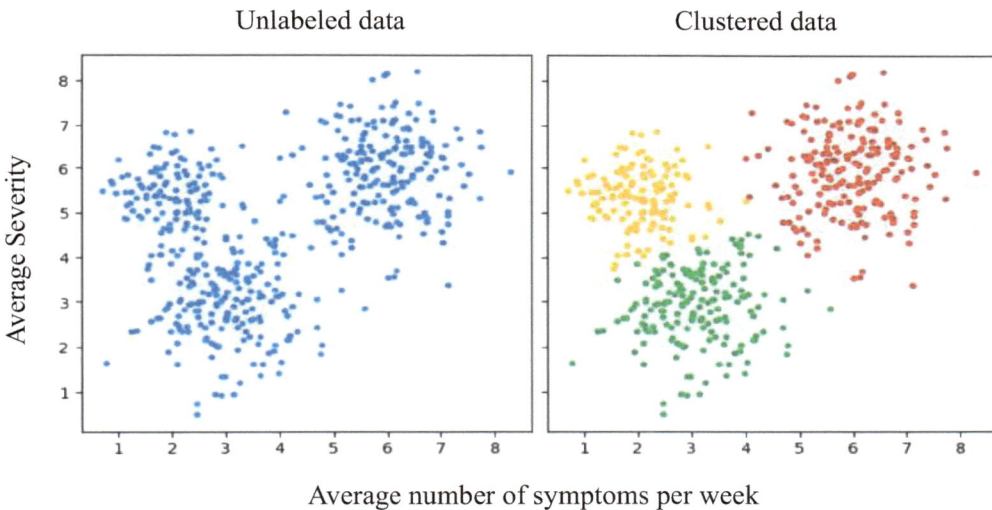

Fig. (13). Showing how clustering can be applied on unlabeled data [reference taken from developers google.com].

1.5.1.1. K-means clustering

This kind of clustering is mainly used in image compression and data segmentation tasks. It partitions the entire dataset into different groups called clusters, where each data point belongs to the cluster with the lowest mean value. The algorithm works in the following steps:

Step1: Initialize the value of K, where K is the number of clusters.

Step 2: Analyze each sample point and assign it to the nearest centroid.

Step 3: Centroid of each cluster is recomputed.

Step 4: Repeat Step 2 and 3 until the change is minimal.

Each centroid represents the centre of the cluster it is assigned to. For a cluster with n sample data points and y features, the centroid can be found as:

$$Centroid\ for\ feature\ k = \frac{1}{n}\sum_{i=1}^{n} x_{ik} \tag{13}$$

Where, xik is the kth feature for i^{th} sample point

1.5.1.2. DBSCAN

It stands for Density-Based Spatial Clustering of Applications with Noise, which performs grouping based on the minimum number of sample points in the region and finding a distance metric. It automatically creates the clusters without specifying the number [19]. As a result, clusters of varying sizes are created with the detection of outliers [20]. Certain parameters are required for the implementation of DBSCAN.

- ε: Epsilon decides the neighbor of a data point. Two points are considered to be neighbours if their separation is less than or equal to ε. A sizable portion of the data will be regarded as anomalies if the eps value is set too low. The clusters will merge and most of the data points will be in the same clusters if it is selected in a very high amount.
- Minpts: It stands for a minimum number of data points within ε radius. If the size of the dataset is large then a large value of minpts should be chosen.

Algorithm

Step1: All neighbor sample points N within ε are found.

Step 2: Form a cluster for each core point if it is not assigned to any cluster.

Step 3: if |N|>= minpts, N=N U N'

Step 4: Traverse the remaining unvisited points in the sample dataset.

K-means clustering and DBSCAN, both are used to create clusters but they are used in different scenarios. DBSCAN is used when clusters are not known in advance whereas k-means is used when we know how many clusters are there in the given dataset.

1.5.2. Association Rules

These are used to establish relationships between variables in large datasets. It is used in the analysis of customer behaviour, recommendation systems, or for other decision-making tasks. It works on the principle of if else statement. Several metrics are used to measure association:

- Support- defines how frequently a data point P is appearing in the dataset.

$$Support(P) = \frac{Frequency(P)}{T}$$

- Confidence- Ratio of transaction that contains P and Q to the total number of occurrences of P.

$$Confidence = \frac{Frequency(P,Q)}{Frequency(P)}$$

- Lift- It is the strength of any rule and can be defined as:

$$Lift = \frac{Support(P,Q)}{Support\ (P) * support(Q)}$$

1.5.2.1. Apriori Algorithm

It finds the frequent item sets from the given data and uses it to generate association rules [21].

Step1: Generate the itemset by counting the occurrence of individual items and discard the items that do not meet the minimum threshold.

Step 2: Prune infrequent item set.

Step 3: Generate association rules by splitting item sets into antecedent and consequent parts.

Step 4: Repeat steps 2 & 3 until no more frequent item sets are found.

1.5.2.2. Eclat Algorithm

Equivalency Class Transformation is referred to as the Eclat algorithm. This approach locates frequently occurring item sets in a transaction database by employing a depth-first search strategy. It executes more quickly than the Apriori Algorithm.

1.5.2.3. FP Growth Algorithm

Frequent Pattern, or F-P growth algorithm, is an enhanced variant of the Apriori Algorithm. It uses a tree structure called a frequent pattern or tree to represent the database. This frequent tree is meant to be used for extracting the most common patterns.

1.6. AI's Impact on Different Sectors: Case Studies and Examples

The following real-world examples and case studies demonstrate the practical applications of foundational technologies of artificial intelligence:

1.6.1. Healthcare

AI is already being applied in the healthcare industry for performing a number of applications and some of them are described below:

- Diagnostic: Nowadays, deep learning models (VGG, ResNet, CNN) are being implemented to create AI systems that can analyse medical images such as MRIs, CT scans, and X-rays with remarkable precision and accuracy [22]. These methods of AI can detect and identify patterns in such images that may be very difficult for human radiologists to detect.
- Drug discovery: In conventional times, drug development and discovery was a very time-consuming and expensive task but due to the introduction of artificial intelligence, the timeline for discovering a drug is decreased. With its help, different compounds can be detected at the molecular level [23, 24]. Generative AI also plays a crucial role in identifying the beneficial compounds for study and clinical trials; for example, the use of AI in expediting the COVID-19 vaccine research cannot be forgotten.

Breast cancer detection, lung disease detection, and retinal disease screening are a few examples where AI is doing really well. Malignant tumours can be detected by analyzing mammograms using CNN, which has shown remarkable results. IBM Watson for oncology is an AI-based model that is used to detect mutations in tumours thereby helping oncologists opt right therapies for the patients. Deep learning methods can also be used to detect or identify COVID-19, and pneumonia from X-ray images of the chest. Another example in the healthcare system is the da Vinci Surgical system (a robotic system), which is used for repairing cardiac valves, and renal and is also used in gynaecologic surgeries. All these examples show how AI is reshaping the healthcare sector and improving patient outcomes.

1.6.2. Finance

Financial markets are also improving trading strategies for the detection of fraud and customer interaction by using artificial intelligence [25, 26]. It is being used by the finance sector to perform algorithmic trading for customer service using chatbots.

- The financial sector generates a huge amount of data on a daily basis, so AI-driven algorithms can analyse this vast data set in real-time to identify the profits trading opportunities. With the advent of technology, frauds are also increasing [27]. AI systems are being utilised to detect and prevent fraud in terms of financial transactions, various machine learning models can analyse the transactions in real-time and can indicate any kind of fraudulent activity. Visa's AI system is one such example of credit card fraud detection. The authors have worked on a fusion model based on logistic regression, random forest, and cat boost. It is observed that the fusion model is giving the best accurate results as compared to the models when implemented individually. Zest AI application came into the picture in 2009 for a loan approval system. Using this application, the customer can predict the loan default risk using data like income, spending patterns, *etc*.
- Chatbots are also used by financial organisations to provide uninterrupted services to customers. This virtual assistant can handle routine tasks such as fund transfer queries, investment decisions, advice regarding which share to purchase, *etc* [28]. The use of natural language processing understands and responds to customer queries in an effective way hence improving the speed of the services. Personal finance management is also possible with AI. Tools like YNAB and Mint are getting popular among users that analyse their expenses and recommend proper financial budget planning. Bloomberg is another application based on machine learning models that forecast price movements and predict market trends. People who are involved in share markets are getting benefits in terms of finance through this application.

1.6.3. Manufacturing and Supply Chain

The manufacturing sector is also transformed by AI in terms of optimizing the production processes [29]. Equipment failures can be detected using AI-empowered predictive maintenance systems. Defects in manufactured products can also be detected in real time and this reduces the maintenance cost. Supply chain operations [30, 31] involve the entire flow of production, and machine learning models can be used to analyze the historical data, to predict weather conditions. This information can be utilized for the smooth delivery of products to the customers.

Deep learning models can analyze defects in products using their videos or images. For example, in a semiconductor manufacturing company, surface defects in metal parts can be identified through real-time inspection. The robotic arms used for manufacturing, are governed by computer vision for precise assembly of the products. In inventory optimization, regression models like multilinear regression, and polynomial regression methods play a significant roles. These methods are used to predict demand patterns from historical data. It has become easy to manage stock levels in warehouses to avoid overstocking.

1.6.4. Retail and Marketing

Recommendation systems, advertisements, and consumer insight are the focused areas of retail and marketing for AI [32]. By using recommendation systems, customer choice, browsing patterns, and behaviour can be analysed to give suggestions to them. Advertisements can be flaunted on the social media platforms of the customer to catch their attention. In this way, AI is reshaping this sector too.

E-commerce websites like Amazon, Flipkart, Netflix, *etc* recommend various products to customers based on their previous purchase history or their content searching behaviour. Neural Collaborative Filtering method, a deep learning model is used for this task. Customer segmentation is the process of identifying target customers based on purchasing behavior, demographics, or their preferences. Clustering algorithms like k-means and DBSCAN of machine learning are applied for this purpose so that potential customers can be grouped to target marketing campaigns more effectively. Dynamic pricing is another real-world example, where airlines and online retailers adjust prices on a daily basis, even on an hourly basis to maximize their revenue. The market basket analysis method helps the retailers to get maximum profit by guiding them on which items should be placed in the store and in which combination with other items. It helps in identifying which products are more in demand by the customers based on the purchase history of different customers.

1.6.5. Education

Adaptive learning platforms are being utilized to analyze the performance of the students in real time [33, 34]. The content is generated as per the IQ level of the student. Platforms like Dreambox provide pathways to students for effective learning. Machine learning models are giving solutions to academic problems as well [35]. Teachers can also use AI to design better curriculums, and custom learning plans for each category of student [36, 37, 38].

Coursera, one of the popular platforms, provides various personalized professional courses to students as well as educational organizations based on their preferences. ML models can analyze the performance of students and provide guidance to them to improvise their performance. Knewton application is a good example, which is an AI-driven application. It enables the students to take tests of the courses being opted for by the students. The score they obtain will decide the tutoring and study plans for them. ChatGPT and BERT are getting popular nowadays to generate quizzes, and assignments for students within a fraction of a second.

1.6.6. Agriculture

The agriculture field is also being transformed by artificial intelligence in a number of ways. Farming techniques like smart irrigation [39], plant disease prediction [40, 41, 42]] soil health monitoring [43], and weather predictions are all necessary for the quantitative and qualitative production of crops. Machine learning techniques such as random forest, SVM, naïve Bayes, and deep learning techniques such as convolutional neural network, ResNet, *etc* are the most commonly used methods for these techniques. Computer vision systems are used for early detection of pests and nutrient deficiencies. Farmers can use handy applications on their mobile phones for better decision-making and automating several tasks.

The real-world examples include CropX, which is used in crop yield production. Data collected by sensors are being used by ML methods to optimize the yield of the crops by monitoring soil conditions and providing actionable insights. Plantix, a mobile application is used for plant disease identification and nutrient deficiency detection from the uploaded images. Some other potential examples are explained in Chapter 3 in detail.

CONCLUSION

AI augmentation is the concept where instead of replacing human workers, AI will enhance human capabilities that consist of the completion of repetitive tasks. This will allow the humans to focus on more complicated and complex tasks efficiently. Human-AI collaboration can bring drastic changes in the world; for example, in the healthcare field, AI can help or assist doctors by analysing medical images, suggesting treatment plans, and diagnosing diseases. It also helps in re-skilling workers. Many conventional jobs require updating of skills specifically the people who work in government or educational institutes. Upskilling is required to stay in the market and it should be the prime responsibility of humans to stay up to date.

AI has automated the world's maximum number of tasks and it is an alarming situation for job displacement across industries or various sectors. Tasks like data entry, transportation, and manufacturing are taken control by automation. The jobs of people working in this area are at stake. The current chapter focused on the evolution of AI techniques, specifically, machine learning algorithms, and how these are utilized in different sectors along with real-world examples. The next chapter is focused on various deep learning models and their working in detail.

REFERENCES

[1]   R. Cioffi, M. Travaglioni, G. Piscitelli, A. Petrillo, and F. De Felice, "Artificial intelligence and machine learning applications in smart production: Progress, trends, and directions", 2020. [http://dx.doi.org/10.3390/su12020492]

[2]   B. hu Li, B. cun Hou, W. tao Yu, X. bing Lu, and C. wei Yang, "Applications of artificial intelligence in intelligent manufacturing: a review", *Zhejiang University,* vol. 2017, Jan. 01. [http://dx.doi.org/10.1631/FITEE.1601885]

[3]   K. Lašas, Uta Užupyt, and T. Krilavičius, "Fraudulent Behaviour Identification in Ethereum Blockchain", 2020. Available from: http://ceur-ws.org

[4]   J. A. Nichols, H. W. Herbert Chan, and M. A. B. Baker, "Machine learning: applications of artificial intelligence to imaging and diagnosis", *Springer Verlag,* vol. Feb. 07, 2019. [http://dx.doi.org/10.1007/s12551-018-0449-9]

[5]   D. Tiozzo Fasiolo, L. Scalera, E. Maset, and A. Gasparetto, "Towards autonomous mapping in agriculture: A review of supportive technologies for ground robotics", *Robot. Auton. Syst.,* vol. 169, p. 104514, 2023. [http://dx.doi.org/10.1016/j.robot.2023.104514]

[6]   A.I. Khan, S.M.K. Quadri, S. Banday, and J. Latief Shah, "Deep diagnosis: A real-time apple leaf disease detection system based on deep learning", *Comput. Electron. Agric.,* vol. 198, p. 107093, 2022. [http://dx.doi.org/10.1016/j.compag.2022.107093]

[7]   M.I. Tarik, S. Akter, A. Al Mamun, and A. Sattar, "Potato disease detection using machine learning", *Proceedings of the 3rd International Conference on Intelligent Communication Technologies and Virtual Mobile Networks, ICICV 2021,* 2021pp. 800-803 [http://dx.doi.org/10.1109/ICICV50876.2021.9388606]

[8]   A. Rastogi, R. Arora, and S. Sharma, "Leaf disease detection and grading using computer vision technology & fuzzy logic", *2nd International Conference on Signal Processing and Integrated Networks, SPIN 2015,* 2015pp. 500-505 [http://dx.doi.org/10.1109/SPIN.2015.7095350]

[9]   M.A.A.S. Ali, "AI-Natural Language Processing (NLP)", *Int. J. Res. Appl. Sci. Eng. Technol.,* vol. 9, no. VIII, pp. 135-140, 2021. [http://dx.doi.org/10.22214/ijraset.2021.37293]

[10]   M. Danilevsky, K. Qian, R. Aharonov, Y. Katsis, B. Kawas, and P. Sen, "A Survey of the State of Explainable AI for Natural Language Processing", 2020. Available from: [http://dx.doi.org/10.18653/v1/2020.aacl-main.46]

[11]   J. Chen, X. Deng, Y. Wen, W. Chen, A. Zeb, and D. Zhang, "Weakly-supervised learning method for the recognition of potato leaf diseases", *Artif. Intell. Rev.,* no. 0123456789, pp. 1-18, 2022. [http://dx.doi.org/10.1007/s10462-022-10374-3] [PMID: 36573133]

[12]   B. Hatuwal, B. Joshi, B. K. Hatuwal, and A. Shakya, "Plant Leaf Disease Recognition Using Random Forest, KNN, SVM and CNN",

[http://dx.doi.org/10.17562/PB-62-2]

[13]   M. Brijain, R. Patel, M. Kushik, and K. Rana, *A Survey on Decision Tree Algorithm For Classification,* 2014. Available from: www.ijedr.org

[14]   B. Charbuty, and A. Abdulazeez, "Classification Based on Decision Tree Algorithm for Machine Learning", *Journal of Applied Science and Technology Trends,* vol. 2, no. 1, pp. 20-28, 2021.
[http://dx.doi.org/10.38094/jastt20165]

[15]   J. L. Speiser, M. E. Miller, J. Tooze, and E. Ip, "A comparison of random forest variable selection methods for classification prediction modeling", *Elsevier Ltd,* vol. Nov. 15, 2019.
[http://dx.doi.org/10.1016/j.eswa.2019.05.028]

[16]   P. Liu, K.K.R. Choo, L. Wang, and F. Huang, "SVM or deep learning? A comparative study on remote sensing image classification", *Soft Comput.,* vol. 21, no. 23, pp. 7053-7065, 2017.
[http://dx.doi.org/10.1007/s00500-016-2247-2]

[17]   S. Kumar Sahu, and M. Pandey, *An optimal hybrid multiclass SVM for plant leaf disease detection using spatial Fuzzy C-Means model*, 2023.
[http://dx.doi.org/10.1016/j.eswa.2022.118989]

[18]   M. Usama, J. Qadir, A. Raza, H. Arif, K.A. Yau, Y. Elkhatib, A. Hussain, and A. Al-Fuqaha, "Unsupervised Machine Learning for Networking: Techniques, Applications and Research Challenges", *IEEE Access,* vol. 7, pp. 65579-65615, 2019.
[http://dx.doi.org/10.1109/ACCESS.2019.2916648]

[19]   D. Deng, "DBSCAN Clustering Algorithm Based on Density", *in Proceedings - 2020 7th International Forum on Electrical Engineering and Automation, IFEEA 2020,* 2020pp. 949-953 Institute of Electrical and Electronics Engineers Inc.
[http://dx.doi.org/10.1109/IFEEA51475.2020.00199]

[20]   N. Gholizadeh, H. Saadatfar, and N. Hanafi, "K-DBSCAN: An improved DBSCAN algorithm for big data", *J. Supercomput.,* vol. 77, no. 6, pp. 6214-6235, 2021.
[http://dx.doi.org/10.1007/s11227-020-03524-3]

[21]   C. Lopez, S. Tucker, T. Salameh, and C. Tucker, "An unsupervised machine learning method for discovering patient clusters based on genetic signatures", *J. Biomed. Inform.,* vol. 85, pp. 30-39, 2018.
[http://dx.doi.org/10.1016/j.jbi.2018.07.004] [PMID: 30016722]

[22]   Ștefan Busnatu, "Clinical Applications of Artificial Intelligence—An Updated Overview", *MDPI,* vol. Apr. 01, 2022.
[http://dx.doi.org/10.3390/jcm11082265]

[23]   M. Javaid, A. Haleem, R. Pratap Singh, R. Suman, and S. Rab, "Significance of machine learning in healthcare: Features, pillars and applications", *International Journal of Intelligent Networks,* vol. 3, pp. 58-73, 2022.
[http://dx.doi.org/10.1016/j.ijin.2022.05.002]

[24]   A. Alanazi, "Using machine learning for healthcare challenges and opportunities", *Elsevier Ltd,* vol. Jan. 01, 2022.
[http://dx.doi.org/10.1016/j.imu.2022.100924]

[25]   J. Lee, "Access to Finance for Artificial Intelligence Regulation in the Financial Services Industry", *Eur. Bus. Organ. Law Rev.,* vol. 21, no. 4, pp. 731-757, 2020.
[http://dx.doi.org/10.1007/s40804-020-00200-0]

[26]   R. Najem, M.F. Amr, A. Bahnasse, and M. Talea, "Artificial Intelligence for Digital Finance, Axes and Techniques", In: *in Procedia Computer Science* Elsevier B.V., 2022, pp. 633-638.
[http://dx.doi.org/10.1016/j.procs.2022.07.092]

[27]   Q. Liu, "Research on Risk Management of Big Data and Machine Learning Insurance Based on Internet Finance", In: *Journal of Physics: Conference Series.* Institute of Physics Publishing, 2019.
[http://dx.doi.org/10.1088/1742-6596/1345/5/052076]

[28]   I. Karachun, L. Vinnichek, and A. Tuskov, "Machine learning methods in finance", *SHS Web of Conferences,* vol. 110, 2021p. 05012
[http://dx.doi.org/10.1051/shsconf/202111005012]

[29]   A. Ahmed, P. He, P. He, Y. Wu, Y. He, and S. Munir, "Environmental effect of agriculture-related manufactured nano-objects on soil microbial communities", *Elsevier Ltd,* vol. Mar. 01, 2023.
[http://dx.doi.org/10.1016/j.envint.2023.107819]

[30]   D. Ni, Z. Xiao, and M.K. Lim, "A systematic review of the research trends of machine learning in supply chain management", *Int. J. Mach. Learn. Cybern.,* vol. 11, no. 7, pp. 1463-1482, 2020.
[http://dx.doi.org/10.1007/s13042-019-01050-0]

[31]   K.J. Park, "Determining the tiers of a supply chain using machine learning algorithms", *Symmetry (Basel),* vol. 13, no. 10, p. 1934, 2021.
[http://dx.doi.org/10.3390/sym13101934]

[32]   A. Haleem, M. Javaid, M. Asim Qadri, R. Pratap Singh, and R. Suman, "Artificial intelligence (AI) applications for marketing: A literature-based study", *KeAi Communications Co,* vol. Jan. 01, 2022.
[http://dx.doi.org/10.1016/j.ijin.2022.08.005]

[33]   F. Ouyang, M. Wu, and L. Zheng, "Integration of artificial intelligence performance prediction and learning analytics to improve student learning in online engineering course", *Int J Educ Technol High Educ,* vol. 20, p. 4, 2023.
[http://dx.doi.org/10.1186/s41239-022-00372-4]

[34]   K. Zhang, and A. B. Aslan, "AI technologies for education: Recent research & future directions", *Elsevier B.V.,* vol. Jan. 01, 2021.
[http://dx.doi.org/10.1016/j.caeai.2021.100025]

[35]   J. Kim, H. Lee, and Y.H. Cho, "Learning design to support student-AI collaboration: perspectives of leading teachers for AI in education", *Educ. Inf. Technol.,* vol. 27, no. 5, pp. 6069-6104, 2022.
[http://dx.doi.org/10.1007/s10639-021-10831-6]

[36]   L. Chen, P. Chen, and Z. Lin, "Artificial Intelligence in Education: A Review", *IEEE Access,* vol. 8, pp. 75264-75278, 2020.
[http://dx.doi.org/10.1109/ACCESS.2020.2988510]

[37]   H.C. Davies, R. Eynon, and C. Salveson, "The Mobilisation of AI in Education: A Bourdieusean Field Analysis", *Sociology,* vol. 55, no. 3, pp. 539-560, 2021.
[http://dx.doi.org/10.1177/0038038520967888]

[38]   K. Okoye, J.T. Nganji, J. Escamilla, and S. Hosseini, "Machine learning model (RG-DMML) and ensemble algorithm for prediction of students' retention and graduation in education", *Computers and Education: Artificial Intelligence,* vol. 6, p. 100205, 2024.
[http://dx.doi.org/10.1016/j.caeai.2024.100205]

[39]   S. R, R. M, V. S, S.K. e, Y. S, A. Kumar, J.R. i, and V. K, "A novel autonomous irrigation system for smart agriculture using AI and 6G enabled IoT network", *Microprocess. Microsyst.,* vol. 101, p. 104905, 2023.
[http://dx.doi.org/10.1016/j.micpro.2023.104905]

[40]   S. Poornima, S. Kavitha, S. Mohanavalli, and N. Sripriya, "Detection and classification of diseases in plants using image processing and machine learning techniques", *AIP Conf. Proc.,* vol. 2095, no. April, p. 030018, 2019.
[http://dx.doi.org/10.1063/1.5097529]

[41]   M. Bala, and V. Mehan, "Metaheuristic Techniques for Classification Used in Identification of Plant Diseases", *ECS Trans.,* vol. 107, no. 1, pp. 13473-13480, 2022.
[http://dx.doi.org/10.1149/10701.13473ecst]

[42]   M. Bala, and S.K. Bansal, "Investigating a Spectrum of Machine Learning Methods for Leaf Disease Detection in Pepper, Potato, and Tomato", *ECS J. Solid State Sci. Technol.,* vol. 13, no. 10, p. 107003,

2024.
[http://dx.doi.org/10.1149/2162-8777/ad83f2]

[43]   M.M. Selim, *Introduction to the Integrated Nutrient Management Strategies and Their Contribution to Yield and Soil Properties*. Hindawi Limited, 2020.
[http://dx.doi.org/10.1155/2020/2821678]

CHAPTER 2

Investigating the Influence of Artificial Intelligence with Deep Learning

Abstract: Artificial Intelligence (AI) and Deep Learning (DL) have emerged as transformative technologies with the potential to revolutionize various domains. This paper explores the fundamental concepts and advancements in AI and DL, highlighting their significance in solving complex problems and enhancing computational efficiency. AI aims to mimic intelligent behavior by enabling machines to think, observe, learn, and adapt, while DL, a subset of AI and machine learning, focuses on algorithms modeled after the architecture and operation of neural networks in the human brain. The development of AI has been driven by the need to handle complex problems involving uncertainty and vast amounts of data, with techniques such as machine learning, deep learning, and pattern recognition showing promise in structural engineering applications. DL models, inspired by the composition and operations of the human brain, excel at processing large datasets to uncover intricate patterns and insights. DL has become the most prominent technology within the fields of machine learning, AI, data science, and big data analytics due to its ability to learn from datasets. The performance of DL algorithms surpasses that of traditional machine learning techniques as the amount of data increases, enabling the solution of more complex problems even with unstructured, diverse, and networked data. This paper emphasizes the importance of understanding AI and DL concepts to navigate the rapidly evolving technological landscape and appreciate their implications across various aspects of society.

Keywords: Artificial Intelligence, Architecture, CNN, Deep learning, GAN, Machine learning, RNN.

1. INTRODUCTION

Artificial Intelligence is the branch of computer science that has a strong impact on multidisciplinary areas such as mathematics, linguistics, philosophy, and psychology or cognitive science. Generating expert systems that can include or display some intelligence is the main objective of artificial intelligence and it is achieved in two ways either by adopting methods which are more suited for computer processing or by modeling how people perform intelligent requiring tasks [1].

AI, which promises to transform industries, improve human capacities, and influence the course of civilization, is at the front of contemporary technological progress. The fundamental goal of artificial intelligence (AI) is to mimic intelligent behaviour by giving machines the ability to think, observe, learn, and adapt in ways that are similar to those of humans. Over the past few decades, research and development on artificial intelligence (AI) have grown rapidly. Expert systems, natural language processing, speech recognition, computer vision, robotics, and other fields have advanced tremendously, while there are still major issues that need to be resolved. Among other things, the current success of AI stems from the creation of novel system designs that may leverage all the knowledge—including human expertise—available in a particular subject. Thus, in order to enhance their performances, these knowledge-based systems consider human expertise [2]. Artificial Intelligence (AI) facilitates machine knowledge, human-machine communication, and human-machine interaction. Machine learning (ML) is an application of artificial intelligence that allows the systems to automatically learn from their past experiences and get better without being explicitly programmed. On the other hand, Deep Learning (DL) learns from inputs such as pictures, text, and sound and responds accordingly (shown in Fig. **1**).

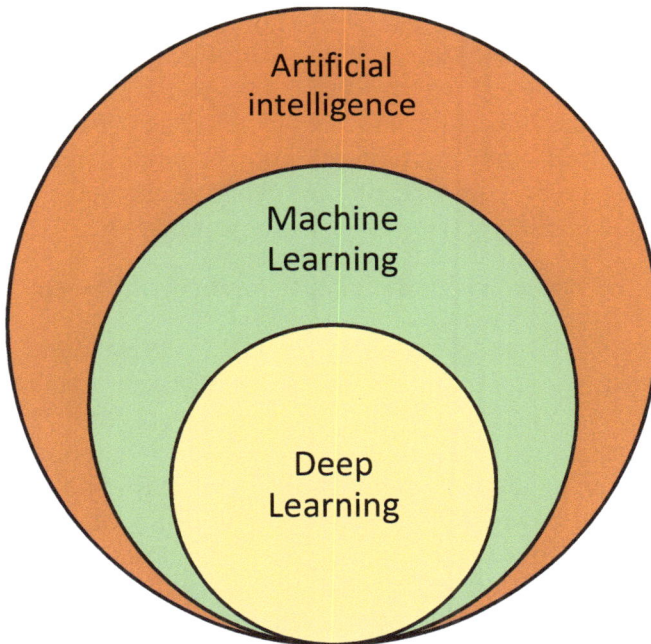

Fig. (1). The circle shows the spheres of Artificial Intelligence (AI), Machine Learning (ML), and Deep Learning (DL). Machine Learning and deep learning are the subsets of Artificial Intelligence. Machine Learning (ML) automatically predicts the results from the given set of input data and Deep Learning (DL) mimics the working of the human brain to incorporate such intelligence into the system.

The necessity to handle complicated problems—especially the ones involving uncertainty and enormous volumes of data—has propelled the development of artificial intelligence. Artificial Intelligence (AI) techniques in structural engineering, including machine learning, deep learning, and pattern recognition, have shown promise in solving problems that traditional models are unable to, increasing computing efficiency and decreasing human labour [3].

1.1. Artificial Intelligence and Deep Learning

Artificial Intelligence (AI) and Deep Learning (DL) have gained widespread recognition over many years, capturing the attention of people and reshaping the field of technology. It is essentially the human thoughts generated by the computers, with the aim of initializing cognitive functions like learning, problem-solving and decision-making.

As Deep Learning (DL) is a subset of artificial intelligence and machine learning that focus on algorithms that are modeled after the architecture and operation of neural networks found in the human brain. Gaining an understanding of ideas generated by the human brain is essential for navigating the constantly changing technology landscape and appreciating the ramifications for many facets of society. It has become a paradigm shift, taking the discipline to previously unheard-of heights. Deep Learning (DL) models, which have their roots in computational artificial neural networks and are inspired by the composition and operations of the human brain, are particularly good at sifting through enormous amounts of data to find complex patterns and insights. These neural networks have the depth to automatically find hierarchical representations, opening up the possibility of amazing achievements across a range of fields [4].

1.2. Delving into the realm of Artificial Intelligence and Deep Learning

Artificial Intelligence (AI) and Deep Learning (DL) represent the zenith of human inventiveness, with the potential to create machines that can occasionally outperform humans in intelligence. These expressions have gained widespread usage in contemporary society, manipulating not only science fiction but also our relationships with one another, the environment, and our jobs. In addition to being tech-savvy, one should have a rudimentary understanding of AI and deep learning since it might be useful in navigating the complex relationship between humans and rapid technological advancement. The goal of artificial intelligence, or AI, is to build computers that are capable of tasks that typically require human intellect, such as pattern recognition, decision-making, and experience-based learning. Deep Learning, a branch of artificial intelligence, employs neural network-inspired algorithms. Deep Learning was introduced in 2006 by Hinton *et al.* based on the concept of artificial neural network (ANN) [5] and it became a "new generation neural network". When deep learning neural networks are trained efficiently, the networks show virtuous results on a wide range of regression and classification problems [6]. Due to the ability to learn from a certain dataset, deep learning has become the most prominent technology within the fields of machine learning, artificial intelligence, data science, and big data analytics [7]. Fig. (**2**) illustrates the performance of deep learning and machine learning models with an increase in the amount of data.

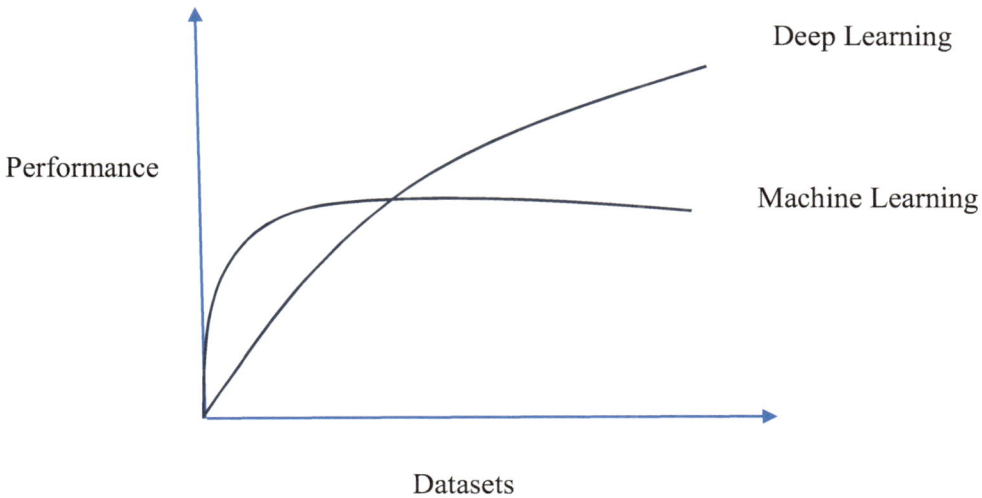

Fig. (2). Performance of deep learning techniques and machine learning techniques w.r.t. the amount of data [8].

Artificial intelligence and deep learning algorithms allow machines to solve more complex problems even when there is unstructured, hugely diverse, and networked data gathering. These algorithms perform well when they learn more with the data. Deep Learning has enhanced machine learning by constructing multiple-layered ("deep") artificial neural networks. This enables computers to learn from enormous volumes of data and provide increasingly intricate forecasts and choices. Artificial Intelligence and Deep Learning are two extremely important technologies that have an influence on many facets of modern society, from tailored online shopping suggestions to self-driving cars. These latest technologies are much more convenient and efficient, but they also bring up significant ethical, social, and financial issues. A deep understanding of these technologies and their implication on society is essential as evidenced by the concerns about bias caused by the algorithms, privacy in data, and effects on employment.

Deep learning has become a cutting-edge method for handling and comprehending complicated data. Fundamentally, deep learning makes use of artificial neural networks—which are designed to mimic the structure and operation of the human brain—to enable autonomous learning from massive amounts of data. The layers of linked nodes, or neurons, that make up these neural networks are designed to extract ever more abstract properties from the incoming data. Deep learning models iteratively modify their parameters to reduce mistakes and maximize performance using a procedure known as backpropagation [9].

1.3. Deep Learning *Vs* Conventional Machine Learning

Deep learning and conventional machine learning are not mutually exclusive methods. Rather, they represent two extremes within the same range of learning abilities. For highly organized types of data, conventional machine learning would often be the best option when it comes to interpretability and computing capacity. Conversely, deep learning is highly proficient in deciphering intricate data, which enables it to recognize certain patterns with remarkable accuracy. They are both able to collaborate harmoniously while working together simultaneously. We can easily train data for deep learning by extracting the standard ML toolkit feature engineering. Moreover, traditional machine learning methods may be employed to do further analysis on the dataset created by deep learning models [9].

While deep learning is different from typical machine learning algorithms (represented in Fig. **3**) in that it can automatically learn hierarchical representations of data, this also removes the requirement for manual feature engineering and makes it possible to infer complex patterns from raw input. Consequently, it has enabled noteworthy advancements in other domains like computer vision, natural language processing, speech recognition, and autonomous driving. Convolutional neural networks, recurrent neural networks, and transformers are examples of deep learning models that have produced previously unheard-of outcomes in sentiment analysis, object identification, language translation, and picture categorization. Deep learning technologies are now more widely available and may be used to build complex artificial intelligence systems because of the development of supporting hardware accelerators like GPUs and TPUs, as well as the extensive use of deep learning frameworks like TensorFlow and PyTorch [10]. Deep learning, however, has been a driving force behind innovation across a wide range of sectors and the cornerstone of future technology and civilization because of its capacity to learn patterns from data and generalize to unforeseen circumstances.

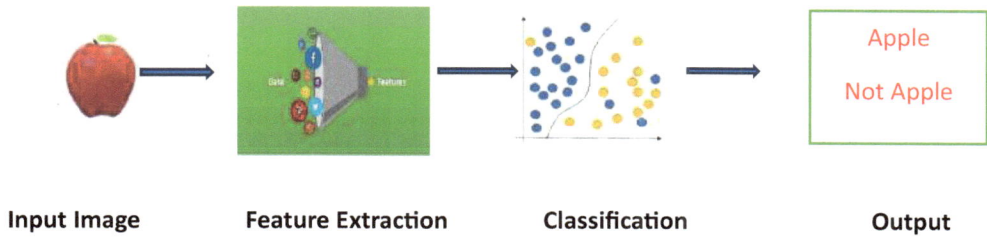

Machine Learning

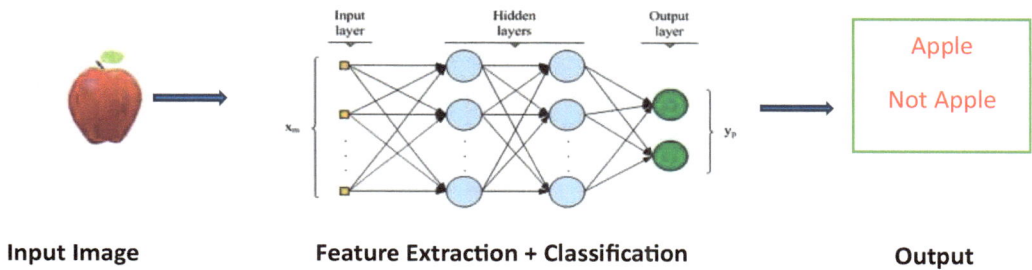

Deep Learning

Fig. (3). Conventional Machine Learning *vs*. deep learning.

In addition to its applications in computer vision, natural language processing, and autonomous systems, deep learning has also found widespread use in fields such as healthcare, finance, and manufacturing. In healthcare, deep learning models are being employed for medical image analysis, disease diagnosis, personalized treatment planning, and drug discovery. For instance, deep learning algorithms can analyse medical images such as X-rays, MRI scans, and CT scans with remarkable accuracy, aiding radiologists in identifying abnormalities and diseases like cancer, pneumonia, and Alzheimer's. Furthermore, deep learning techniques are being utilized to analyse genomic data, enabling researchers to identify genetic variations associated with diseases and develop targeted therapies. In finance, deep learning algorithms are utilized for fraud detection, risk assessment, algorithmic trading, and customer service automation. These models can analyse vast amounts of financial data, including transaction records, market trends, and customer behavior, to detect fraudulent activities, predict market movements, and optimize investment strategies. Moreover, in manufacturing, deep learning is being used for quality control, predictive maintenance, supply chain optimization, and process automation. For example, deep learning models can analyse sensor data from industrial machinery to predict equipment failures before they occur, minimizing downtime and optimizing production efficiency. Additionally, deep learning techniques are being employed for computer-aided design (CAD) and generative design, enabling engineers to create innovative designs and optimize product performance. As deep learning continues to advance, its impact across diverse industries is expected to grow exponentially, driving innovation, efficiency, and competitiveness in the global economy. Furthermore, with ongoing research in areas such as explainable AI, lifelong learning, and neuro-symbolic AI, deep learning holds the potential to unlock new capabilities and address complex challenges, paving the way for a future where intelligent machines augment human capabilities and improve lives worldwide.

Beyond its practical applications, deep learning has also catalysed significant advancements in fundamental research areas such as reinforcement learning, unsupervised learning, and multimodal learning. Reinforcement learning, a paradigm where an agent learns to interact with an environment to achieve specific goals, has seen remarkable progress with deep learning techniques, leading to breakthroughs in areas like game playing, robotics, and autonomous systems. Deep reinforcement learning algorithms have achieved superhuman performance in games like Go, Atari, and Dota 2, showcasing their ability to learn complex behaviors and strategies through trial and error. Furthermore, unsupervised learning techniques, such as autoencoders, variational autoencoders (VAEs), and generative adversarial networks (GANs), have enabled the discovery of hidden structures and patterns in data without the need for labeled examples. GANs, in particular, have garnered attention for their ability to generate realistic synthetic data, leading to applications in image synthesis, style transfer, and data augmentation. Moreover, multimodal learning, which involves processing and integrating information from multiple modalities such as text, images, and audio, has emerged as a promising research direction. Multimodal deep learning models can learn to understand and generate content across different modalities, enabling tasks like image captioning, video understanding, and audio-visual speech recognition [11].

1.4. Significance of Deep Learning

The significance of deep learning lies in its transformative impact on various fields and its ability to tackle complex problems that were previously considered intractable. Here are several key aspects highlighting its significance:

- **Unprecedented Performance**: Deep learning models have proven to be incredibly effective in applications like speech synthesis, picture recognition, and natural language understanding. In some fields, these models can outperform humans by directly learning complex patterns and representations from data using deep neural networks.

- **Automation and Efficiency**: Deep learning enables automation of tasks that were traditionally labor-intensive and time-consuming. By automating processes such as data analysis, image classification, and language translation, deep learning technologies enhance efficiency, reduce costs, and accelerate decision-making across various industries.

- **Perception Discovery**: Deep learning facilitates the discovery of insights and patterns in large datasets that would be impractical or impossible to discern using conventional methods. By extracting complex features and relationships from data, deep learning models uncover hidden structures and correlations, enabling better understanding and decision-making.

- **Personalization and Adaptation:** Deep learning enables personalized experiences and adaptive systems by learning from user interactions and feedback. Recommendation systems, virtual assistants, and personalized marketing campaigns leverage deep learning algorithms to tailor content and services to individual preferences and behaviors, enhancing user satisfaction and engagement.

- **Scientific Discovery**: Deep learning has the potential to revolutionize scientific research by accelerating discovery and innovation across diverse domains. From drug discovery and genomics to climate modeling and material science, deep learning techniques enable researchers to analyse vast amounts of data, simulate complex systems, and generate novel hypotheses, leading to breakthroughs and advancements.

- **Empowerment and Accessibility:** Deep learning democratizes access to AI tools and capabilities, empowering individuals, businesses, and organizations to leverage the power of artificial intelligence. Open-source deep learning frameworks, cloud-based services, and pre-trained models make it easier for developers, researchers, and practitioners to build and deploy AI applications, fostering innovation and collaboration.

- **Addressing Societal Challenges:** Deep learning has the potential to address some of the most pressing societal challenges, including healthcare disparities, environmental sustainability, and social inequality. By enabling advancements in precision medicine, climate modeling, and predictive analytics, deep learning technologies contribute to improving human health, protecting the environment, and promoting social equity [12 - 14].

2. FOUNDATION OF DEEP LEARNING

The creation of sophisticated neural networks that can recognize complicated patterns in data to address real-world issues is the cornerstone of deep learning in artificial intelligence. Because deep learning models, such as deep neural networks, allow for in-context learning—a process in which models may learn from sparse instances without explicit training—they have transformed a number of fields, including computer vision and natural language processing. Deep learning concentrates on utilizing many layers of artificial neurons to extract characteristics from input data. These models are a component of the larger field of machine learning and are continually improving *via* experience [15 - 19].

2.1. Artificial Neural Networks (ANN)

Artificial Neural Networks (shown in Fig. **4**), generally abbreviated as ANNs are an interesting concept that brings us closer to the functioning of the human brain in computer science. Unlike traditional programming in which humans set out specific instructions that the computer then follows, ANNs have instead learned a series of examples and can adapt. These systems replicate the network of billions of interconnected neurons in our brains, neurons that constantly exchange information and communicate.

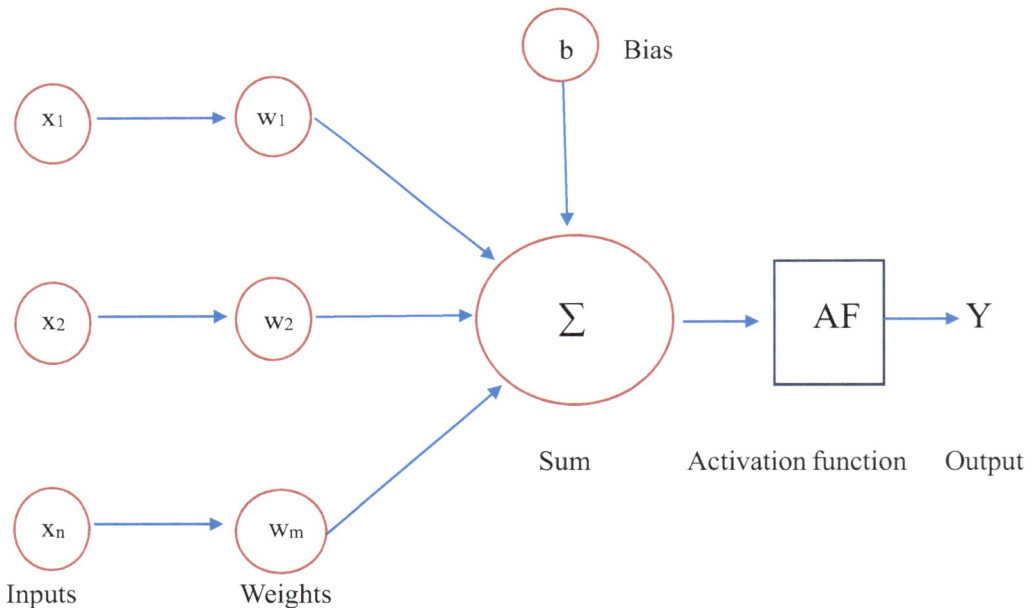

Fig. (4). Basic architecture of the artificial neural network.

These ANNs are constructed by basic units, which are known as artificial neurons. Consider these neurons as little computational devices. One neuron is connected to others, receives input, the other's signal processes it mathematically and then passes its output signal on. Every neuron takes in information from other neurons, processes it mathematically, and then transmits its signal. These artificial neurons are interconnected and have weights applied to them that affect the signal intensity. These ANN weights are modified throughout training, just as the connections between actual neurons are stronger or weaker as humans learn.

The power of neural networks comes from their architecture and the ability to learn from data through a process called training. During training, the network adjusts the weights of connections between neurons based on the error in its predictions, a method known as backpropagation. This iterative process fine-tunes the network, enabling it to make increasingly accurate predictions.

Neural network architecture can be as simple as a feedforward network where data flows from input to output (possibly through a few hidden layers), up to something quite complex like convolutional neural networks (CNNs) and recurrent neural networks. CNNs are good at processing images because they can capture spatial hierarchies using convolutional layers. On the other hand, RNNs are an architecture specifically built for sequential data which in turn makes it an ideal choice for the analysis of time series data as well as natural language processing. On the other hand, these networks have loops and information can get carried over neurons which is essential to model temporal dynamics [20].

The most interesting thing about neural networks is that they can be used to accomplish things that are hard for regular computers, such as recognizing images or translating language. Or even playing games. For example, Deep Learning, which is the neural network with many layers has revolutionizedimage recognition. Neural networks have already achieved superhuman performance in complex games such as Go, played by a network developed by Google's DeepMind, offering proof-of-concept of sorts for what neural nets can achieve in decision-making.

Neural networks play an important role in natural language processing (NLP), image and video recognition, and de-noising filter algorithms for other types of data, A common application is an input associated with identifying voice as a human attribute. Such techniques, where words are represented as vectors in a continuous vector space, such as word embeddings have been one of the key breakthroughs to discern contextual meaning and semantics within the text. Models such as the transformer that uses attention mechanisms to determine how much importance each word in a sentence has, started an NLP revolution all by themselves. These advances have enabled applications like real-time language translation, sentiment analysis, *etc*. Artificial neural networks have a wide range of expanding uses. ANNs are the driving force behind facial recognition software in the field of image recognition, which enables our gadgets to recognize us in pictures or unlock our phones with a grin. Additionally, they are transforming natural language processing, allowing machines to produce realistic dialogue, translate between languages, and even compose other forms of creative material.

However, it is crucial to recognize that there are difficulties with artificial neural networks. It can be computationally costly to train neural networks since they need a lot of computing power and data. Furthermore, it might be challenging to comprehend precisely how complicated ANNs arrive at their judgments due to the opaque nature of their inner workings. Particularly when ANNs are utilized for crucial jobs like loan approvals or criminal justice forecasts, this lack of transparency might give rise to ethical questions.

Artificial neural networks are a major advancement in artificial intelligence despite these difficulties. Their capacity for learning and adaptation makes them effective instruments for resolving challenging issues in a variety of fields. We may anticipate that ANNs will become much more influential in determining the direction of technology and society as we continue to improve and enhance them [21].

2.2. Neurons

The basic units of the nervous system and brain, neurons. Fig. (5) are the building blocks of the neuronal architecture that supports our emotions, thoughts, and behaviors. From basic reflexes to intricate cognitive functions, the body's ability to transfer information is facilitated by these specialized cells. The cell body, also known as the soma, dendrites, and axon are the three primary components of a neuron. The nucleus is located in the cell body, which is crucial for the metabolic processes of the neuron. As they extend from the cell body, dendrites pick up signals from neighboring neurons and send them back to the cell body. A long, thin projection called an axon is responsible for sending messages from the cell body to neighboring neurons, muscles, or glands. Both chemical and electrical signals are used by neurons to communicate.

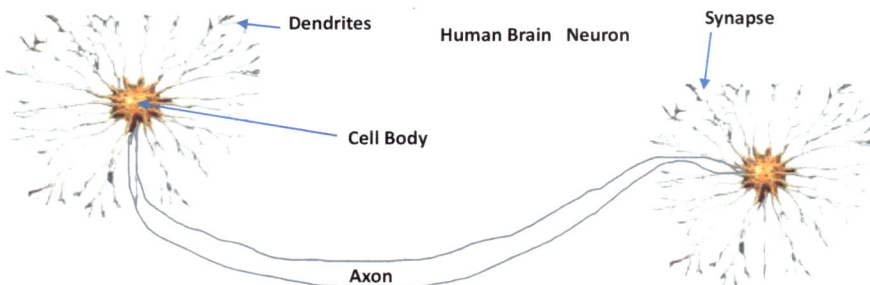

Fig. (5). Structure of a human brain neuron.

An action potential is an electrical signal that is produced and travels down an axon when a neuron is stimulated. Ions travel across the membrane of the neuron during this process, a procedure that is precisely controlled by voltage-gated ion channels. The release of neurotransmitters, which are chemical messengers that traverse synapses—the spaces between neurons—to interact with receptors on the dendrites of nearby neurons, is triggered after the action potential reaches the end of the axon. The information flow is sustained by this chemical signaling, which enables the impulse to be sent to the subsequent cell.

The complexity of these neuronal functions is, indeed, vast Sensory neurons, such as light, sound or touch receptors respond to the outside world and send information back to the brain and spinal cord. These impulses are sent to muscles by motor neurons, which cause movement and connect the brain and spinal cord. Interneurons are mainly found in the brain and spinal cord, where they provide essential links between sensory and motor neurons. They can also create conveying reflex pathways so that neural circuits assist complex acts like thinking, learning, or remembering. An estimate of about 100 trillion synapses connect more than 86 billion neurons that make up the human brain's complex and ever-growing network. These connections, and the ability for them to change, also called synaptic plasticity, are needed for memory and learning [22, 23].

2.3. Role of Neurons in ANN

The idea of a neuron is fundamental to artificial neural networks (ANNs), which use biological neurons as inspiration to build systems that can learn and carry out challenging tasks. Often called a node or a unit, an artificial neuron is a condensed representation of a real neuron that is intended to mimic its essential characteristics and operations. The fundamental components of artificial neural networks (ANNs) are these artificial neurons, which provide the networks the ability to analyse input, learn from it, and generate predictions.

Input signals, which can be either raw data or the outputs of other neurons, are received by each artificial neuron. Usually, these inputs are expressed as numerical quantities. Every input in an ANN has a weight, which is a parameter that indicates how important the input is to the neuron's operation. After computing a weighted sum and adding a bias factor, the neuron runs the total through an activation function to process the inputs. In terms of math, this is expressed as:

$$Y = \sum (W_i . X_i) + b$$

where Y is the weighted sum output, W_i represents the weights, X_i denotes the input values, and b is the bias.

Layers of artificial neurons are arranged to form a network. An input layer, one or more hidden layers, and an output layer make up a standard ANN. The first layer of the network gets the data, which is then processed further by each layer that comes after it, culminating in the final output layer, which presents the network's prediction or verdict. While neurons in the same layer function in parallel, weighted connections allow the outputs of one layer's neurons to affect those in lower levels. Deeper layers in the structure capture more abstract information, enabling ANNs to learn hierarchical representations of the input [24].

In artificial neural networks (ANNs), learning entails modifying the weights and biases of the neurons in response to the prediction error of the network. This is usually accomplished by combining an optimization approach such as gradient descent with a technique known as backpropagation. Across the training process, the network generates predictions, determines the error by contrasting the expected results with the real targets, and then propagates this mistake across the network. After that, the biases and weights are adjusted to reduce the error, enhancing the network's functionality repeatedly [25, 26].

2.4. Activation Functions

Artificial neural networks (ANNs) rely heavily on activation functions because they add non-linearity to the model, which helps the network recognize and interpret complicated patterns. These are a few of the activation functions in ANNs that are most often used:

- **Sigmoid (Logistic) Function**: Input values are mapped to a range between 0 and 1 *via* the sigmoid function. It is frequently applied to binary classification issues. But it has problems like vanishing gradients, which can cause backpropagation to lag in learning.
- **Hyperbolic Tangent (tanh) Function**: The input values are mapped by the tanh function to a range of -1 to 1. Because it is zero-centred, training can benefit from its convergence. Even with this benefit, it still has the vanishing gradient issue.
- **Rectified Linear Unit (ReLU)**: One of the most often used activation functions in deep learning is the ReLU function. By maintaining all positive values constant and setting all negative values to zero, it creates non-linearity. ReLU can suffer from the "dying ReLU" problem, in which neurons might go dormant and cease learning if they only output zero. Despite its computational efficiency, ReLU cannot solve the vanishing gradient problem [27].

- **Leaky ReLU**: When the input is negative (with α usually set to a tiny value like 0.01), the Leaky ReLU solves the dying ReLU problem by permitting a modest, non-zero gradient.
- **Parametric ReLU (PReLU)**: It is more flexible, α is a learnable parameter that changes throughout training, much to Leaky ReLU.
- **Softmax**: For multi-class classification tasks, neural networks mainly utilize the Softmax function in the output layer [28]. To make comparing classes easier, it transforms logits raw prediction values into probabilities that add up to 100%.
- **Gaussian (Radial Basis Function, RBF)**:Support vector machines and radial basis function networks are the primary applications for this function [29]. It simulates a Gaussian distribution by mapping inputs to a range between 0 and 1, with a peak at 1 when the input is zero.

2.5. Loss Functions

In deep learning models, loss functions are essential because they affect the training and assessment procedures. Deep learning uses a variety of loss functions, each having advantages and disadvantages. For example, studies have looked at popular loss functions like focal loss and cross-entropy and have suggested novel strategies like fuzzy adaptive loss function and IDID-loss. The IDID loss concurrently mitigates data scarcity, data density, and data overlapping to handle class-imbalance learning difficulties. Conversely, the fuzzy adaptive loss function improves classification accuracy by using fuzzy logic and aggregation operators, especially when class-level noise circumstances and class imbalance are present. It is crucial for practitioners to comprehend the features and uses of various loss functions in order to select the approach that best fits their particular needs [30 - 32]. Some common loss functions in deep learning are:

Mean Squared Error (MSE): Used for regression tasks, where the goal is to predict continuous values.

Mean Absolute Error (MAE): Used for regression tasks, less sensitive to outliers compared to MSE.

Binary Cross-Entropy Loss: Used for binary classification tasks.

Categorical Cross-Entropy Loss: Used for multi-class classification tasks where each instance belongs to one of the C classes.

3. DEEP LEARNING ARCHITECTURES

Deep learning, a kind of machine learning, allows computers to simulate the way the human brain processes information and generates patterns for decision-making, it has revolutionized a number of industries. Deep learning models' multi-layered design, which is frequently modeled after the neural networks found in the human brain, allows for the extraction of ever more sophisticated characteristics from unprocessed input data. There are different types of deep learning networks (shown in Fig. **6**). Artificial neural networks (ANNs), in particular deep neural networks (DNNs), which are distinguished by their depth, and the number of layers through which input passes, are at the heart of deep learning. Typically, these designs consist of an output layer, many hidden layers, and an input layer. Each layer is made up of neurons, which are the basic building blocks of computing [33].

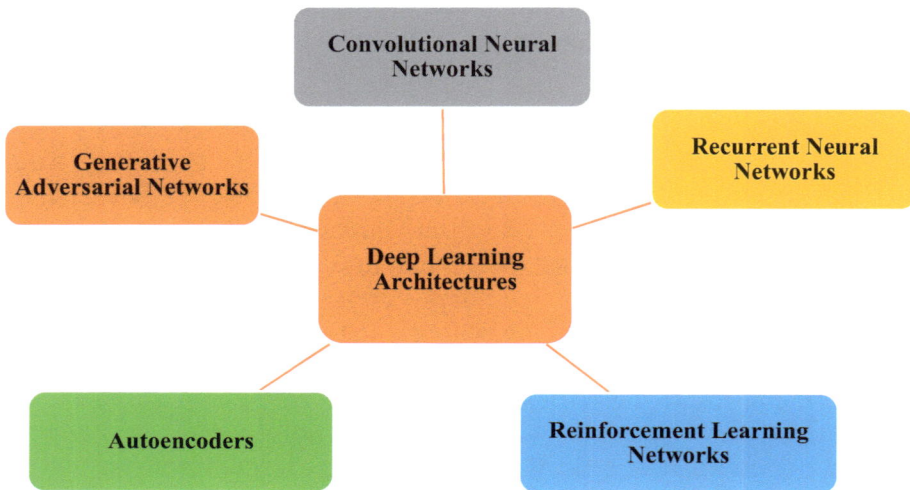

Fig. (6). Different types of deep learning architectures

3.1. Convolutional Neural Networks (CNNs)

A type of deep learning model called convolutional neural networks (CNNs) is made especially for handling structured grid data, mostly picture data. Drawn inspiration from the structure of the animal visual brain, they excel at tasks including object identification, picture segmentation, and recognition. CNNs are extensively utilized in many different sectors and have completely changed computer vision.

3.1.1. CNNs Architecture

A typical CNN has several layers (shown in Fig. **7**) in its design, including activation functions, pooling layers, convolutional layers, and fully connected layers. It is the advanced version of an artificial neural network.Convolution basically refers to a mathematical function where two different functions are multiplied to generate a third function. This is done to know how one function affects or changes the other function. Convolutional layers extract characteristics like edges and textures from input data by applying learnable filters. The feature maps are down-sampled by pooling layers, which lowers computational complexity without sacrificing crucial information. Classification is carried out by fully linked layers using the characteristics that have been retrieved, and the model may learn intricate patterns because activation functions provide the model with non-linearity [34, 35].

3.1.2. Components of CNNs

Convolutional Layers: These layers use kernels or learnable filters to apply convolution operations on the input data. As filters are applied to the input picture, local patterns and characteristics are extracted. Convolutional layers enable the network to learn increasingly complicated representations by capturing the spatial hierarchies of data. Mathematically, the operation of a convolutional layer is specified by equation 1.

$$y[i,j] = \Sigma_{m,n} x[i+m, j+n] . k[m,n] \qquad (1)$$

where x is the input, k is the kernel, and y is the output feature map.

Pooling Layers: Convolutional layers provide feature maps, which are then down-sampled by pooling layers to reduce their spatial dimensions. Average and maximum pooling are two common pooling procedures. By keeping relevant data and eliminating unnecessary features, pooling helps lower computing complexity and manage overfitting.

Fully Connected Layers: Fully connected layers, link every neuron in one layer to every other layer's neuron. The high-level characteristics that the convolutional and pooling layers extracted are used by these layers to conduct classification. The final output predictions are generated by fully linked layers, which are normally located at the conclusion of the CNN design.

To efficiently train and extract features from input data and provide correct predictions and classifications in a variety of tasks, including object detection, semantic segmentation, and picture recognition, each of these elements is essential to the design of CNNs.

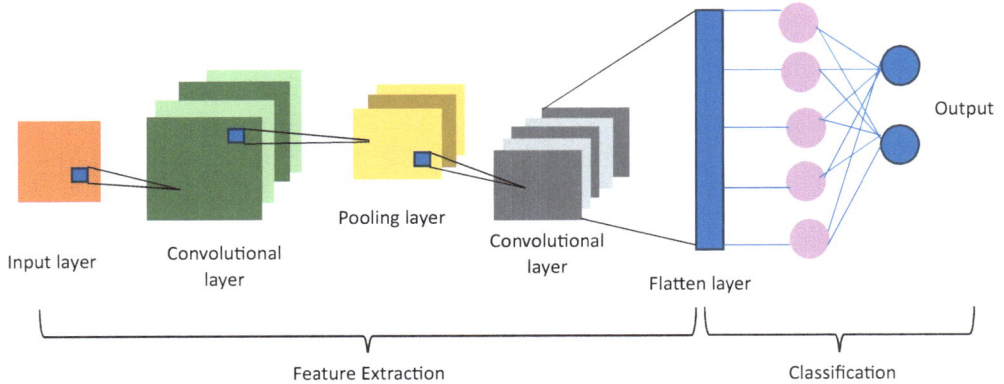

Fig. (7). Architecture of convolutional neural network.

3.1.3. Types of CNNs

LeNet: The first CNN design, LeNet was put out by Yann LeCun *et al*. and was mainly intended for handwritten digit recognition. Convolutional layers make up the first three layers, then pooling layers and fully linked layers. LeNet popularized the idea of employing pooling layers to reduce dimensionality and convolutional layers to extract features. LeNet, however simple in comparison to contemporary designs, is nonetheless a major player in the deep learning space and set the stage for further advancements in convolutional neural networks [36].

AlexNet: In 2012, AlexNet—introduced by Alex Krizhevsky *et al*.—won the ImageNet Large Scale Visual Recognition Challenge (ILSVRC), signaling a significant advancement in picture categorization. It has a deep network consisting of several pooling and convolutional layers, then fully linked layers. Large-scale image recognition tasks performed better once CNN architectures were made far more complicated and deep by AlexNet. Due to its success, convolutional neural networks have been the subject of more study, demonstrating the promise of deep learning [36].

VGGNet: The University of Oxford's Visual Geometry Group created VGGNet, which is renowned for its consistent architecture and ease of use. Multiple convolutional layers with tiny 3x3 filters make up this structure, which is then followed by fully linked and pooling layers. Easy implementation and comprehension are made possible by VGGNet's uniform structure, which has a constant kernel size and stride. The relevance of depth in convolutional neural networks is demonstrated by VGGNet, which demonstrated competitive performance in image classification tests despite having a high number of parameters, increasing its computing cost [36].

ResNet: Kaiming He *et al.* proposed ResNet, short for Residual Network, to solve the problem of training very deep networks by including residual connections, also known as skip connections. Through these connections, the network may avoid particular levels, which helps mitigate the issue of vanishing gradients and makes it easier to train very deep networks that have hundreds of layers. ResNet's architecture is made up of residual blocks that have identity mappings after several convolutional layers. ResNet performed at the cutting edge in a variety of image recognition tasks and had a major impact on later advancements in convolutional neural networks by making it possible for deeper networks to be trained successfully [37].

Inception (GoogLeNet): Within the same layer, inception modules conduct simultaneous convolutions of varying kernel sizes. Inception is commonly referred to as GoogLeNet. The network's representational strength is increased while preserving computational efficiency because of its architecture, which allows it to simultaneously record information at several sizes. Inception modules are made up of max pooling operations and convolutional layers with 1x1, 3x3, and 5x5 filters. Utilizing multi-scale features effectively allowed Inception to save processing resources while attaining state-of-the-art performance on many picture classification benchmarks. Its original modules served as an inspiration for later architectures that maximized convolutional neural networks' ability to use computing resources [37].

MobileNet: Designed for effective inference on mobile and embedded devices with limited processing resources, is a MobileNet. Depthwise separable convolutions are employed, which divide the typical convolution into depthwise and pointwise convolutions, hence lowering the computational cost without sacrificing accuracy. Applicable to a range of applications on devices with limited resources, MobileNet designs like MobileNetV1, MobileNetV2, and MobileNetV3 provide distinct trade-offs between efficiency and accuracy [38].

EfficientNet: To improve performance, Efficient Net offers a revolutionary compound scaling technique that consistently increases the depth, breadth, and resolution of the network. EfficientNet surpasses prior networks in efficiency while achieving state-of-the-art accuracy on image classification tasks by striking a balance between model size and computational cost. A range of models with varying depth, width, and resolution are represented by EfficientNet-B0 through EfficientNet-B7, giving customers the option to select the right model size depending on their computing needs and performance specifications [39].

DenseNet: The highly linked layers of DenseNet, also known as Dense Convolutional Network, are distinguished by the feed-forward connections between each layer and every other layer. Features propagate more widely and parameters operate more efficiently because of this connection structure, which also promotes feature reuse and improves gradient flow across the network. Because of DenseNet's dense connection, deeper networks may be built with fewer parameters by promoting feature reuse and mitigating the vanishing gradient issue. Strong performance has been shown by DenseNet designs, including DenseNet-121, DenseNet-169, and DenseNet-201, on a variety of image classification and detection tasks [40].

SqueezeNet: Compared to conventional CNN designs, SqueezeNet seeks to achieve great performance with a comparatively small number of parameters. It uses a unique design with fire modules, which reduce the amount of parameters while maintaining accuracy. They are made up of squeeze layers followed by expand layers. Due to its small design, SqueezeNet may be used for real-time applications and devices with limited resources. SqueezeNet provides an effective solution for problems like object identification and picture classification in contexts with constrained computing resources by striking a balance between model size and performance [41].

NASNet: Neural Architecture Search Network, or NASNet is a family of CNN designs that are automatically found using neural architecture search (NAS) methods. In order to find network topologies that yield high accuracy on picture classification tasks, NASNet searches a broad search area. It presents cell-based topologies in which the final network is formed by stacking repeated cells. The architectures of NASNet perform well across a range of datasets and show how automated architectural search techniques may be used to create CNNs that are efficient for a given set of requirements [42].

3.1.4. Use Cases of CNNs

The CNNs are used in a wide range of applications, including:

- Image Classification: Identifying objects or patterns within images.
- Object Detection: Locating and classifying objects within images or videos.
- Semantic Segmentation: Assigning a class label to each pixel in an image, enabling a detailed understanding of its contents.
- Image Captioning: Generating natural language descriptions of images.
- Face Recognition: Identifying and verifying individuals based on facial features.

Further, CNNs have become a cornerstone of computer vision technology, providing unmatched performance in a variety of applications across several fields. Their capacity to autonomously derive hierarchical representations from unprocessed data has propelled progress in picture interpretation, opening doors for inventive uses in robotics, healthcare, and other fields.

3.2. Recurrent Neural Networks (RNNs)

Neural networks that handle sequential input while preserving an internal state or memory are known as recurrent neural networks or RNNs for short. With connections that create directed cycles, RNNs, as opposed to feedforward neural networks, are able to identify temporal relationships in the input. For jobs where the sequence of inputs counts, such as time series prediction, natural language processing (NLP), and speech recognition, this makes them ideal.

3.2.1. RNNs Architecture

An input layer, recurrent connections, and an output layer make up the three primary parts of an RNN's design (shown in Fig. **8**). Sequential data, such as timestamps in a time series or words in a phrase, is transmitted to the input layer. Unlike feed-forward networks, in RNNs, each input depends on the previously generated output from another layer to make decisions. Equal weight and bias value are added for each layer of the network. The network can keep track of previous inputs through recurrent connections, which spread information across time. The loops make sure that the information generated by these layers is preserved in the memory. Based on the acquired representations, the output layer produces predictions or classifications. During the training of the network, backpropagation is used, such that if an error is found, weights can be adjusted accordingly. Variations such as Gated Recurrent Units (GRUs) and Long Short-Term Memory (LSTM) networks address the shortcomings of ordinary RNNs, such as the vanishing gradient problem, in addition to the fundamental design [43, 44].

3.2.2. Types of RNNs

Long Short-Term Memory (LSTM): LSTM introduces gating methods and memory cells to alleviate the vanishing gradient problem and better capture long-term relationships in the data.

Gated Recurrent Unit (GRU): It works like an LSTM, but with a more straightforward design that combines the input and forget gates into a single update gate.

Bidirectional RNN: It captures information from past and future inputs by processing sequential data in both forward and backward directions.

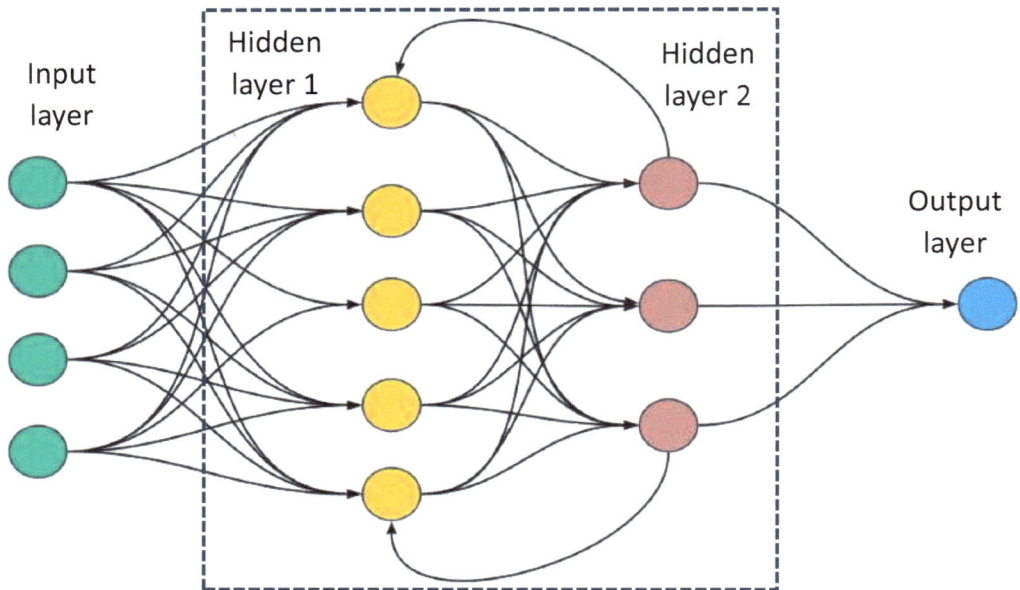

Fig. (8). Basic architecture of RNN.

Deep RNN: It learns hierarchical representations of sequential data by piling up layers of recurrent units.

3.2.3. Use Cases of RNNs

RNNs are used for a variety of sequential data-related activities, such as [45]:

1. Language modelling: LM is the process of creating text or foretelling a sentence's following word.
2. Machine translation: It is the process of translating text across languages.
3. Text-to-speech conversion: It is known as speech recognition.
4. Time series prediction: It is the process of estimating future values from past data.
5. Generating new musical sequences from pre-existing works is known as music generation.

3.3. Generative Adversarial Networks (GANs)

In 2014, Ian Goodfellow and associates presented it. GANs are made up of a generator and a discriminator neural network, which are trained concurrently *via* adversarial competition. The discriminator's job is to separate authentic data samples from those generated by the generator, whereas the generator's job is to make synthetic data that mimics actual data. Training helps the discriminator grow more adept at spotting fakes while teaching the generator how to provide data that is more realistic. Until the generator generates data that is identical to actual data and the discriminator is unable to discriminate between the two with any degree of reliability, this adversarial process is repeated.

In order to extract spatial hierarchies and patterns from picture input, convolutional layers are commonly used in GAN architectures. A sequence of up-sampling layers and activation functions are used by the generator to convert an input of a random noise vector into a structured output, such as a picture. The discriminator, on the other hand, processes generated and actual input *via* convolutional layers in order to provide binary classifications [46].

Many disciplines have advanced significantly as a result of GANs. They are utilized in computer vision for picture production, super-resolution, and style transfer, which involves transforming images from one style to another or producing high-quality images from low-resolution inputs. GANs are used in natural language processing for machine translation and text synthesis, resulting in content that is comprehensible and appropriate for its context. In the field of medicine, GANs are also used to forecast the course of disease and to generate medical pictures for training data augmentation. They are also employed in the entertainment sector to provide lifelike special effects and animations. Training GANs is still difficult despite their success because of problems including mode collapse and instability, although research is still being done to improve these models' resilience and generalizability [47, 48].

3.4. Autoencoders

An artificial neural network type called an autoencoder is used in unsupervised learning to acquire effective data representations, usually for feature extraction or dimensionality reduction. The encoder and the decoder are the two primary components that make up an autoencoder's architecture. By compressing the input data into a latent-space representation, the encoder effectively lowers the dimensionality of the data. The most notable aspects of the incoming data are captured by this condensed form, also known as the bottleneck. Next, using this compressed representation as a starting point, the decoder reconstructs the original data with the goal of generating an output that closely resembles the original input [49].

For applications like data denoising, anomaly detection, and picture compression, autoencoders are very helpful. Through the process of learning to ignore noise and concentrate on the underlying patterns found in the data, undesired variations may be efficiently removed. By evaluating reconstruction error, autoencoders may find anomalous patterns in data that considerably depart from the norm in anomaly detection. A prominent form that introduces a probabilistic method to encoding and enables the creation of fresh data samples is called Variational Autoencoders (VAEs). Because of this, VAEs are very useful in applications such as data augmentation and picture production. All things considered, autoencoders are an effective tool in the deep learning toolbox that promotes improvements across a range of fields and allows for effective data representation [50].

3.5. Reinforcement Learning Networks

A key field in deep learning is called reinforcement learning (RL), which focuses on teaching agents to interact with their surroundings and make a series of decisions. RL's core tenet is that ideal behaviors are discovered *via* trial and error, with incentives and punishments serving as guides. In reinforcement learning (RL), an agent learns directly from the results of its actions with the goal of maximizing cumulative reward over time. This is in contrast to supervised learning, where models learn from a dataset of labeled instances.

A policy network and a value network are common components of an RL network's design. In essence, the policy network directs the agent's behavior by mapping states to actions. The value network helps the agent assess the long-term advantages of its actions by estimating the expected reward of a state or state-action pair.

Uses: RL is utilized in autonomous cars for navigation and decision-making, in robots for control tasks, and in finance for portfolio management. Because RL can learn complicated behaviors and adapt to changing settings, it is an effective tool for tackling real-world issues where making the best decisions is essential [51, 52].

2.3.6 Transformers

In 2017, another architecture of deep networks came into the picture, called transformers. These networks are based on an attention mechanism, which is so powerful that they have replaced RNNs and CNNs. The input is divided into a number of tokens and through the self-attention mechanism, the model finds the most relevant input sequence. All the identified tokens are then processed in parallel, making these networks more efficient and computationally faster. The transformers also consist of the encoder-decoder phase as mentioned below:

• Encoder: The input sequence is processed by this phase and then contextual representations are generated.

- Decoder: Based on the encoded and previous outputs, the decoder generates the output sequence.

The final layer of the decoder uses the softmax function and generates predictions token-wise.

The potential applications of transformers are- BERT and GPT models, which are popularly being utilized by almost every sector like sentiment analysis, google translators, SQuAd benchmarks, *etc*. In 2018, google introduced bidirectional encoder representation from transformers, known as BERT for processing natural languages. It has the potential to perform processing of the text bi-directionally making it understand the context of words in an efficient way. It is used in a Google search engine to improve the search query and to generate more meaningful and relevant results. At the same time, this model has a major challenge in that it is computationally expensive due to its complex nature and large size.

Another advanced version of transformers is large language models that are trained on huge amounts of text data such that they can understand and generate human language. GPT (generative pre-trained transformer) was developed by OpenAI and is extremely popular among users because it has solution to every question being asked. Still, work is going on to improve the functionality of GPT.

4. DEEP LEARNING FRAMEWORKS FOR MODEL DEVELOPMENT

To create, train, and implement deep learning models, deep learning frameworks are necessary resources. By offering pre-built modules and APIs, these frameworks make it easier to create complicated neural networks, freeing up researchers and developers to concentrate more on experimentation and creativity rather than the complexities of creating algorithms from the ground up. The following are a few of the most widely used deep learning frameworks:

- **TensorFlow**: TensorFlow is one of the most popular deep learning frameworks, developed by Google Brain. A wide range of machine learning and deep learning methods are supported, and it provides adaptable, powerful tools for model building. TensorFlow is renowned for its scalability, which enables the deployment of models on a range of platforms, including large-scale distributed systems and mobile devices. Additionally, TensorFlow Serving for model deployment in production and TensorFlow Lite for mobile and embedded devices are included.
- **PyTorch**: PyTorch, developed by Facebook's AI Research team, is well-known for its dynamic computational graph, which, in contrast to static graphs, enables

more flexible and intuitive model creation. PyTorch's simplicity and ease of use make it perfect for research and quick prototyping, which is why it is so popular in both academia and industry. Hugging Face's Transformers for natural language processing and TorchVision for computer vision tasks are just two examples of the vast ecosystem of libraries and tools that the framework offers, along with support for distributed training.

- **Keras**: Keras, which was first created as a stand-alone project, is now incorporated as TensorFlow's high-level API. Keras's modular architecture and user-friendly interface make neural network construction and training easier. Recurrent networks, convolutional networks, and mixtures of the two are supported, and it is frequently used for quick experimentation and prototyping. Keras is easy to use even for novices, and its extensive features allow for a sophisticated study.

- **MXNet**: MXNet is an open-source deep learning framework with scalability and efficiency built in by the Apache Software Foundation. It offers flexibility for model building by supporting imperative and symbolic programming. Large-scale deep learning applications can benefit from MXNet's support for distributed computing and effective memory use. Also, it is the selected deep learning.

- **Deeplearning4j (DL4J)**: A deep learning framework designed for the Java Virtual Machine (JVM) is called DL4J. It works well with large data frameworks like Apache Spark and Hadoop and is intended for usage in the industry. DL4J may be used to deploy deep learning models in commercial settings and supports distributed training on both CPUs and GPUs.

Each of these frameworks has advantages over the others and serves a variety of purposes, ranging from large-scale production deployment to research and quick prototyping. The selection of a framework is typically contingent upon the particular project specifications, level of experience, and available computing resources [53 - 55].

5. APPLICATIONS OF AI AND DEEP LEARNING MODELS

Deep learning models and artificial intelligence (AI) are automating processes, improving decision-making, and offering deeper insights, transforming a number of sectors as depicted in Fig. (**9**). They support illness diagnosis, patient outcome prediction, and therapy personalization in the healthcare industry. Through the analysis of massive datasets, they enhance risk management, algorithmic trading, and fraud detection in the financial industry. Deep learning is used by the car industry to improve efficiency and safety in autonomous vehicles. AI helps retail through dynamic pricing, inventory control, and tailored suggestions. Applications of natural language processing (NLP), such as chatbots and virtual assistants, enhance information availability and consumer interactions. Artificial intelligence (AI) in agriculture helps with precision farming, crop health monitoring, and yield prediction, which increases sustainability and production. In general, deep learning and AI outgrowth innovation in a variety of fields by resolving challenging issues and generating new opportunities [56, 57].

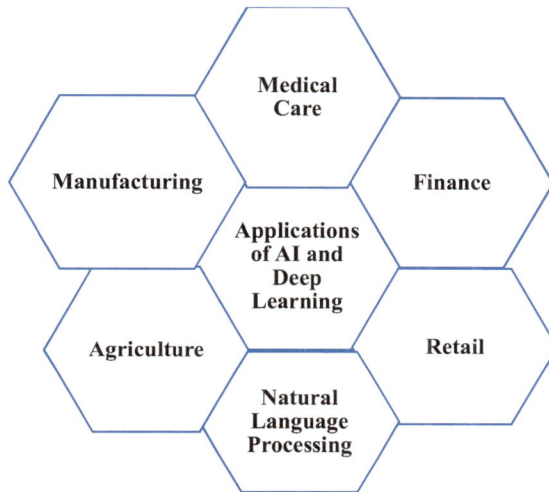

Fig. (9). Showing different application areas of artificial intelligence and machine learning.

6. FUTURE TRENDS AND CHALLENGES OF AI AND DEEP LEARNING

Deep learning and artificial intelligence (AI) are developing quickly, spurring innovation in many industries. Explainable AI (XAI), which improves openness and confidence in AI judgments, particularly in healthcare and finance, is one of the major themes. Edge AI is emerging to facilitate real-time decision-making necessary for applications such as smart homes and autonomous driving. Edge AI processes data locally on devices. By using dispersed devices to train models without exchanging raw data, federated learning improves privacy. AI is becoming more and more involved in customized medicine, helping to customize care for each patient. Through prediction and optimization applications, artificial intelligence (AI) is progressively tackling environmental concerns and climate change. Advanced Natural Language Processing (NLP) also enhancing human-computer interactions.

Deep learning and AI are facing a number of difficulties despite their encouraging developments. Because large volumes of data are needed, strong anonymization and handling techniques are essential, making data privacy and security crucial. AI decision-making's bias and fairness are important concerns, particularly in delicate domains like recruiting and law enforcement, where equitable solutions are needed. Scalability is a problem as well since training models require a lot of processing power, necessitating the use of increasingly advanced hardware and methods. Ethical issues necessitate precise rules and procedures, including employment displacement and improper use of AI. Innovation and safety must be balanced in the development of legislation and standards. Technical challenges still include ensuring model generality and robustness and incorporating AI into current infrastructures can be expensive and time-consuming.

CONCLUSION

Deep learning is one quickly developing field in machine learning. Its rapid development over a few years is attested to by the multitude of applications stated above. The range of industries that utilize these algorithms attests to their versatility. Deep learning has the potential to be an important security tool in the future since it integrates facial and speech recognition. Beyond this, the study of digital image processing has other uses. For these reasons, along with the fact that deep learning has shown to be a really optimized process, deep learning is a cutting-edge field in artificial intelligence research. In the next chapters, potential applications of these networks are defined in different sectors-agriculture, cybersecurity, healthcare, and education.

REFERENCES

[1]   F.J. Kurfess, *Artificial Intelligence.* Encycl. Phys. Sci. Technol, 2003, pp. 609-629.
      [http://dx.doi.org/10.1016/B0-12-227410-5/00027-2]

[2]   M.H. Huang, and R.T. Rust, "Artificial Intelligence in Service", *J. Serv. Res.,* vol. 21, no. 2, pp. 155-172, 2018.
      [http://dx.doi.org/10.1177/1094670517752459]

[3]   H. Salehi, and R. Burgueño, "Emerging artificial intelligence methods in structural engineering", *Eng. Struct.,* vol. 171, pp. 170-189, 2018.
      [http://dx.doi.org/10.1016/j.engstruct.2018.05.084]

[4]   Z. Gao, and X. Wang, *Deep learning,* 2019.
      [http://dx.doi.org/10.1007/978-981-13-9113-2_16]

[5]   G.E. Hinton, S. Osindero, and Y.W. Teh, "A fast learning algorithm for deep belief nets", *Neural Comput.,* vol. 18, no. 7, pp. 1527-1554, 2006.
      [http://dx.doi.org/10.1162/neco.2006.18.7.1527] [PMID: 16764513]

[6]   J. Karhunen, T. Raiko, and K.H. Cho, *Unsupervised deep learning: A short review.* Adv. Indep. Compon. Anal. Learn. Mach, 2015, pp. 125-142.
      [http://dx.doi.org/10.1016/B978-0-12-802806-3.00007-5]

[7]   I.H. Sarker, "Deep Cybersecurity: A Comprehensive Overview from Neural Network and Deep Learning Perspective", *SN Computer Science,* vol. 2, no. 3, p. 154, 2021.
      [http://dx.doi.org/10.1007/s42979-021-00535-6] [PMID: 33778771]

[8]   I.H. Sarker, "Deep Learning: A Comprehensive Overview on Techniques, Taxonomy, Applications and Research Directions", *SN Computer Science,* vol. 2, no. 6, p. 420, 2021.
      [http://dx.doi.org/10.1007/s42979-021-00815-1] [PMID: 34426802]

[9]   G.D. Kovacs, L.F. Tepelea, and C. Cret, "A Comparative Study of Traditional and Deep Learning Methods in Image Depth Measuring", *2023 17th Int. Conf. Eng. Mod. Electr. Syst. EMES 2023,* pp. 1-4, 2023.
[http://dx.doi.org/10.1109/EMES58375.2023.10171686]

[10]   X. Xie, W. He, Y. Zhu, and H. Xu, "Performance Evaluation and Analysis of Deep Learning Frameworks", *ACM Int. Conf. Proceeding Ser,* pp. 38-44, 2022.
[http://dx.doi.org/10.1145/3573942.3573948]

[11]   "A Comprehensive Overview and Comparative Analysis on Deep Learning Models: CNN, RNN, LSTM, GRU",
[http://dx.doi.org/10.48550/ARXIV.2305.17473]

[12]   M.M. Najafabadi, F. Villanustre, T.M. Khoshgoftaar, N. Seliya, R. Wald, and E. Muharemagic, "Deep learning applications and challenges in big data analytics", *J. Big Data,* vol. 2, no. 1, p. 1, 2015.
[http://dx.doi.org/10.1186/s40537-014-0007-7]

[13]   S. Surya, and A. Muthukumaravel, "Significance of Deep Learning in Artificial Intelligence Systems", *2023 9th Int. Conf. Adv. Comput. Commun. Syst.,* pp. 2220-2223, 2023.
[http://dx.doi.org/10.1109/ICACCS57279.2023.10112723]

[14]   T. Räz, and C. Beisbart, "The Importance of Understanding Deep Learning", *Erkenn,* vol. 89, pp. 1823-1840, 2024.
[http://dx.doi.org/10.1007/s10670-022-00605-y]

[15]   I. Drori, "Foundations", *Sci. Deep Learn.,* no. Aug, pp. 1-2, 2022.
[http://dx.doi.org/10.1017/9781108891530.002]

[16]   S. Pattanayak, "Mathematical Foundations", *Pro Deep Learn. with TensorFlow,* vol. 2, no. 0, pp. 1-108, 2023.
[http://dx.doi.org/10.1007/978-1-4842-8931-0_1]

[17]   A. Delgado, and D. M. Rius, *Foundations of artificial intelligence and machine learning.*

[18]   J. Schneider, "Foundation models in brief: A historical, socio-technical focus", Accessed: May 25, 2024. Available from: https://lambdalabs.com/blog/demystifying-gpt-3

[19]   S. Skansi, and M. Kardum, "A Prolegomenon on the Philosophical Foundations of Deep Learning as Theory of (Artificial) Intelligence", *Disputatio philosophica,* vol. 23, no. 1, pp. 89-99, 2022.
[http://dx.doi.org/10.32701/dp.23.1.6]

[20]   M.D. Sadanand, and D. Sachin Bhosale, "Basic of Artificial Neural Network", *International Journal of Advanced Research in Science, Communication and Technology,* vol. 3, no. 3, pp. 299-303, 2023.
[http://dx.doi.org/10.48175/IJARSCT-8159]

[21]   S. Chakraverty, D.M. Sahoo, and N.R. Mahato, *Artificial Neural Network Terminologies.* Concepts Soft Comput, 2019, pp. 153-165.
[http://dx.doi.org/10.1007/978-981-13-7430-2_10]

[22]   https://www.khanacademy.org/science/biology/human-biology/neuron-nervous-system/a/overview of-neuron-structure-and-function

[23]   M. Hanani, "Satellite glial cells in sensory ganglia: from form to function", *Brain Res. Rev.,* vol. 48, no. 3, pp. 457-476, 2005.
[http://dx.doi.org/10.1016/j.brainresrev.2004.09.001] [PMID: 15914252]

[24]   S. Kollmannsberger, D. D'Angella, M. Jokeit, and L. Herrmann, "Neural Networks", *Studies in Computational Intelligence,* vol. 977, pp. 19-45, 2021.
[http://dx.doi.org/10.1007/978-3-030-76587-3_3]

[25]   M. Aggarwal, and M.N. Murty, *Deep Learning.* SpringerBriefs Appl. Sci. Technol, 2021, pp. 35-66.
[http://dx.doi.org/10.1007/978-981-33-4022-0_3]

[26]   O.A. Montesinos López, A. Montesinos López, and J. Crossa, *Fundamentals of Artificial Neural Networks and Deep Learning.* Multivar. Stat. Mach. Learn. Methods Genomic Predict, 2022, pp. 379-425.
        [http://dx.doi.org/10.1007/978-3-030-89010-0_10]

[27]   S. Sharma, S. Sharma, and A. Athaiya, "Activation functions in neural networks", *International Journal of Engineering Applied Sciences and Technology,* vol. 4, no. 12, pp. 310-316, 2020.
        [http://dx.doi.org/10.33564/IJEAST.2020.v04i12.054]

[28]   A.S. Tomar, A. Sharma, A. Shrivastava, A.S. Rana, and P. Yadav, "A Comparative Analysis of Activation Function, Evaluating their Accuracy and Efficiency when Applied to Miscellaneous Datasets", *Proc. 2nd Int. Conf. Appl. Artif. Intell. Comput. ICAAIC 2023,* pp. 1035-1042, 2023.
        [http://dx.doi.org/10.1109/ICAAIC56838.2023.10140823]

[29]   G. Chakraborty, N. Shiratori, and S. Noguchi, "A quickly trained ANN with single hidden layer Gaussian units", pp. 466–472, Mar. 1993.
        [http://dx.doi.org/10.1109/ICNN.1993.298602]

[30]   S. Maldonado, C. Vairetti, K. Jara, M. Carrasco, and J. López, "OWAdapt: An adaptive loss function for deep learning using OWA operators", 2023.

[31]   J. Du, X. Zhang, P. Liu, C. M. Vong, and T. Wang, "An Adaptive Deep Metric Learning Loss Function for Class-Imbalance Learning via Intraclass Diversity and Interclass Distillation", *IEEE Trans. neural networks Learn. Syst.,* pp. 466-472, 1993.
        [http://dx.doi.org/10.1109/TNNLS.2023.3286484]

[32]   "Loss Functions and Metrics in Deep Learning. A Review", 2023
        [http://dx.doi.org/10.48550/ARXIV.2307.02694]

[33]   M. Almasi, "Deep Learning and Neural Networks: Methods and Applications", *Innov. Comput. Sci. Eng.,* no. Jun, 2023.
        [http://dx.doi.org/10.59646/csebookc8/004]

[34]   A. Zarándy, A. Horváth, and P. Szolgay, "CNN Technology-Tools and Applications", *IEEE Circuits Syst. Mag.,* vol. 18, no. 2, pp. 77-89, 2018.
        [http://dx.doi.org/10.1109/MCAS.2018.2821771]

[35]   S. Laroui, H. Omara, M. Lazaar, and O. Mahboub, "Comparative study of performing features applied in CNN architectures", 2019.
        [http://dx.doi.org/10.4108/eai.24-4-2019.2284238]

[36]   Y. Lecun, L. Bottou, Y. Bengio, and P. Haffner, *A B7CEDGF HIB7PRQTSUDGQICWVYX HIB edCdSISIXvg5r ` CdQTw XvefCdS,* 1998. http://ieeexplore.ieee.org/document/ 726791/#full-tex--section

[37]   K. He, X. Zhang, S. Ren, and J. Sun, "Deep residual learning for image recognition", *Proc. IEEE Comput. Soc. Conf. Comput. Vis. Pattern Recognit.,* pp. 770-778, 2016.
        [http://dx.doi.org/10.1109/CVPR.2016.90]

[38]   "MobileNetV1 Explained | Papers With Code." Accessed: May 25, 2024. [Online]. Available: https://paperswithcode.com/method/mobilenetv1

[39]   "EfficientNet Explained | Papers With Code." Accessed: May 25, 2024. [Online]. Available: https://paperswithcode.com/method/efficientnet

[40]   "DenseNet Explained | Papers With Code." Accessed: May 25, 2024. [Online]. Available: https://paperswithcode.com/method/densenet

[41]   "SqueezeNet Explained | Papers With Code." Accessed: May 25, 2024. [Online]. Available: https://paperswithcode.com/method/squeezenet

[42]   "NASNet | Papers With Code." Accessed: May 25, 2024. [Online]. Available: https://paperswithcode.com/model/nasnet?variant=nasnetalarge

[43]   S. Ahlawat, *Recurrent Neural Networks.* Reinf. Learn. Financ, 2023, pp. 177-232.
[http://dx.doi.org/10.1007/978-1-4842-8835-1_4]

[44]   S. Ahlawat, "Reinforcement Learning for Finance", *Reinf. Learn. Financ,* 2023.
[http://dx.doi.org/10.1007/978-1-4842-8835-1]

[45]   https://www.researchgate.net/publication/277603865_A_Critical_Review_of_Recurrent_Neural_Netw
orks_for_Sequence_Learning

[46]   X. Bi, K. Guo, J. He, and X. Jing, "Application and review of generative adversarial networks", , vol.
12348, pp. 1234809-1234809, 2022.
[http://dx.doi.org/10.1117/12.2641605]

[47]   K.Y. Hsieh, H.C. Tsai, and G.Y. Chen, "Generation of High-resolution Lung Computed Tomography
Images using Generative Adversarial Networks", *Proc. Annu. Int. Conf. IEEE Eng. Med. Biol. Soc.
EMBS,* pp. 2400-2403, 2020.
[http://dx.doi.org/10.1109/EMBC44109.2020.9176064]

[48]   T. Karras, S. Laine, and T. Aila, "A style-based generator architecture for generative adversarial
networks", *Proc. IEEE Comput. Soc. Conf. Comput. Vis. Pattern Recognit.,* pp. 4396-4405, 2019.
[http://dx.doi.org/10.1109/CVPR.2019.00453]

[49]   Y. Bengio, *Autoencoders, Unsupervised Learning, and Deep Architectures Pierre,* 2009.

[50]   A. Makandar, and K. Wangi, "Comparison and Analysis of Various Autoencoders", *Advances in
Intelligent Systems and Computing,* vol. 1348, no. Sep, pp. 67-76, 2023.
[http://dx.doi.org/10.1007/978-981-19-4676-9_6]

[51]   M. Beeks, R.R. Afshar, Y. Zhang, R. Dijkman, C. van Dorst, and S. de Looijer, "Deep Reinforcement
Learning for a Multi-Objective Online Order Batching Problem", *Proc. Int. Conf. Autom. Plan. Sched.
ICAPS,* vol. vol. 32, pp. 435-443, 2022.
[http://dx.doi.org/10.1609/icaps.v32i1.19829]

[52]   R.R. Afshar, J. Rhuggenaath, Y. Zhang, and U. Kaymak, "An Automated Deep Reinforcement
Learning Pipeline for Dynamic Pricing", *IEEE Trans. Artif. Intell.,* vol. 4, no. 3, pp. 428-437, 2023.
[http://dx.doi.org/10.1109/TAI.2022.3186292]

[53]   D.Y. Perwej, "An Evaluation of Deep Learning Miniature Concerning in Soft Computing", *Int. J. Adv.
Res. Comput. Commun. Eng.,* no. Feb, pp. 10-16, 2015.
[http://dx.doi.org/10.17148/IJARCCE.2015.4203]

[54]   https://typeset.io/papers/deep-learning-frameworks-1l4zrpn5

[55]   "Deep Learning Frameworks", *Artif. Intell. Technol.,* no. Oct, pp. 123-135, 2023.
[http://dx.doi.org/10.1007/978-981-19-2879-6_4]

[56]   M. Vogt, "An Overview of Deep Learning and Its Applications", *Proceedings,* no. Jan, pp. 178-202,
2019.
[http://dx.doi.org/10.1007/978-3-658-23751-6_17]

[57]   R. Sharma, and V. Mehan, "Skin Disease Detection Using Image Processing and Soft Computing",
ECS Trans., vol. 107, no. 1, pp. 17051-17061, 2022.
[http://dx.doi.org/10.1149/10701.17051ecst]

CHAPTER 3

Smart Fields: Revolutionizing Agriculture with Artificial Intelligence

Abstract: Artificial intelligence has embarked on significant changes in various fields and agriculture is one of them. This chapter is focused on the transformative effects of artificial intelligence (AI) on modern agriculture with an emphasis on how it has improved sustainability and completely disrupted farming methods. Precision agriculture is the second name given to modern farming that includes various tools and technologies to monitor and optimize agricultural production processes. It helps farmers to maximise crop yields, and environmental impact, and use resources more efficiently. Soil analysis, crop monitoring, disease and pest detection, and autonomous machinery are some of the major applications that are covered here. AI-powered imaging systems are essential for early disease diagnosis and management in crop management. These technologies enable prompt actions *via* early detection of disease or pest infestation indicators. In order to ensure improved crop health and increased yields, machine learning algorithms examine trends in plant health and suggest suitable remedies. AI models also help farmers plan more efficiently for storage, marketing, and distribution by predicting crop yields based on a variety of parameters, including weather data, soil conditions, and plant health. Also, Artificial Intelligence (AI) guarantees that crops are transported and sold efficiently, decreasing waste and increasing farmer profitability by anticipating demand and optimising logistics and distribution. Supply chain optimisation powered by AI improves agricultural operations' overall sustainability and efficiency. The chapter explores computer vision, predictive analytics, and machine learning algorithms, showing how these technologies support real-time interventions and data-driven decision-making.

Keywords: Crop monitoring, Plant diseases, Predictive analysis, Robotic farming, Sowing seeds, Smart irrigation.

1. INTRODUCTION

It is expected that by the year 2050, the population of the planet will become 10 billion approximately. It will put tremendous pressure on the agricultural industry so as to boost up yields of the crops and productivity [1 - 4]. There are two possible strategies that can be adopted to find the solution to this problem. Either the land size can be increased or implement large-scale farming to foster the production on current farmland. Both solutions can be used to fulfill the growing food demand of the increasing population. Artificial Intelligence (AI) has emerged as a new wave of innovation in the past few decades that has the capability to completely transform this sector [5]. It has shown itself to be a transformative force that can address many issues faced by modern agriculture through its ability to process huge amounts of data and streamline processes. It can be applied in various applications of agriculture as shown in Fig. (**1**).

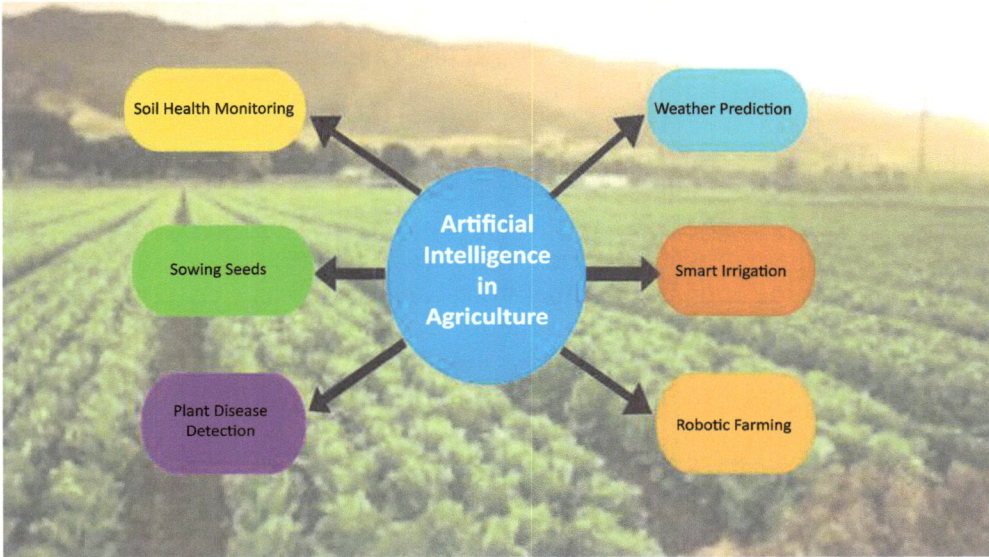

Fig. (1). Applications of AI in Agriculture.

AI has the capability to process huge amounts of data coming from various sources in real-time to give farmers important insights about crop health and soil conditions. In this manner, precision agriculture is brought into a more workable approach that allows maximum resource use of fertilizers and water in the process. AI can analyze big data sets from different sensors and satellites to enable farmers to gain useful insights regarding crop health [6 - 8], quality of soil, and weather conditions [9, 10]. This makes it possible to make precise decisions regarding fertilization, irrigation, and pesticide use to maximize the effectiveness of resources, while at the same time minimizing their effect on the environment. Another crucial application of AI in agriculture is crop monitoring, which provides in-the-moment field condition analysis and surveillance. Through the analysis of images obtained by drones or ground-based sensors, machine-learning algorithms can identify early indicators of diseases, insect infestations, and nutritional deficits. Early detection of these problems allows farmers to take focused measures to stop them from spreading, which lowers the need for chemical treatments and maintains crop quality [11 - 13]. In addition, farmers may track yields more precisely and optimise harvesting schedules for maximum freshness and market demand with the use of AI-enabled monitoring systems.

By offering precise weather forecasts and encouraging adaptable farming methods, AI strengthens resistance against climate change. AI-driven automation also takes care of the demand for productive and self-sufficient farm operations as labour shortages become more common. In addition, labour-intensive operations throughout the agricultural value chain are being revolutionised by AI-driven robotics and automation [14]. AI navigation algorithms in autonomous cars enable previously unheard-of levels of efficiency and precision when carrying out a variety of field tasks, including planting, weeding, and harvesting. Because these robotic solutions work for long hours without the need for human interaction, they not only improve productivity but also help address the labour problem on farms [15]. Furthermore, in smart irrigation systems, AI models can predict weather patterns with the help of which farmers can decide when and how much to irrigate based on upcoming rainfall, temperature, and humidity. AI-powered smart controllers can adjust the irrigation schedules automatically depending upon the data received in real-time. This ensures optimal water delivery without any human intervention.

AI is also revolutionising logistics and supply chain management in the agriculture industry. Predictive analytics algorithms are utilised to optimise distribution routes, storage facilities, and inventory levels by analysing past data, market trends, and external factors such as weather patterns. Artificial Intelligence (AI) helps minimise transportation costs, eliminate food spoilage, and assure timely delivery of agricultural products to customers worldwide by precisely anticipating demand and identifying potential bottlenecks [16].

1.2. Soil Health Monitoring

Good crops come from good soils, and healthy crops feed people and other animals. There is a direct correlation between food quality and quantity and soil quality. The food-producing plants depend on soil for vital nutrients, water, oxygen, and root support to grow and thrive (depicted in Fig. **2**). One or more soil issues may contribute to plant issues and poor development. Three major issues with soil are erosion, topsoil removal, and compaction (dense soil that drains water slowly). It will save you time and money and provide a healthier landscape if you assess your soil and make the required corrections and enhancements before planting [17, 18]. Once an area is planted, it is difficult to go back and fix bad soil conditions. Using artificial intelligence tools to monitor and control soil health in agricultural contexts is known as soil health monitoring with AI [19]. Informed decisions that can increase crop yields, maximise resource use, and support sustainable agricultural practices are made possible by the useful insights on soil quality that this technology provides to farmers and land managers.

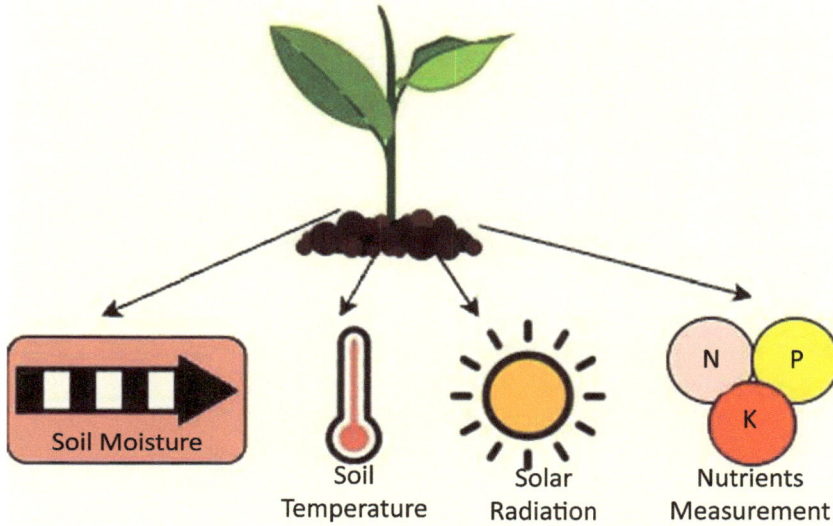

Fig. (2). AI in soil health monitoring.

Using sensor networks to gather data in real-time on soil moisture, temperature, pH, nutrient concentrations, and microbial activity is a crucial aspect of AI-powered soil health monitoring [20]. To capture geographical variability and guarantee thorough coverage, these sensors are frequently positioned strategically around the field or implanted in the soil. Farmers can detect possible problems like fertiliser shortages, compaction, or salinity accumulation by using AI algorithms to continuously monitor these factors and analyse patterns and trends. The enormous amounts of data produced by soil sensors are interpreted in large part by machine learning algorithms. These algorithms are used to build predictive models that can precisely assess soil health and forecast future results based on previous data on soil, crop performance, and environmental conditions. Farmers may make data-driven decisions about soil management practices by using AI algorithms that recognise patterns and run correlation analyses to uncover intricate links between crop performance and soil attributes [21 - 23].

Remote sensing is another area that can be used to monitor soil health [24]. Using various wavelengths, satellites fitted with sensors may take pictures of farmland. With the use of AI algorithms, these photos may be used to evaluate the health of the vegetation, spot nutrient shortages, locate erosion-prone locations, and track variations in soil moisture over time.

1.3. Plant Disease Detection

Plant diseases are a significant threat to agricultural productivity and food security worldwide. The early detection and identification of these diseases are crucial to prevent significant crop losses and ensure sustainable agricultural practices [25 - 27]. Traditional methods of plant disease detection rely on manual inspections, which can be time-consuming, error-prone, and often lead to delayed treatment. Table **1** represents the difference between plant disease detection using AI and conventional practices. This difference self explains why AI is coming into the picture. The advent of artificial intelligence (AI) and machine learning (ML) has revolutionized the field of plant disease detection by providing accurate, efficient, and scalable solutions.

Table 1. represents the difference between conventional and AI-based plant disease detection techniques.

Characteristics	Conventional Techniques	AI-Based Techniques
Speed	Time-consuming and labor-intensive	Fast and efficient.
Accuracy	Prone to human error	High accuracy and reliability.
Scalability	Limited to small-scale inspections	Scalable for large-scale agricultural operations.
Cost-Effectiveness	Resource-intensive and expensive	Cost-effective and efficient.
Real-Time Monitoring	Periodic inspections only	Real-time monitoring and early detection.
Integration with Other Technologies	Limited integration	Integrated with IoT sensors, drones, and satellite imaging.
Data Analysis and Insights	Limited data analysis	Provides detailed insights into disease patterns and environmental factors.
Early Detection and Prevention	Late detection and treatment	Early detection and prevention of disease spread.
Specialized Expertise	Requires extensive knowledge of plant pathology	Does not require specialized expertise.
Continuous Improvement	Static knowledge and methods	Continuously learns and improves from new data.

Diseases in plants are caused by various agents (shown in Fig. **3**). Biotic agents include various pathogens, nematodes and other insects.

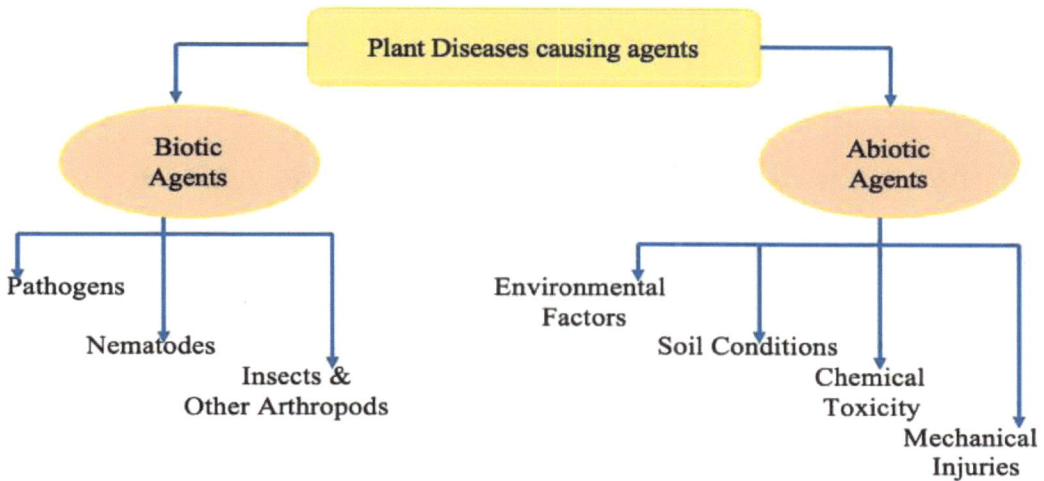

Fig. (3). Agents causing plant diseases.

- Pathogens: Fungi, bacteria, viruses, and protozoa can cause infectious diseases in plants. These pathogens can reproduce in the plant or on its surface, leading to the spread of disease [28 - 30].
- Nematodes: These microscopic worms can cause root damage, leading to symptoms like stunting, yellowing, and wilting.
- Insects and Other Arthropods: Insects and other arthropods can transmit diseases and cause physical damage to plants [31].

Abiotic agents [32, 33]include environmental conditions and several other factors mentioned below:

- Environmental Factors: Weather conditions like temperature, humidity, light, and water can contribute to plant stress and disease. For example, high temperatures can lead to heat stress, while excessive water can cause root rot.
- Soil Conditions: Soil structure, pH, and nutrient availability can affect plant health. Compaction, nutrient deficiencies, and toxicities can all lead to abiotic disease.
- Chemical Toxicity: Exposure to chemicals like pesticides, herbicides, and heavy metals can cause plant injury and disease.
- Mechanical Injuries: Physical damage from wind, hail, or other forces can cause injuries that can lead to diseases.

AI-based techniques, such as deep learning (DL) [34, 35], and computer vision (CV), have shown promising results in identifying plant abnormalities and infestations. These technologies can analyze digital images of plant leaves to detect diseases at an early stage, enabling farmers to take prompt action and prevent the spread of diseases. The integration of AI with other technologies such as IoT sensors, drones, and satellite imaging has further enhanced the accuracy and efficiency of disease detection.

1.3.1. Different Methods of AI Used in the Detection of Plant Diseases.

For the purpose of controlling and reducing the impact on agricultural output and quality, plant disease detection is essential. Plant diseases are diagnosed using a variety of approaches, from conventional visual inspection to sophisticated molecular and sensor-based procedures. A few commonly used techniques are depicted in Fig. (**4**).

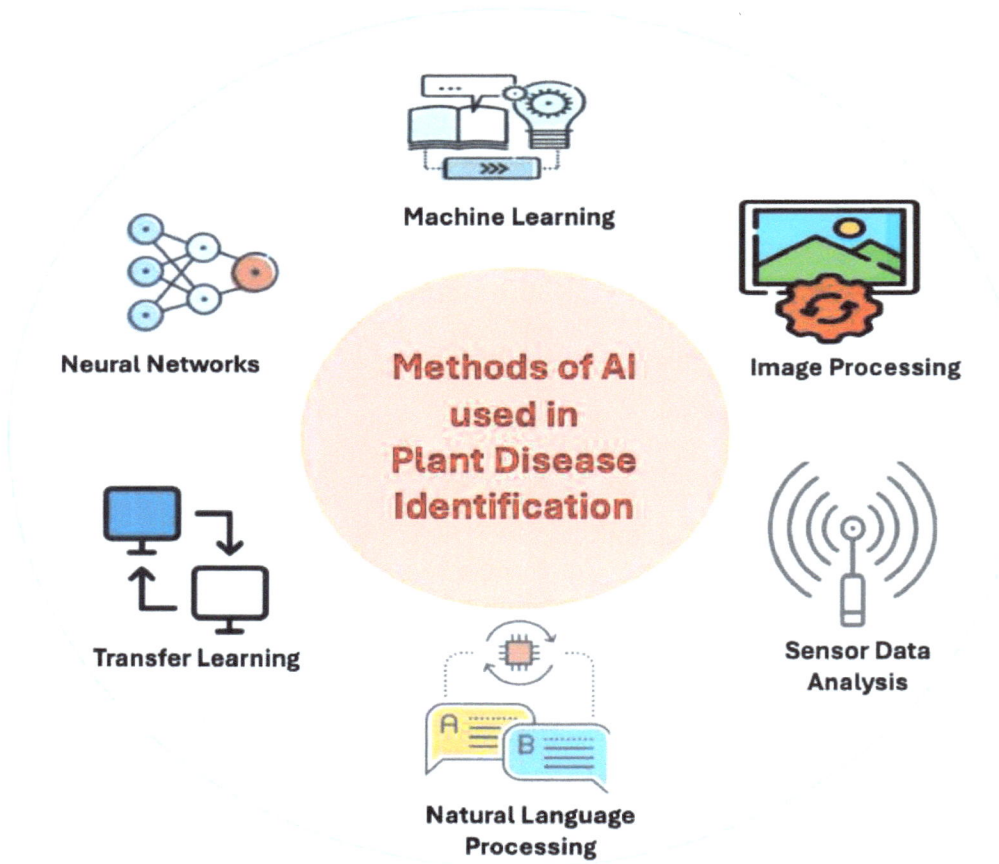

Fig. (4). Methods used in the detection of plant diseases.

Machine learning includes various algorithms which are trained on labelled datasets of healthy and diseased plants so that patterns can be identified and new data can be classified. Some commonly used algorithms are: Support Vector Machines (SVM) [36], Decision Trees [37], Random Forests [38], and K-Nearest Neighbours (KNN). These algorithms have shown promising results in classifying images of plant leaves to detect diseases, and predicting disease outbreaks based on environmental data [39, 40].

Image Processing [41 - 43]involves techniques for processing and analyzing images to extract meaningful information. Image segmentation, feature extraction, and texture analysis are the main techniques that help in identifying disease symptoms like spots, lesions, and discoloration on plant surfaces [44, 45]. AI models have the ability to analyze data from various sensors (*e.g.*, spectral, thermal, moisture) to detect anomalies indicative of disease. Early detection of stress or infection before visible symptoms appear is thereby predicted. Transfer Learning uses pre-trained models on large datasets and their fine-tuning is done for specific tasks. Its application involves adapting models trained on general plant disease datasets to specific crops or regions.

Natural Language Processing (NLP) helps in analyzing textual data such as scientific literature, farmer reports, and social media for disease surveillance. It also helps in identifying emerging disease threats and summarizing current knowledge on plant diseases. Convolutional Neural Networks (CNNs) are a type of deep learning model particularly effective for image analysis [46]. It helps in detecting and classifying diseases from images of leaves, stems, and fruits. Recurrent Neural Networks (RNNs) are another form of deep learning models that are suitable for sequential data and time-series analysis. Its application includes predicting disease spread over time based on historical data.

1.4. Sowing seeds

AI's incorporation into the planting procedure is revolutionary for modern farming. AI-driven solutions ensure that seeds are sown under ideal conditions by improving precision, efficiency, and sustainability, opening the door for greater agricultural yields and more resilient farming systems [47].

Fig. (**5**) is self-explanatory and shows how AI is being utilized in sowing seeds resulting in good and effective crop yield. To find the best time and place to plant, AI-driven algorithms examine large datasets that include crop requirements, weather patterns, and soil attributes. This guarantees that seeds are sown in an environment that optimises their growth potential.

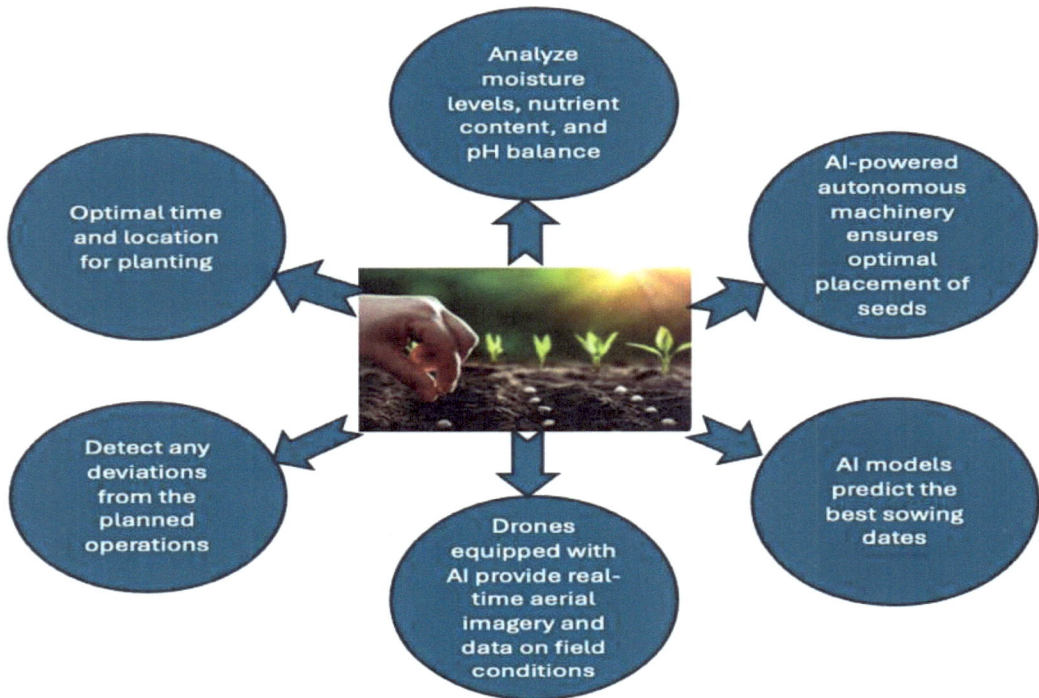

Fig. (5). How AI helps in sowing seeds.

- Machine learning algorithms evaluate pH balance, nutrient content, and moisture levels by processing data from soil sensors. Artificial Intelligence facilitates farmers' understanding of field variability by producing comprehensive soil maps. These realisations enable variable rate seeding, in which the density of the seeds is modified based on the properties of the soil to guarantee consistent growth and economical utilisation of resources.
- AI-powered machines are equipped with GPS and computer vision technologies to navigate fields with high precision. AI algorithms control the depth and spacing of seeds, ensuring optimal placement.
- AI models forecast the ideal planting dates to minimise bad weather and maximise germination rates by examining past data and the state of the environment today. By assisting farmers in scheduling their plantings, these forecasts lower the possibility that crops would fail due to unanticipated weather.

1.5. Weather Prediction

Two important aspects of agriculture are decision and planning which are directly related to good crop yield. However, abrupt changes in the climate or weather conditions directly affect these two aspects. Farmers depend on fast and accurate weather forecasts to help them make well-informed decisions about planting, irrigation, harvesting, and pest management. They can optimise their operations and reduce the risks associated with unfavourable weather conditions by utilising AI-driven weather prediction models, which provide accuracy and dependability. A fuzzy logic model was developed [48] to examine the effects of climate change on agricultural output. It was designed so that farmers can make quick decisions at the right time to prevent any kind of damage to crops due to extremely bad weather conditions and achieved a 97% judgement rate.Some author worked on AI-enabled wind power forecasting system that enhances deterministic prediction and offers probabilistic information[49]. Estimates of extreme events, such as icing, strong winds, and extremely high temperatures, are provided by other modules. Similarly, a study showed that the application of AI approaches combined with a physical understanding of the environment can lead to a significant improvement in the ability to predict various high-impact weather types [50]. The workflow diagram depicted in Fig. (**6**) tells how AI can be used to predict weather conditions.

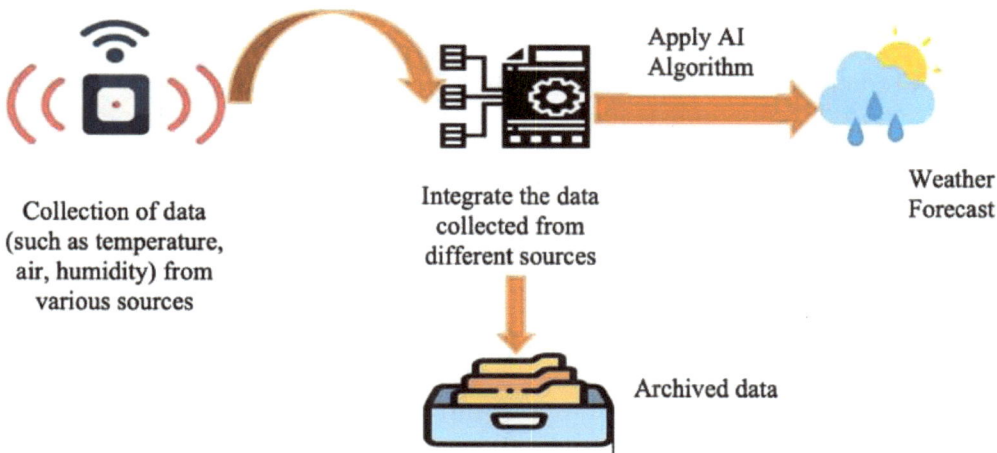

Fig. (6). Generalized method to predict weather conditions using AI.

A few research works are also carried out where accurate weather forecasts help farmers to manage their crops more effectively, by providing information regarding plant density, crop rotation, and soil management techniques. It can help farmers in choosing the ideal times to carry out different tasks such as planting seeds, applying fertiliser, and carrying out other crucial chores. Weather monitoring can be done in different ways mentioned below:

1.5.1. Monitoring the Weather in Real Time

Real-time weather monitoring and updates can be provided by AI-powered systems, giving farmers early warning of shifting weather patterns. Making quick decisions, like modifying irrigation schedules in the event of unexpected rain or shielding crops from sharp temperature decreases, depends on this real-time information. Crop resilience and productivity can be greatly increased by having the capacity to react swiftly to changes in the weather.

1.5.2. Long-Term and Seasonal Forecasting

By examining past climatic data and present weather trends, AI models are skilled at producing seasonal and long-term weather forecasts. Farmers may better plan their agricultural cycles, choose suitable crop kinds, and choose the best dates to plant and harvest their crops with the aid of these forecasts. For example, farmers may grow crops resistant to drought or make investments in effective irrigation systems if they anticipate a dry season.

1.5.3. Using Predictive Analytics to Manage Risk

AI can assist farmers in evaluating and managing the risks associated with extreme weather events, such as floods, droughts, and storms, by combining weather prediction with predictive analytics. AI algorithms can forecast the possibility and possible consequences of these occurrences, enabling farmers to take precautionary action. AI, for instance, can predict when a drought will start, allowing farmers to conserve water or postpone planting until the weather improves.

1.6. Smart Irrigation

A healthy economy requires effective water management as a fundamental component. All across the globe, people are working on sustainable agriculture practices. Irrigation system is one of the important tasks performed by farmers. The conventional methods of an irrigation system require a lot of effort and wastage of water too. A greater awareness of the operation environment and the operation activities is made possible by the data generated by modern agricultural operations from a number of sensors. Smart irrigation [51 - 53] is an innovative technology for controlling water use in gardening, landscaping, and agriculture. It helps in reducing water application by using a variety of sensors, data analytics, and automated systems to make sure plants get the proper amount of water at the right time. Enhancing crop yields, lowering environmental impact, increasing water use efficiency, and reducing water-related expenditures are the main objectives of smart irrigation. AI algorithms analyze data from various sources, including soil moisture sensors [54, 55], weather forecasts, and crop health monitors, to determine the precise amount of water needed by plants. This data-driven approach ensures that crops receive the right amount of water at the right time, preventing both under- and over-irrigation. A study developed a 6G IoT-based smart irrigation system, which achieved an accuracy of 86.34% with a precision of 91% [[56]]. This model is capable of finding environmental conditions and depending on the prediction, it irrigates the fields accordingly. To build a smart irrigation system, different sensors are used as shown in Table **2**.

Table 2. Various types of sensors are used in smart irrigation systems.

Sensor Type	Name of the sensor	Pros	Cons
Soil Moisture Sensors	Decagon GS3, Vegetronix VH400	- Provides real-time soil moisture data. Helps optimize water usage. - Reduces water waste.	Can be expensive. Requires proper calibration. Sensor maintenance and replacement costs.
Weather Sensors	Davis Vantage Pro2, Netatmo Weather Station	Provides data on temperature, humidity, and rainfall. Helps predict irrigation needs. Reduces water usage during rainy conditions.	Can be affected by local microclimates. Initial setup can be costly Requires integration with irrigation system.
Flow Sensors	Toro TFS Series, Hunter HC Flow Meter	Toro TFS Series, Hunter HC Flow Meter. Detects leaks and system inefficiencies.	Can be challenging to install in existing systems. May require professional installation.
Rain Sensors	Rain Bird RSD-BEx, Hunter Mini-Clik	Prevents irrigation during rain. Easy to install and integrate.	Can sometimes give false readings. Limited to sensing rain, not overall weather.
Evapotranspiration (ET) Sensors	Toro Precision Soil Sensor, Hunter ET System	Measures water loss through evaporation and transpiration. Provides precise irrigation scheduling.	Can be expensive. Requires calibration and maintenance.

Using past data and weather forecasts, artificial intelligence (AI) uses predictive analytics to forecast future water demand. Because of their forethought, farmers can set irrigation plans ahead of time and guarantee that water will be accessible when crops want it the most. Additionally, predictive models can foresee drought conditions, assisting farmers in proactively implementing water-saving measures. Artificial intelligence-driven irrigation systems can modify watering schedules in response to anticipated rainfall by using weather forecasting data. For example, the system can limit or skip irrigation if rain is expected, saving water and avoiding soil oversaturation. The alignment of irrigation with natural patterns of precipitation is ensured by this integration.

Farmers may better adjust to climate change with the help of AI-driven smart irrigation systems, which offer adaptable and responsive water management options. AI can adapt irrigation systems to changing conditions as climatic patterns become more unpredictable, ensuring that crops stay productive and healthy even in the face of environmental obstacles.

1.7. Robotic Farming

The application of robots and automated systems to improve various agricultural operations is known as robotic farming, often referred to as automated farming or precision farming [57, 58].

- Ploughing, planting, and harvesting can be done by autonomous tractors with GPS and artificial intelligence (AI) without the need for human assistance. The precise field navigation that these devices are configured to do ensures reliable and effective functioning.
- Drones used in agriculture can be used for seed planting, pesticide application, crop health monitoring, and aerial surveillance. They support farmers in making wise decisions by offering high-resolution pictures and real-time data.
- Specified crops, fruits, and vegetables are harvested by robotic harvesters. They carefully harvest ripe food, minimising damage, and waste, by using computer vision and artificial intelligence.
- Welding robots with sensors and artificial intelligence (AI) can detect and eradicate weeds manually or by applying herbicide selectively, which minimises the requirement for chemical inputs.
- After harvest, robots can sort and pack produce based on size, ripeness, and quality, streamlining the post-harvest process and maintaining consistency.

Robotic farming has many advantages, but it also has drawbacks, including expensive startup costs, complicated technology, and the requirement for a strong infrastructure. Ongoing developments in robotics, AI, and machine learning, however, should solve these issues and improve the usability and effectiveness of robotic farming.

7.1.1. Extraordinary Aspects of Robotic Farming

Even while robotic farming is already outstanding, there are a number of remarkable elements (depicted in Fig. **7**) that show how it can revolutionise agriculture in ways that were before unthinkable.

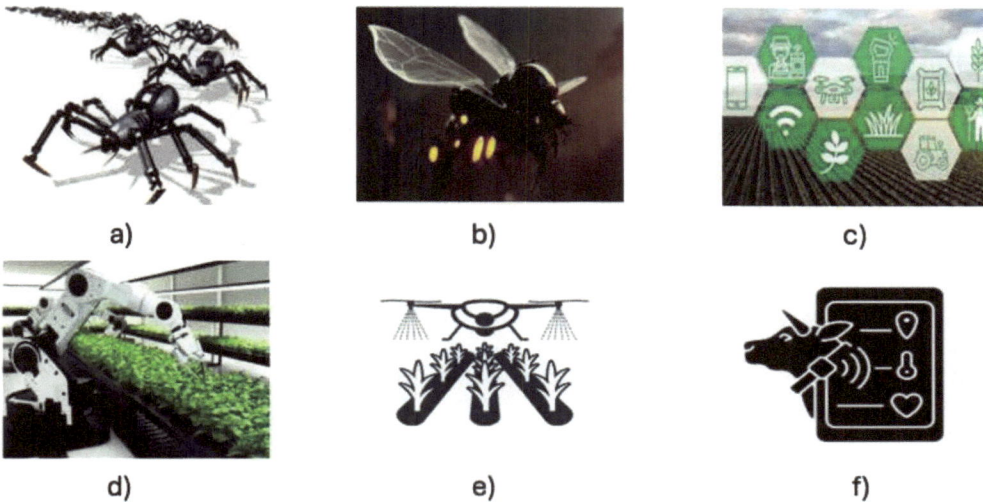

a)   b)   c)

d)   e)   f)

Fig. (7). a) Swarm Robotics **b**) Robotic Pollinators c)Hyper-precision Agriculture d)Vertical Farming Robots **e**) Scouting Drones **f**) Autonomous Livestock Management.

Swarm Robotics: Inspired by the behavior of social insects like ants and bees, swarm robotics involves deploying a large number of small, inexpensive robots that work together to achieve a common goal. In agriculture, swarm robots can collectively perform complex tasks such as planting, weeding, and monitoring crops. These robots communicate and collaborate, covering large areas more efficiently than single, larger robots.

Robotic Pollinators: With the decline in bee populations, robotic pollinators have been developed to assist in the pollination of crops. These small drones mimic the action of bees, transferring pollen from one flower to another. They can significantly enhance crop yields, especially in regions where natural pollinators are scarce.

Hyper-Precision Agriculture: Using advanced AI and machine learning algorithms, robots can analyze vast amounts of data to make hyper-precise adjustments to farming practices. This includes the exact placement of seeds, precise application of fertilizers and pesticides, and targeted irrigation [59]. Such precision minimizes resource usage and maximizes crop health and yield.

Crop Scouting Drones: Drones equipped with advanced sensors and AI analyze fields in detail to detect issues before they become significant problems. These drones can identify plant diseases, nutrient deficiencies, and pest infestations early, allowing for timely interventions. They provide data that can be used to improve farming practices continuously.

Autonomous Livestock Management: Robots and drones manage livestock, ensuring their health and well-being. Autonomous systems can monitor the health of animals, manage feeding schedules, and even assist in herding. They reduce labor needs and ensure that livestock are cared for efficiently and humanely.

Vertical Farming Robots: In urban areas, vertical farming involves growing crops in stacked layers or vertically inclined surfaces, often within controlled environments. Robots manage every aspect of these farms, from planting and watering to harvesting. They operate in confined spaces and optimize growth conditions, making urban agriculture highly productive and sustainable.

1.8. Examples of AI Applications in Agriculture

- **John Deere's See & Spray:** Uses computer vision and machine learning to distinguish between crops and weeds, applying herbicides only where needed. It has revolutionized herbicide application through a combination of high-resolution cameras, machine vision, and AI algorithms. As the sprayer moves through the field, cameras capture detailed images of the ground. These images are processed in real-time by AI algorithms, which distinguish between crops and weeds. The system then makes immediate decisions, controlling individual nozzles on the sprayer to apply herbicide precisely to the weeds, minimizing wastage and avoiding crop exposure. This selective spraying significantly reduces herbicide use, lowering costs and environmental impact while promoting healthier crop growth. Advanced versions of See & Spray can even differentiate between crops and weeds in green-on-green scenarios, offering even greater precision. By automating weed detection and application, See & Spray enhances operational efficiency and provides valuable data for future field management. This technology exemplifies how modern agriculture is leveraging AI and machine vision to achieve greater sustainability and productivity.
- **IBM Watson Decision Platform for Agriculture:** Provides weather forecasts, disease risk assessments, and crop health monitoring to help farmers make data-driven decisions. The platform provides comprehensive insights into crop health and field conditions by combining data from multiple sources, such as satellite imaging, soil sensors, weather forecasts, and Internet of Things devices. Watson's artificial intelligence (AI) uses this data to regulate irrigation, optimise planting schedules, forecast results, and manage pests and diseases. Farmers

may make well-informed decisions that improve productivity, efficiency, and sustainability with the help of the platform's real-time recommendations and actionable insights. Furthermore, it facilitates stakeholder engagement by exchanging insights along the agricultural supply chain, so aiding in the resolution of issues like resource management and climatic variability. By using a comprehensive strategy, farmers are equipped with the knowledge and resources they need to increase agricultural output and sustainability.

- **Blue River Technology:** Uses machine learning for precision weed control, enabling targeted herbicide application. Being a John Deere subsidiary, it leads the way in agricultural innovation with its state-of-the-art computer vision and machine learning tools. The business is most recognised for creating the precision agricultural tool See & Spray, which targets and identifies weeds inside crops using cutting-edge cameras and artificial intelligence. With the use of this technology, herbicides can be applied precisely, cutting expenses, minimising the impact on the environment, and eliminating the need for chemicals. See & Spray can distinguish between weeds and crops using real-time picture analysis, ensuring that only undesirable plants are treated. The advancements of Blue River Technology are transforming weed control and improving the efficiency and sustainability of farming methods. Their dedication to utilising robotics and AI is opening the door for a more intelligent and sustainable agricultural future, which will eventually enable farmers to produce more with fewer resources.

CONCLUSION

AI is bringing significant changes in every field and also helping in sustainable farming practices. Through the integration of AI technologies, people related to the agriculture sector can enhance the efficiency and sustainability of their tasks. The role of AI in precision agriculture cannot be ignored. AI-enabled drones, machinery, sensors, etc. providereal-time monitoring of soil health, weather prediction, irrigation systems, and crop conditions. It will help farmers to make decisions and act accordingly. Predictive analysis is another aspect of AI that analyzes historical data and recommends proactive measures to reduce losses, save crops, and ensure a stable food supply.

Advanced AI systems are being utilized to create efficient irrigation schedules. Such systems are able to analyze soil moisture data and predict weather conditions thereby helping in building intelligent water management systems. Robotics has automated labor-intensive tasks such as planting, weeding, and harvesting. The burden of the farmers has been reduced and productivity has been increased.

In the research area, AI has also made a significant contribution. Machine learning and deep learning algorithms can analyze huge datasets to identify patterns and correlations that are overlooked by humans. This can help in developing new crop varieties, pest resistance, and other sustainable farming practices. Furthermore, a notable point is that the adoption of AI in agriculture is not without challenges. Initially incorporating AI into existing systems is costly and several security issues also persist. Predictive analysis and other techniques have revolutionized the agricultural sector but at the same time, there are some challenges for small-scale farmers that need to be focused on as they may lack the financial resources to make use of these technologies. The high-end sensors cost several hundred dollars, which is not in the range of every farmer. Digital literacy is also a challenge for these farmers. Farmers in remote areas may not have access to cloud-based platforms or mobile apps that rely on consistent internet connectivity. But these challenges can be outweighed with time. It is a continuously evolving field and its integration in agriculture will undoubtedly play an important role in sustainable development.

REFERENCES

[1]   S. Zürner, L.P. Deutschländer, M. Schieck, and P.D.B. Franczyk, "Sustainable Development of AI applications in Agriculture: A Review", *Procedia Comput. Sci.,* vol. 225, pp. 3546-3553, 2023.
        [http://dx.doi.org/10.1016/j.procs.2023.10.350]

[2]   S. Zürner, L.P. Deutschländer, M. Schieck, and B. Franczyk, "Sustainable Development of AI applications in Agriculture: A Review", In: *Procedia Computer Science.* Elsevier B.V., 2023, pp. 3546-3553.
        [http://dx.doi.org/10.1016/j.procs.2023.10.350]

[3]   H.T. Thai, K.H. Le, and N.L.T. Nguyen, "Towards sustainable agriculture: A lightweight hybrid model and cloud-based collection of datasets for efficient leaf disease detection", *Future Gener. Comput. Syst.,* vol. 148, pp. 488-500, 2023.
        [http://dx.doi.org/10.1016/j.future.2023.06.016]

[4]   M. Bala, R. Sharma, and S. Gupta, *Integration of Hybrid Nanomaterials and Artificial Intelligence for Sustainable Agriculture.* 2024.
        [http://dx.doi.org/10.4018/979-8-3693-1261-2.ch004]

[5]   S. Divya, *Smart data processing for energy harvesting systems using artificial intelligence.* 2023.
        [http://dx.doi.org/10.1016/j.nanoen.2022.108084]

[6]   Y. Kurmi, and S. Gangwar, "A leaf image localization based algorithm for different crops disease classification", *Inf. Process. Agric.,* vol. 9, no. 3, pp. 456-474, 2022.
        [http://dx.doi.org/10.1016/j.inpa.2021.03.001]

[7]   M. Agarwal, S.K. Gupta, and K.K. Biswas, "Development of Efficient CNN model for Tomato crop disease identification", *Sustain. Comput.,* vol. 28, p. 100407, 2020.
        [http://dx.doi.org/10.1016/j.suscom.2020.100407]

[8]   A.S. Paymode, and V.B. Malode, "Transfer Learning for Multi-Crop Leaf Disease Image Classification using Convolutional Neural Network VGG", *Artificial Intelligence in Agriculture,* vol. 6, pp. 23-33, 2022.
        [http://dx.doi.org/10.1016/j.aiia.2021.12.002]

[9]   R. Thangaraj, S. Anandamurugan, P. Pandiyan, and V.K. Kaliappan, "Artificial intelligence in tomato

leaf disease detection: a comprehensive review and discussion", *J. Plant Dis. Prot.,* vol. 129, no. 3, pp. 469-488, 2022.
[http://dx.doi.org/10.1007/s41348-021-00500-8]

[10]   É. Lutz, and P. C. Coradi, "Applications of new technologies for monitoring and predicting grains quality stored: Sensors, Internet of Things, and Artificial Intelligence", *Elsevier B.V.,* vol. Jan. 01, 2022.
[http://dx.doi.org/10.1016/j.measurement.2021.110609]

[11]   S. Kaur, S. Pandey, and S. Goel, "Plants Disease Identification and Classification Through Leaf Images: A Survey", *Arch. Comput. Methods Eng.,* vol. 26, no. 2, pp. 507-530, 2019.
[http://dx.doi.org/10.1007/s11831-018-9255-6]

[12]   S. Poornima, S. Kavitha, S. Mohanavalli, and N. Sripriya, "Detection and classification of diseases in plants using image processing and machine learning techniques", *AIP Conf. Proc.,* vol. 2095, no. April, p. 030018, 2019.
[http://dx.doi.org/10.1063/1.5097529]

[13]   M. Iftikhar, I.A. Kandhro, and N. Kausar, "Plant disease management: a fine-tuned enhanced CNN approach with mobile app integration for early detection and classification", *Artif Intell Rev,* vol. 57, no. 167, 2024.
[http://dx.doi.org/10.1007/s10462-024-10809-z]

[14]   A. A. Basheer, "Graphene materials for fabrication of robots", *Elsevier Ltd,* vol. 01, 2023.
[http://dx.doi.org/10.1016/j.matchemphys.2023.127781]

[15]   D. Tiozzo Fasiolo, L. Scalera, E. Maset, and A. Gasparetto, "Towards autonomous mapping in agriculture: A review of supportive technologies for ground robotics", *Robot. Auton. Syst.,* vol. 169, p. 104514, 2023.
[http://dx.doi.org/10.1016/j.robot.2023.104514]

[16]   D. Danai-Varsou, P. Zhang, A. Afantitis, Z. Guo, I. Lynch, and G. Melagraki, "Nanoinformatics and artificial intelligence for nano-enabled sustainable agriculture", In: *Nano-Enabled Sustainable and Precision Agriculture.* Elsevier, 2023, pp. 503-531.
[http://dx.doi.org/10.1016/B978-0-323-91233-4.00015-6]

[17]   R.M. Shepherd, and A.M. Oliverio, "Micronutrients modulate the structure and function of soil bacterial communities", *Soil Biol. Biochem.,* vol. 192, p. 109384, 2024.
[http://dx.doi.org/10.1016/j.soilbio.2024.109384]

[18]   D. S. Powlson, "Soil management in relation to sustainable agriculture and ecosystem services", *Food Policy,* vol. 36, no. 1, Jan, 2011.
[http://dx.doi.org/10.1016/j.foodpol.2010.11.025]

[19]   K.M. Eltohamy, S. Khan, S. He, J. Li, C. Liu, and X. Liang, "Prediction of nano, fine, and medium colloidal phosphorus in agricultural soils with machine learning", *Environ. Res.,* vol. 220, p. 115222, 2023.
[http://dx.doi.org/10.1016/j.envres.2023.115222] [PMID: 36610537]

[20]   M.A. Raja, and A. Husen, "Role of nanomaterials in soil and water quality management", In: *Nanomaterials for Agriculture and Forestry Applications.* Elsevier, 2020, pp. 491-503.
[http://dx.doi.org/10.1016/B978-0-12-817852-2.00020-2]

[21]   M. Bala, S. Kumar Bansal, and F. Fatima, "Nanotechnology: A boon for agriculture", *Mater. Today Proc.,* vol. 73, no. October, pp. 267-270, 2023.
[http://dx.doi.org/10.1016/j.matpr.2022.09.498]

[22]   J.A. Malik, "Implementing Fog Computing in Precision Agriculture for Real-Time Soil Health Monitoring and Data Management", In: Sumithra, M.G., Sathyamoorthy, M., Manikandan, M., Dhanaraj, R.K., Ouaissa, M. (eds) Computational Intelligence in Internet of Agricultural Things. Studies in Computational Intelligence. vol 1170. 2024. Springer, Cham.
[http://dx.doi.org/10.1007/978-3-031-67450-1_14]

[23]   J. Nepal, W. Ahmad, F. Munsif, A. Khan, and Z. Zou, *Advances and prospects of biochar in improving soil fertility, biochemical quality, and environmental applications.* Frontiers Media S.A., 2023.
[http://dx.doi.org/10.3389/fenvs.2023.1114752]

[24]   V.A. Gontijo da Cunha, J. Hariharan, Y. Ampatzidis, and P.D. Roberts, "Early detection of tomato bacterial spot disease in transplant tomato seedlings utilising remote sensing and artificial intelligence", *Biosyst. Eng.,* vol. 234, pp. 172-186, 2023.
[http://dx.doi.org/10.1016/j.biosystemseng.2023.09.002]

[25]   J.G.A. Barbedo, "Detection of nutrition deficiencies in plants using proximal images and machine learning: A review", *Comput. Electron. Agric.,* vol. 162, no. May, pp. 482-492, 2019.
[http://dx.doi.org/10.1016/j.compag.2019.04.035]

[26]   T. Chen, W. Yang, H. Zhang, B. Zhu, R. Zeng, X. Wang, S. Wang, L. Wang, H. Qi, Y. Lan, and L. Zhang, "Early detection of bacterial wilt in peanut plants through leaf-level hyperspectral and unmanned aerial vehicle data", *Comput. Electron. Agric.,* vol. 177, p. 105708, 2020.
[http://dx.doi.org/10.1016/j.compag.2020.105708]

[27]   A.O. Anim-Ayeko, C. Schillaci, and A. Lipani, *Automatic blight disease detection in potato (Solanum tuberosum L.) and tomato (Solanum lycopersicum, L. 1753) plants using deep learning*, 2023.
[http://dx.doi.org/10.1016/j.atech.2023.100178]

[28]   A.O. Anim-Ayeko, C. Schillaci, and A. Lipani, "Automatic blight disease detection in potato (Solanum tuberosum L.) and tomato (Solanum lycopersicum, L. 1753) plants using deep learning", *Smart Agricultural Technology,* vol. 4, p. 100178, 2023.
[http://dx.doi.org/10.1016/j.atech.2023.100178]

[29]   M. Bala, and V. Mehan, "Metaheuristic Techniques for Classification Used in Identification of Plant Diseases", *ECS Trans.,* vol. 107, no. 1, pp. 13473-13480, 2022.
[http://dx.doi.org/10.1149/10701.13473ecst]

[30]   P.K. Sethy, N.K. Barpanda, A.K. Rath, and S.K. Behera, *Image Processing Techniques for Diagnosing Rice Plant Disease: A Survey*, 2019.
[http://dx.doi.org/10.1016/j.procs.2020.03.308]

[31]   M. Bala, and S. Bansal, "Review—Unveiling the Power of Deep Learning in Plant Pathology: A Review on Leaf Disease Detection", *ECS J. Solid State Sci. Technol.,* vol. 13, no. 4, p. 047003, 2024.
[http://dx.doi.org/10.1149/2162-8777/ad3981]

[32]   S. C. A. Houetohossou, V. R. Houndji, C. G. Hounmenou, R. Sikirou, and R. L. G. Kakaï, "Deep learning methods for biotic and abiotic stresses detection and classification in fruits and vegetables: State of the art and perspectives", *KeAi Communications Co.,* vol. Sep. 01, 2023.
[http://dx.doi.org/10.1016/j.aiia.2023.08.001]

[33]   K. Kanchanadevi, N. R. Rajalakshmi, and G. Arulkumaran, "An Improved Deep Residual Convolutional Neural Network for Plant Leaf Disease Detection,"", *Comput. Intell. Neurosci.,* vol. 2022, 2022.
[http://dx.doi.org/10.1155/2022/5102290]

[34]   G. Geetharamani, *Comput. Electr. Eng.,* vol. 76, pp. 323-338, 2019.
[http://dx.doi.org/10.1016/j.compeleceng.2019.04.011]

[35]   P. Bedi, and P. Gole, "Plant disease detection using hybrid model based on convolutional autoencoder and convolutional neural network", *Artificial Intelligence in Agriculture,* vol. 5, pp. 90-101, 2021.
[http://dx.doi.org/10.1016/j.aiia.2021.05.002]

[36]   B. Hatuwal, B. Joshi, B. K. Hatuwal, and A. Shakya, *Plant Leaf Disease Recognition Using Random Forest, KNN, SVM and CNN.*

[37]   B. Charbuty, and A. Abdulazeez, "Classification Based on Decision Tree Algorithm for Machine Learning", *Journal of Applied Science and Technology Trends,* vol. 2, no. 1, pp. 20-28, 2021.

[http://dx.doi.org/10.38094/jastt20165]

[38]   J. L. Speiser, M. E. Miller, J. Tooze, and E. Ip, *A comparison of random forest variable selection methods for classification prediction modeling* Elsevier Ltd, 2019.
[http://dx.doi.org/10.1016/j.eswa.2019.05.028]

[39]   M. Bala, and S.K. Bansal, "Investigating a Spectrum of Machine Learning Methods for Leaf Disease Detection in Pepper, Potato, and Tomato", *ECS J. Solid State Sci. Technol.,* vol. 13, no. 10, p. 107003, 2024.
[http://dx.doi.org/10.1149/2162-8777/ad83f2]

[40]   M. Suresha, K.N. Shreekanth, and B.V. Thirumalesh, "Recognition of diseases in paddy leaves using knn classifier", *2017 2nd International Conference for Convergence in Technology, I2CT 2017,* vol. 2017-Janua, pp. 663-666, 2017.
[http://dx.doi.org/10.1109/I2CT.2017.8226213]

[41]   M. Bala, and V. Mehan, "Identification of Rice Plant Diseases Using Image Processing, Machine Learning & Deep Learning: A Review", *CEUR Workshop Proc,* vol. 3058, pp. 0-3, 2021.

[42]   A. Chug, A. Bhatia, A.P. Singh, and D. Singh, "A novel framework for image-based plant disease detection using hybrid deep learning approach", *Soft Comput.,* vol. 27, no. 18, pp. 13613-13638, 2023.
[http://dx.doi.org/10.1007/s00500-022-07177-7]

[43]   H. El Akhal, A. Ben Yahya, N. Moussa, and A. El Belrhiti El Alaoui, "A novel approach for image-based olive leaf diseases classification using a deep hybrid model", *Ecol. Inform.,* vol. 77, p. 102276, 2023.
[http://dx.doi.org/10.1016/j.ecoinf.2023.102276]

[44]   T. Wiesner-Hanks, E.L. Stewart, N. Kaczmar, C. DeChant, H. Wu, R.J. Nelson, H. Lipson, and M.A. Gore, "Image set for deep learning: field images of maize annotated with disease symptoms", *BMC Res. Notes,* vol. 11, no. 1, p. 440, 2018.
[http://dx.doi.org/10.1186/s13104-018-3548-6] [PMID: 29970178]

[45]   M. Masood, "MaizeNet: A Deep Learning Approach for Effective Recognition of Maize Plant Leaf Diseases", *in IEEE Access,* vol. 11, pp. 52862-52876, 2023.
[http://dx.doi.org/10.1109/ACCESS.2023.3280260]

[46]   W.B. Demilie, "Plant disease detection and classification techniques: a comparative study of the performances", *J Big Data,* vol. 5, p. 11, 2024.
[http://dx.doi.org/10.1186/s40537-023-00863-9]

[47]   S.M. Javidan, A. Banakar, K. Rahnama, K.A. Vakilian, and Y. Ampatzidis, "Feature engineering to identify plant diseases using image processing and artificial intelligence: A comprehensive review", *Smart Agricultural Technology,* vol. 8, no. 100480, 2024.
[http://dx.doi.org/10.1016/j.atech.2024.100480]

[48]   M.Z. Chowdhury, M. Shahjalal, S. Ahmed, and Y.M. Jang, "6G Wireless Communication Systems: Applications, Requirements, Technologies, Challenges, and Research Directions", *IEEE Open J. Commun. Soc.,* vol. 1, pp. 957-975, 2020.
[http://dx.doi.org/10.1109/OJCOMS.2020.3010270]

[49]   B. Kosovic, S.E. Haupt, D. Adriaansen, S. Alessandrini, G. Wiener, L. Delle Monache, Y. Liu, S. Linden, T. Jensen, W. Cheng, M. Politovich, and P. Prestopnik, "A comprehensive wind power forecasting system integrating artificial intelligence and numerical weather prediction", *Energies,* vol. 13, no. 6, p. 1372, 2020.
[http://dx.doi.org/10.3390/en13061372]

[50]   A. McGovern, K.L. Elmore, D.J. Gagne, S.E. Haupt, C.D. Karstens, R. Lagerquist, T. Smith, and J.K. Williams, "Using artificial intelligence to improve real-time decision-making for high-impact weather", *Bull. Am. Meteorol. Soc.,* vol. 98, no. 10, pp. 2073-2090, 2017.
[http://dx.doi.org/10.1175/BAMS-D-16-0123.1]

[51]   S. R, R. M, V. S, S.K. e, Y. S, A. Kumar, J.R. i, and V. K, "A novel autonomous irrigation system for smart agriculture using AI and 6G enabled IoT network", *Microprocess. Microsyst.,* vol. 101, p. 104905, 2023.
[http://dx.doi.org/10.1016/j.micpro.2023.104905]

[52]   Nishu, and S. Kumar, "Smart and innovative nanotechnology applications for water purification", *Hybrid Advances,* vol. 3, p. 100044, 2023.
[http://dx.doi.org/10.1016/j.hybadv.2023.100044]

[53]   R.P. Ramachandran, C. Erkinbaev, and C. Vellaichamy, "Smart nano-biosensors in sustainable agriculture and environmental applications", In: *Food, Medical, and Environmental Applications of Nanomaterials.* Elsevier, 2022, pp. 527-542.
[http://dx.doi.org/10.1016/B978-0-12-822858-6.00019-4]

[54]   J-Y. Yoon, "Use of machine learning/artificial intelligence in chemical sensors and biosensors", In: *Machine Learning and Artificial Intelligence in Chemical and Biological Sensing.* Elsevier, 2024, pp. 71-81.
[http://dx.doi.org/10.1016/B978-0-443-22001-2.00003-2]

[55]   M. Pirzada, and Z. Altintas, "Recent progress in optical sensors for biomedical diagnostics", *MDPI AG,* vol. Apr. 01, 2020.
[http://dx.doi.org/10.3390/mi11040356]

[56]   F.E. Oguz, M.N. Ekersular, K.M. Sunnetci, and A. Alkan, "Enabling Smart Agriculture: An IoT-Based Framework for Real-Time Monitoring and Analysis of Agricultural Data", *Agric. Res.,* vol. 13, no. 3, pp. 574-585, 2024.
[http://dx.doi.org/10.1007/s40003-024-00705-x]

[57]   J. S. Duhan, R. Kumar, N. Kumar, P. Kaur, K. Nehra, and S. Duhan, "Nanotechnology: The new perspective in precision agriculture", *Elsevier B.V.,* vol. Sep. 01, 2017.
[http://dx.doi.org/10.1016/j.btre.2017.03.002]

[58]   P. Zhang, Z. Guo, S. Ullah, G. Melagraki, A. Afantitis, and I. Lynch, "Nanotechnology and artificial intelligence to enable sustainable and precision agriculture", *Nature Research,* vol. Jul. 01, 2021.
[http://dx.doi.org/10.1038/s41477-021-00946-6]

[59]   J. Abdulridha, Y. Ampatzidis, S.C. Kakarla, and P. Roberts, "Detection of target spot and bacterial spot diseases in tomato using UAV-based and benchtop-based hyperspectral imaging techniques", *Precis. Agric.,* vol. 21, no. 5, pp. 955-978, 2020.
[http://dx.doi.org/10.1007/s11119-019-09703-4]

CHAPTER 4

Enhancing Cybersecurity through Intelligent Defence

Abstract: In the modern era, everything is transformed onto online platforms whether it is a transaction of money, sending information from one system to another, e-mails, business plans, trading, *etc.* Every passing minute, a huge amount of data is generated, processed, and executed. Cybersecurity is a field of computer science that deals with the protection of all these things over the internet and machine learning techniques are playing an important role in identifying threats. This chapter is focused on describing the role of machine learning in the detection of intrusions present in the system so that sensitive data can be protected. By analysing a huge amount of data, AI can identify hidden patterns and behaviours that help in building more proactive measures.

Keywords: Cybersecurity, DoS attack, Intrusion detection system, Malware, Machine learning, Signature-based detection.

1. INTRODUCTION

In the conventional period, computers were isolated machines used for specific purposes. However, as technology advances in terms of networking, computers are connected forming a large network, leading to the development of the Internet [1, 2]. Nowadays, the Internet has become a necessity for everyone. People have become so dependent on the Internet to carry out various tasks such as online banking, online payments, shopping, education, *etc.* In a study [3], it was found that the internet usage rate in 2017 was 48% but now it is increased to more than 90% in developing countries. These kinds of work have become so easy and faster. But at the same time, the need to protect and secure the data from unauthorized access has also arisen. Point-to-point data transfer has become a challenge because the rate of fraud, intrusions, and other malware attacks has also increased. Various types of threats such as phishing attacks [4], data breaches [5], denial of service attacks [6], *etc.* are coming into the picture on a daily basis. In the year 2000, companies like amazon.com and ebay.com got affected by cyber-attacks where the intruders made modifications in the program coding. As a result, companies declared shutdown to remove this anomaly [7]. In May 2005, a professional criminal obtained confidential information belonging to 500,000 clients of Wachovia Inc. Instead of using an advanced hacking method, the thief used conventional bribery to recruit. Ethereum theft [8] took place in July 2017 where 150 USD were stolen from an Ethereum application within a few minutes. The outdated and conventional techniques of detection such as firewalls, and antivirus systems are not sufficient enough to tackle these kinds of problems. Fig. (**1**) shows the rate of increase in cybercrimes in India from 2012 to 2022 [9]. From this, it can be analysed that there has been a significant jump in the number of such crimes over the past few years.

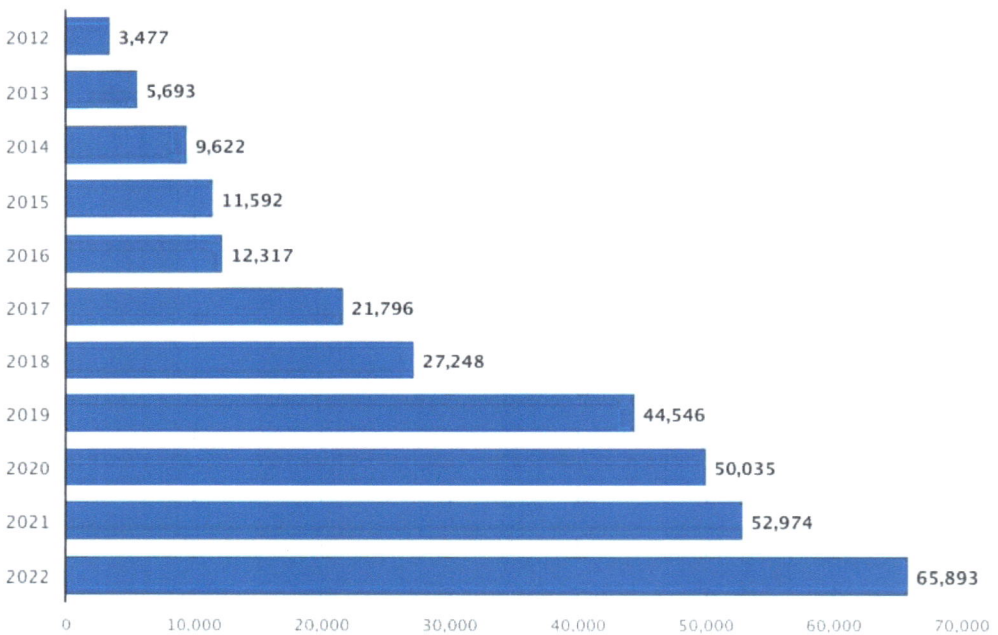

Fig. (1). Rate of increase of cybercrimes in India from 2012 to 2022 [9].

Cybersecurity is composed of two words-cyber and security. The cyber term is related to computers, information technology, and digital systems such as networks programs systems, and data. Security is concerned with the protection of applications, data, system, and networks [10 - 12]. It is also termed as electronic information security and is needed to protect:

- private data,
- intellectual data,
- banking and financial data,
- channel security.

Machine learning techniques can be applied to applications that deal with different transactions over the internet to make the system more robust, secure, and reliable. To maintain cybersecurity, it is mandatory to have fundamental knowledge of risks and threats that one can encounter while using internet services, making transactions, and any other related tasks.

1.2. Cyber-attacks and Malware

Cyber-attack refers to the process of gaining unauthorized access to someone's system through the introduction of any malicious act. This results in disruption of the computer system and the information contained inside it. These attacks can come from various modes- business competitors, terrorists, secret agents, and hackers. On the other hand, malware is malicious software used to gain access to someone's computer so that either the information can be retrieved or the data stored in the system can be disrupted. Malware can be in the form of code, software, links or any other kind of active content that can be spread or distributed through e-mails, social networking sites, downloads, or websites. Some commonly found malware are shown in Fig. (**2**).

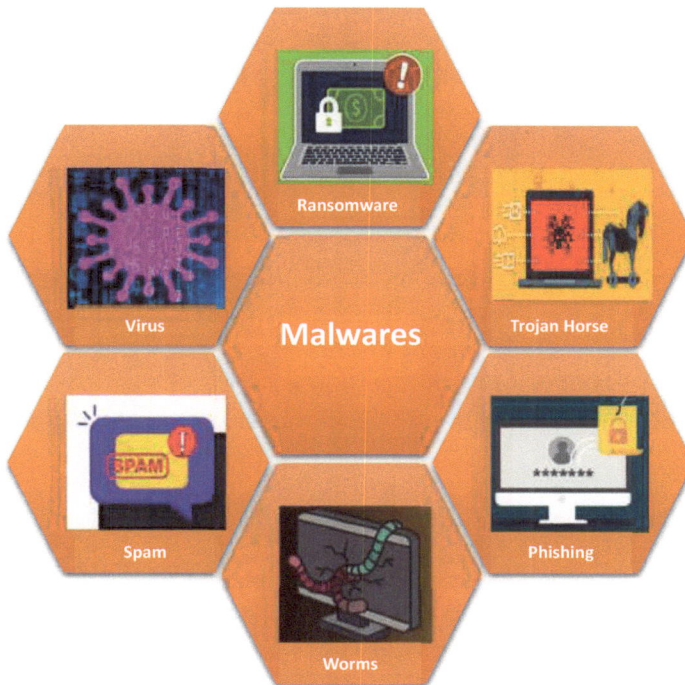

Fig. (2). Types of malware.

- **Virus:** It is also known as a vital information resource under seizure that spreads through any external media, pen drive, or internet. Basically, it is a piece of code that can be inserted into the system without authorized access. These are human-made and have the capability of copying themselves so as to destroy the contents stored in the system. Macro viruses, logical bomb viruses, and boot viruses are the commonly found viruses that may harm systems.
- **Trojan Horses:** These appear as useful programs but in actuality, they are not. The main purpose of this malware is to capture somebody's login credentials which include username and password. These must be sent by some outside means. If a system is attacked by a trojan horse then there are some signs from where its existence can be found. The indicators are- the blinking of a computer screen, the mouse pointer disappears, the background setting changes on its own, the appearance of sudden pop-ups on the screen, *etc.*
- **Worms:** It is a kind of self-replicating program that does not require any medium to get transferred. Through the network, it can easily be sent from one system to another, and from there, it further gets transferred to some other systems as well that are connected to the network.
- **Phishing:** It is an attack in the form of a message asking for some information like a social security number or PAN number with the intention of stealing crucial data. The message claims that if the information is not provided by the user then the account will be blocked. Examples of this kind of attack are: malicious or fake links for subscriptions, links in emails from banks, *etc.*
- **Adware:** These are advertisement-supported software that by default delivers advertisements without the consent of the user. These are some of the major sources of cyber-attacks, wherein a user clicks on the advertisement by mistake and gets trapped.
- **Spam:** Spam mails are often received by users that contain unwanted information. Hackers use these emails to spread viruses, trojan horses, and other kinds of malware. In emails, spam emails are found often that contain emails that a user did not request and does not want to access. However, it is always advisable not to open spam emails if it has been received from some unknown person.
- **Ransomware:**These kinds of attacks are very dangerous where the attackers gain access to the systems and demand ransom to release control. Such attacks are done on a large scale, and the companies that are famous in their fields are generally the target.

1.3. AI in Cybersecurity

Artificial intelligence (AI) algorithms are essential for spotting irregularities in system logs, user activity, and network traffic because they can analyze enormous volumes of data and spot patterns that could indicate security risks.

1.3.1. Detection of DoS

A denial of service attack (shown in Fig. **3**) is a kind of attack where the attackers prevent legitimate users from accessing or availing services from the network [13]. The victim's computer is flooded with so many messages that create congestion in the network and restrict all other nodes connected to the victim node from gaining access to the information [14].

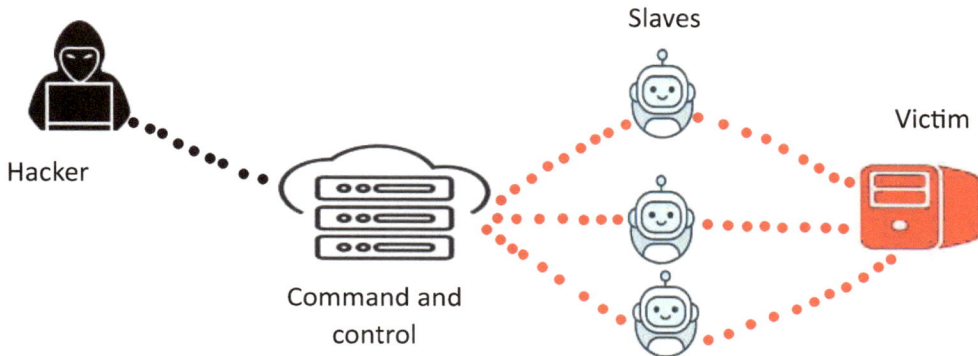

Fig. (3). Distributed denial of service attack.

The authors [15] worked on the CAIDA 2007 dataset to implement machine learning models so that distributed denial of service attacks can be detected. Logistic regression and naïve Bayes were used for classification and prediction. It was found that logistic regression performed better than naive Bayes. Saini *et al.* [16] used WEKA as a machine learning tool to detect distributed denial of service attacks(DDoS). Three classifiers random forest, multi-layer perceptron, and J48 were used and from their investigation, it was found that J48 gave 98.64% accuracy.

1.3.2. Phishing attack detection

Phishing attacks are done by attackers with the intention of stealing crucial information and taking monetary benefits from the victim either through email spoofing or through creating dummy websites [17]. The victim is not able to identify the real or genuine site and gets trapped. Such attacks can be divided into the following categories:

• DNS blacklist
• Web crawler
• Heuristic approach

The domain name system blacklist approach is used by attackers where a large number of IP addresses are generated and these addresses can be mounted on the browser for programming. Furthermore, these IP addresses are used for spamming, and the DNS system is updated frequently. A web crawler is a kind of program that begins to access web pages on its own through links in the web index. Gori *et al.* [18] proposed a heuristic-based algorithm to detect phishing emails and phishing or non-phishing sites. The generalized model for the detection of phishing attacks is depicted in (Fig. **4**).

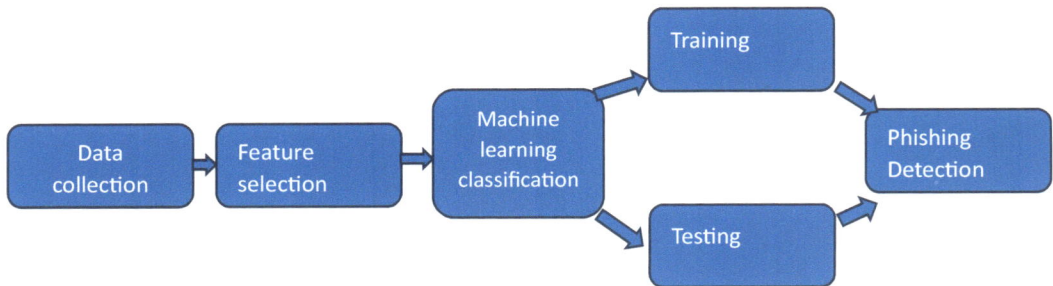

Fig. (4). Basic architecture of detecting phishing attack.

1.3.3. Real-time network monitoring

Real-time network traffic monitoring is possible because of AI algorithms, which can spot abnormalities in communication patterns, packet headers, and data payloads [19]. Artificial intelligence (AI) systems can identify anomalous spikes in traffic volume, anomalous communication patterns, or unexpected connections to dubious IP addresses by creating baselines of typical network traffic patterns [20]. Network anomalies can be automatically detected using machine learning algorithms, which can then be flagged for additional examination by security experts.

Examples of these algorithms include clustering, classification, and anomaly detection approaches. Intrusion detection and prevention systems (IDPS) with AI capabilities can improve network security by continually analyzing network traffic and instantly responding to possible attacks [21]. Potential benefits of using AI algorithms are:

- Analyzing access patterns, authentication data, and user activity logs to create baselines of typical behavior for both individuals and groups.
- Identify departures from pre-established behavioral patterns, like irregular file access patterns, unlawful resource access, or unusual login timings, by utilizing machine learning algorithms.

- Evaluate behavioural biometrics, like typing patterns, mouse movements, and keystroke dynamics, to authenticate users and find anomalies that could indicate compromised accounts or unwanted access.
- User and Entity Behaviour Analytics (UEBA) solutions powered by artificial intelligence (AI) can correlate various data sources in order to detect unusual behaviour across networked systems and applications. This capability facilitates the early detection and remediation of both external and insider threats.

In order to identify unusual activity that may be a sign of a security problem, artificial intelligence (AI) algorithms can examine system logs, event records, and audit trails produced by servers, apps, and security devices.

1.4. Machine Learning Algorithms for the Detection of Attacks

1.4.1. Random Forest

AI algorithms play a significant role in identifying abnormalities in network traffic by examining patterns, behaviours, and departures from typical network activity. Intrusion detection systems (IDS) are used to detect malicious activities in computer networks. Random forest is one of the popular ML algorithms that can be applied to detect cyber threats by learning patterns from the network [22]. The model works in the following steps:

Step 1: It constructs multiple decision trees during the training of labeled data having features such as IP addresses, protocols, packet sizes, and network flow metadata.

Step 2: The decision trees in the forest learn various patterns of attacks like DoS, R2L (root to local) attacks, U2R (user to root) attacks, and many more.

Step 3: During the testing phase, random forest evaluates incoming traffic based on the features it has learned during training.

1.4.2. Naive Bayes (NB)

It is a probabilistic classifier based on Bayes' theorem, which assumes that all the attributes in a given dataset are independent. In case of cyber security, suppose a dataset with network traffic parameters is given to detect an attack. Naive Bayes will classify new traffic by calculating the posterior probabilities of the type of attacks and assign the class that would have the highest probability.

NB model can be applied in a real-time IDS environment where classification needs to be done at a frequent rate. It can detect threats present in the network by using the following steps:

- **Data pre-processing:** Data cleaning is done such that all missing values are treated first with an appropriate method. Data of network traffic is converted into feature vectors. Each feature represents the details of a network packet such as network packet, protocol type, connection type, connection duration, *etc.*
- **Training:** Labeled data is used to train the model. Probability values of normal and attack classes are calculated. The likelihood of normal *versus* attacked traffic is learned by the model during this phase.
- **Classification:** When new data is given as input to the model, posterior probability is calculated by the model, and classification is done based on the highest posterior probability.

The strength of the model lies in the environment where the independence assumption between features holds well. It also scales well with large datasets and is easy to implement.

1.4.3. Support Vector Machine(SVM)

It is another powerful supervised machine learning algorithm used in intrusion detection systems, classifications of malware, detection of phishing attacks, and spam detection. This model works well in high-dimensional spaces and is capable of handling both linear and non-linear data effectively [23].

Using a hyperplane, SVM divides data into different classes. It aims to increase the difference between two groups of malicious and legitimate traffic. The data points that are closest to the hyperplane are known as support vectors, and they are essential in determining the hyperplane's location. Kinan *et al.* [24] used SVM for network intrusion and cyber-attack detection. False alarms are reduced in this work by using linear and non-linear forms of SVMs. Another work [25] used SVM for the reduction of dimensions to extract only important features from the dataset so that the accuracy of the model can be enhanced. Further, they combined filter and wrapper models to select the best feature for the detection of intrusion. Training and testing time was also reduced using this feature. Each model has its strength depending upon the context of cybersecurity. A comparative analysis of RF, NB, and SVM is depicted in Table **1**.

1.5. Adversarial Attacks

Adversarial assaults are conscious attempts to exploit cybersecurity protocol weaknesses in machine learning or any computational framework to mislead models or systems by generating inaccurate forecasting or evoking unintended activity [26]. The most common adversarial attacks in cybersecurity are:

Table 1. Comparison of random forest, naive Bayes, and support vector machine classifiers.

Aspects	Random Forest	Naive Bayes	Support Vector Machine
Algorithm type	Ensemble of decision trees	Probabilistic (Bayesian)	Linear or Non-linear Classifier
Working principle	Combines multiple decision trees to form a majority vote, which results in better classification.	Based on Bayes' theorem, calculates the probability of a class given certain features.	Finds a hyperplane to best separate classes with maximum margin.
Suitability in cybersecurity	Effective for detecting complex attacks (*e.g.*, DoS, DDoS) and versatile for various types of threats.	Best for tasks like spam filtering, phishing detection, or malware classification with simple data distributions.	Well-suited for high-dimensional data like malware classification, intrusion detection, and network anomalies.
Handling Non-linearity	Can handle non-linearity through decision tree splitting.	Assumes feature independence, which makes it less flexible for non-linear relationships.	Handles non-linear data with kernels (*e.g.*, RBF, Polynomial).
Training Speed	Slower than NB, especially with large datasets due to multiple trees.	Extremely fast, especially with large datasets.	Moderate, though kernel tricks can be computationally expensive for large datasets.
Prediction Speed	Moderate, due to the need to aggregate results from multiple decision trees.	Very fast, suitable for real-time systems.	Moderate to slow depending on the complexity of the kernel.
Feature Importance	Can rank features by importance, making it easy to interpret which features are key for detection.	Does not provide feature importance insights, and assumes equal contribution from features.	Can handle high-dimensional data but does not inherently provide feature importance.
Overfitting	Less prone to overfitting due to averaging multiple trees.	Prone to underfitting if the independence assumption does not hold.	Can overfit on small datasets, but regularization helps to control it.
Real-time Application	Suitable for offline detection, though may be slow in real-time depending on the number of trees.	Ideal for real-time applications due to its speed.	May be slower than NB but can be optimized for near-real-time applications.
Scalability	Handles large datasets well by parallelizing tree construction.	Scales easily to large datasets.	Handles large datasets moderately, but can be slow if complex kernels are used.
Strengths	-High accuracy -Robust to noise -Handles missing data well	- Fast training and prediction - Works well with small datasets - Simple to implement	- Good for high-dimensional data - Effective with both linear and non-linear classification.

(Table 1) cont.....

Aspects	Random Forest	Naive Bayes	Support Vector Machine
Weaknesses	- Slower for large datasets - Can be difficult to interpret	- Assumes feature independence, which often doesn't hold true in real data.	- Can be slow with large datasets and complex kernels. - Sensitive to parameter selection.

- **Evasion Attacks:** Attackers design inputs meant to evade the detection of a system or model without raising suspicions [27]. For example, 1. Include variable network traffic to bypass an intrusion detection system or altered images to trick computer vision systems. 2. Slightly modified malware in order not to be caught by antivirus software using signatures.

  Target: Antivirus software, spam filters, and intrusion detection systems (IDS).

- **Poisoning Attacks:** The attackers introduce malicious data into a system in the training phase with the aim of distorting the learning process to cause flawed behavior in the future [28]; for example, one can lower the accuracy of a spam filter by tainting training data for it by classifying certain spam emails as authentic.

  Target: Machine learning models in the training phase.

- **Model Inversion Attacks:** These attacks infer private information about the training set by using the output of the model [29]; for instance, recovering private data from a healthcare prediction model.

  Target: Predictive models that have been trained on sensitive data sets.

- **Backdoor Attacks:** Attackers inject "triggers" or backdoors into a machine learning model, which invokes under certain conditions [30]. For instance, a face recognition system that, under specific conditions, misrecognizes a person only when that person is wearing a particular thing, such as a scarf with patterns.

  Target: AI and deep learning technology used in vital applications for national security.

- **AI-Powered Phishing Attacks:** To produce highly personalized phishing emails, criminals are now relying on artificial intelligence [31]. Since such AI-generated messages are customized by using data from social media, they can be as difficult to differentiate from real conversations as it is challenging to distinguish real from fake friends. To defeat sophisticated social engineering attacks, this trend underlines the need for even more attention and sophisticated detection [32].

1.6. Malware Detection and Mitigation

Mitigation is the process of fixing software vulnerabilities and preventing them from unauthorized access. In order to recognize and eliminate harmful software threats, malware detection and mitigation are crucial components of cybersecurity

[33]. Signature-based detection method compares files or processes to a database of known malware signatures. The file or process is marked malicious by the system if a match is found. This approach might not work against fresh or emerging threats and is only capable of identifying known malware. Conventional signature-based methods are now outpaced by new techniques like AI, ML, and deep learning techniques.

1.6.1. Machine Learning and Artificial Intelligence

By examining enormous volumes of data to find patterns and abnormalities linked to malicious activity, machine learning, and artificial intelligence approaches can improve malware detection [34, 35]. With time, these systems will be able to adjust and advance to recognize new and emerging dangers.

- **Quarantine and Removal:** In order to stop malware from spreading further, compromised systems or files must be isolated as soon as it is discovered. Before being removed, quarantined files can undergo additional analysis to determine the full scope of the infection.
- **Patch Management:** A lot of malware attacks take advantage of well-known flaws in systems or software. By patching known security flaws, maintaining systems updated with security patches and updates helps reduce the chance of exploitation.
- **Endpoint Protection:** By monitoring and thwarting suspicious activity, endpoint protection solutions such as antivirus software and endpoint detection and response (EDR) systems—can aid in the prevention of malware infestations on individual machines.
- **Network Segmentation:** By breaking up large networks into smaller, more isolated sections, malware outbreaks can be stopped in their tracks and their effects on important systems and data are lessened.

1.6.2. Awareness and Education of Users

By lowering the possibility that users would unintentionally download or run harmful software, educating users about the dangers of malware, typical infection vectors (like phishing emails and malicious websites), and best practices for cybersecurity hygiene can help avoid malware infestations [36].

Incident Response: By creating and putting into practice an incident response plan, businesses can make sure they are prepared to handle malware attacks when they arise. This plan should outline how to contain and lessen the impact of malware events, as well as how to restore data and systems that have been impacted.

1.7. AI Tools for Cybersecurity

In today's digital era, technology is growing at a very fast rate and so the threat landscape for cybersecurity is also changing quickly. Most of the organizations are now using AI-based tools to protect their assets from increasing cyberattacks. Some of the commonly used tools (shown in Fig. **5**) are:

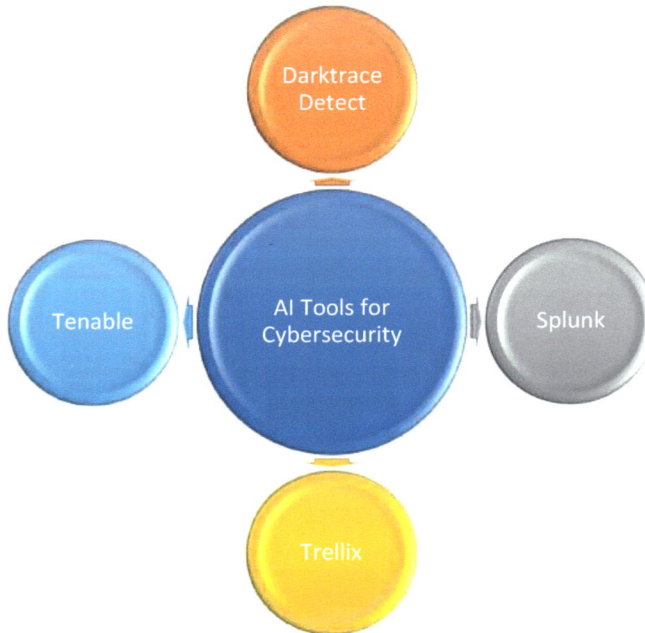

Fig. (5). Various tools used in cybersecurity.

Darktrace Detect:

It is used to identify any ongoing threat in the network. An interesting fact about this tool is that it behaves like an immune system of a human that detects anomalies by learning the normal patterns of behaviour within a network. If any threat is present, it can be detected easily. Basically, it uses an unsupervised machine learning algorithm to model the behaviour of the network. A suspicious activity is detected by this tool by continuously monitoring devices, users, and systems.

Benefits:

• Requires minimal human intervention.
• Identifies previously unknown or stealthy threats.
• Provides real-time alerts and autonomous response capabilities.

Limitations:

- AI-based systems can generate false positives if not carefully tuned.
- Requires time to adapt and learn network behaviors after deployment.

Splunk:

This tool works on data aggregation, where data from multiple sources like servers, databases, and cloud platforms is collected. It is used for security information and event management for real-time detection. With its help, security analysts can create real-time alerts and generate reports on health and security incidents.

Benefits:

- Flexible and scalable, works with both on-premise and cloud infrastructure.
- Strong search, analysis, and reporting capabilities.
- Integration with many third-party security tools and threat intelligence platforms.

Limitations:

- Can be expensive for larger data volumes.
- Requires skilled professionals to write queries and manage configurations.

Trellix:

Trellix provides extended detection and response (XDR) solutions to detect diseases. Formerly, it was part of McAfee and FireEye. It protects endpoints such as computers, servers or mobile devices from suspicious activities and malware. Its ability to detect and block ransomware before it can encrypt files is making it popular among organizations.

Benefits:

- Unified detection across various layers (endpoint, network, cloud).
- Automation of routine security tasks and responses.
- Comprehensive threat intelligence integration.

Limitations:

- Requires significant setup and tuning for large environments.
- May need integration with other security tools to provide full coverage.

Tenable:

It is giving good results for vulnerability management and cyber exposure solutions. Nessus (tenable tool) is a kind of vulnerability scanner that scans the network, systems, and applications to find insecure protocols. Tenable.io can create a holistic view of an organization such that potential attack paths can be predicted and security teams can take preventive actions in advance. In cloud environments like AWS, and Azure, it ensures that infrastructure is compliant and secure.

Benefits:

- It provides significant vulnerability management across different environments.
- In case of a number of vulnerabilities, it can prioritize those based on the risk.
- Works well in cloud environments and hybrid infrastructures.

Limitations:

- May require integration with other tools for full cybersecurity coverage.
- Some complex environments may need custom configurations for effective scanning.

AI is transforming the cybersecurity landscape by providing more advanced tools that result in faster and more accurate malware detection. The summary of these tools is mentioned in Table **2**.

Table 2. Purpose and strengths of AI tools used for cybersecurity.

Tool	Purpose	Strengths	Suitable for
Darktrace detect	AI-powered threat detection via anomaly detection.	Autonomous response, AI-based detection of zero-day attacks.	Internal threat detection, anomaly detection.
Splunk	Data aggregation, SIEM, real-time monitoring	Centralized logging, advanced search, and reporting.	Log management, incident detection.
Trellix	XDR platform for unified threat detection	Endpoint, network, and cloud detection, threat intelligence.	Multi-stage attack detection, ransomware protection.
Tenable	Vulnerability management and cyber exposure	Vulnerability scanning, risk prioritization	Patch management, risk assessment

1.8. Emerging Cybersecurity Ethical Dilemmas

- **Privacy *vs.* Security:** A major ethical dilemma is how to balance the privacy of the individual with our collective security [37]. An example is that of user consent and data privacy when using AI tools that track user activity, such as Microsoft's Recall, which takes a snapshot every five seconds. Since attackers can easily get this information, it is why security experts showed the importance of clear data-gathering procedures and tight security measures that have to be taken in place for user privacy.

- **Ethical Use of AI in Cybersecurity:** Transparency, accountability, privacy, biases, and economic effects are but a few of the complex ethical considerations that AI use in cybersecurity raises. To ensure that AI technology is applied in an ethical manner to protect digital assets, cybersecurity experts must overcome these hurdles.
- **Supply Chain Vulnerabilities:** The vulnerability in the supply chain was exploited to upload malicious packages to a popular repository. Supply chain attacks of this nature call for an ethical discussion of responsibilities among software developers and platform maintainers toward securing and protecting the integrity of their products. It brings forth an issue that has to be brought under scrutiny in the software development practice [38].

1.9. Implementation of AI Solutions in Real-World

In many areas, artificial intelligence is now becoming an essential aspect of enhancing cybersecurity measures [39, 40]. Here are some real-life applications of AI solutions in cybersecurity and tactics that businesses can use to successfully implement these technologies:

- The AI-Powered Cybersecurity Platform from Siemens: A cybersecurity platform based on AI was developed by the world leader in automation and electrification, Siemens, on Amazon Web Services (AWS). It enhances the ability of the business to protect its vast digital infrastructure by using AI for the instant detection and response of cyber threats.

Implementation Methods:

I. Cloud Integration: AI systems can be scaled and made more flexible by using cloud services such as AWS.
II. Real-time monitoring: Monitor continuously through AI tools and identify any kind of anomalies on time.
   ○ Fortinet's AI-Powered Security Solutions: Cybersecurity company Fortinet has adopted the use of artificial intelligence in its security products, making it possible for advanced threat detection and response. Its AI-based product solutions enhance the security features of data centers through the analysis of network traffic into likely breaches.

Implementation Methods:

I. Unified Dashboard: Monitor and manage security notifications using a single interface.
II. AI Integration: Use AI to enhance the effectiveness and accuracy of threat detection.
   ○ Cyber Defense Using AI:

Numerous organizations have managed to implement AI into cyber defense as a way to combat threats. Real-world case studies expose state-of-the-art detection, analytics, and strategies that have improved cybersecurity.

Implementation Methods:

I. Advanced Analytics: Utilize AI in advanced security data analysis for the identification of sophisticated threats.
II. Strategic Planning: Craft comprehensive strategies that integrate AI within the current security frameworks [41].

CONCLUSION

The integration of AI and its tools in cybersecurity has brought a paradigm shift in the detection of threats, malware, and the identification of vulnerabilities in the network. These methods offer a high level of speed and accuracy that are much better than the conventional approaches. It not only detects threats but also aims at the management of vulnerability and behavioral analysis thereby allowing cyber security teams to take preventive measures on time. However, the implementation of AI tools also comes with several challenges such as adversarial attacks and the need for large datasets that need innovative approaches and essential refinements. In conclusion, AI is transforming cybersecurity by providing more proactive, autonomous, and intelligent defenses, offering an essential advantage in an ever-evolving threat landscape.

REFERENCES

[1]   F. Cremer, B. Sheehan, M. Fortmann, A.N. Kia, M. Mullins, F. Murphy, and S. Materne, "Cyber risk and cybersecurity: a systematic review of data availability", *Geneva Pap. Risk Insur. Issues Pract.,* vol. 47, no. 3, pp. 698-736, 2022.
        [http://dx.doi.org/10.1057/s41288-022-00266-6] [PMID: 35194352]

[2]   J. Martínez Torres, C. Iglesias Comesaña, and P.J. García-Nieto, "Review: machine learning techniques applied to cybersecurity", *Int. J. Mach. Learn. Cybern.,* vol. 10, no. 10, pp. 2823-2836, 2019.
        [http://dx.doi.org/10.1007/s13042-018-00906-1]

[3]   K. Shaukat, *Performance comparison and current challenges of using machine learning techniques in*

cybersecurity. 2020.
[http://dx.doi.org/10.3390/en13102509]

[4]   Z. Alkhalil, C. Hewage, L. Nawaf, and I. Khan, "Phishing Attacks: A Recent Comprehensive Study and a New Anatomy", *Frontiers Media S.A.,* 2021.
[http://dx.doi.org/10.3389/fcomp.2021.563060]

[5]   S. Khan, I. Kabanov, Y. Hua, and S. Madnick, "A Systematic Analysis of the Capital One Data Breach: Critical Lessons Learned", *ACM Transactions on Privacy and Security,* vol. 26, no. 1, pp. 1-29, 2023.
[http://dx.doi.org/10.1145/3546068]

[6]   A. Cetinkaya, H. Ishii, and T. Hayakawa, "An overview on denial-of-service attacks in control systems: Attack models and security analyses", *MDPI AG,* 2019.
[http://dx.doi.org/10.3390/e21020210]

[7]   Smith, Katherine Taken and Smith, Murphy and Smith, Jacob Lawrence, Case Studies of Cybercrime and its Impact on Marketing Activity and Shareholder Value (December 13, 2010). Academy of Marketing Studies Journal, 2011, Available at SSRN: https://ssrn.com/abstract=1724815

[8]   K. Lašas, Uta Užupyt, and T. Krilavičius, "Fraudulent Behaviour Identification in Ethereum Blockchain", http://ceur-ws.org 2020.

[9]   https://www.statista.com/statistics/1097071/india-number-of-cyber-crimes-by-leading-state/

[10]   D. Dasgupta, Z. Akhtar, and S. Sen, "Machine learning in cybersecurity: a comprehensive survey", *The Journal of Defense Modeling and Simulation,* vol. 19, no. 1, pp. 57-106, 2020.
[http://dx.doi.org/10.1177/1548512920951275]

[11]   A. Mishra, Y.I. Alzoubi, A.Q. Gill, and M.J. Anwar, "Cybersecurity Enterprises Policies: A Comparative Study", *Sensors (Basel),* vol. 22, no. 2, p. 538, 2022.
[http://dx.doi.org/10.3390/s22020538] [PMID: 35062504]

[12]   A. Sulich, M. Rutkowska, A. Krawczyk-Jezierska, J. Jezierski, and T. Zema, "Cybersecurity and sustainable development", In: *Procedia Computer Science.* Elsevier B.V., 2021, pp. 20-28.
[http://dx.doi.org/10.1016/j.procs.2021.08.003]

[13]   F. Musumeci, A.C. Fidanci, F. Paolucci, F. Cugini, and M. Tornatore, "Machine-Learning-Enabled DDoS Attacks Detection in P4 Programmable Networks", *J. Netw. Syst. Manage.,* vol. 30, no. 1, p. 21, 2022.
[http://dx.doi.org/10.1007/s10922-021-09633-5]

[14]   S.A. Khanday, H. Fatima, and N. Rakesh, "Implementation of intrusion detection model for DDoS attacks in Lightweight IoT Networks", *Expert Systems with Applications,* vol. 215, p. 119330, 2023.
[http://dx.doi.org/10.1016/j.eswa.2022.119330]

[15]   K. Kumari, and M. Mrunalini, "Detecting Denial of Service attacks using machine learning algorithms", *J. Big Data,* vol. 9, no. 1, p. 56, 2022.
[http://dx.doi.org/10.1186/s40537-022-00616-0]

[16]   P.S. Saini, S. Behal, and S. Bhatia, "Detection of DDoS Attacks using Machine Learning Algorithms", *2020 7th International Conference on Computing for Sustainable Global Development (INDIACom), New Delhi, India,* pp. 16-21, 2020.
[http://dx.doi.org/10.23919/INDIACom49435.2020.9083716]

[17]   K.L. Chiew, K.S.C. Yong, and C.L. Tan, "A survey of phishing attacks: Their types, vectors and technical approaches", *Expert Systems with Applications,* vol. 106, no. 1, p. 20, 2018.
[http://dx.doi.org/10.1016/j.eswa.2018.03.050]

[18]   G. Mohamed, J. Visumathi, M. Mahdal, J. Anand, and M. Elangovan, "An Effective and Secure Mechanism for Phishing Attacks Using a Machine Learning Approach", *Processes (Basel),* vol. 10, no. 7, p. 1356, 2022.
[http://dx.doi.org/10.3390/pr10071356]

[19]   M.Q. Kheder, and A.A. Mohammed, "Real-time traffic monitoring system using IoT-aided robotics and deep learning techniques", *Kuwait Journal of Science,* vol. 51, no. 1, p. 100153, 2024.
[http://dx.doi.org/10.1016/j.kjs.2023.10.017]

[20]   Smith, Katherine Taken, *et al.* "Examination of cybercrime and its effects on corporate stock value." Journal of Information, Communication and Ethics in Society 17.1 (2019): 42-60.

[21]   L. Ashiku, and C. Dagli, "Network Intrusion Detection System using Deep Learning", *Procedia Computer Science,* vol. 185, pp. 239-247, 2021.
[http://dx.doi.org/10.1016/j.procs.2021.05.025]

[22]   Y. Xin, L. Kong, Z. Liu, Y. Chen, Y. Li, H. Zhu, M. Gao, H. Hou, and C. Wang, "Machine Learning and Deep Learning Methods for Cybersecurity", *IEEE Access,* vol. 6, pp. 35365-35381, 2018.
[http://dx.doi.org/10.1109/ACCESS.2018.2836950]

[23]   P. Hadem, D.K. Saikia, and S. Moulik, "An SDN-based Intrusion Detection System using SVM with Selective Logging for IP Traceback", *Computer Networks,* vol. 191, p. 108015, 2021.
[http://dx.doi.org/10.1016/j.comnet.2021.108015]

[24]   K. Ghanem, F.J. Aparicio-Navarro, K.G. Kyriakopoulos, S. Lambotharan, and J.A. Chambers, "Support Vector Machine for Network Intrusion and Cyber-Attack Detection", 2017.
[http://dx.doi.org/10.1109/SSPD.2017.8233268]

[25]   J. Jha, and L. Ragha, *ISSN : 2249-0868 Foundation of Computer Science FCS,* 2013.www.ijais.org

[26]   H. Lu, J. Liu, J. Peng, and J. Lu, "Adversarial attacks based on time-series features for traffic detection", *Comput. Secur.,* vol. 148, p. 104175, 2025.
[http://dx.doi.org/10.1016/j.cose.2024.104175]

[27]   M. Malatji, "Comparative analysis of adversarial AI injection attacks: A preliminary study", In: *2024 International Conference on Artificial Intelligence, Computer, Data Sciences and Applications (ACDSA)* IEEE, 2024, pp. 1-5.
[http://dx.doi.org/10.1109/ACDSA59508.2024.10467951]

[28]   R. Hamon, and H. Junklewitz, *Exploring the Feasibility of Physical Adversarial Attacks: A Cybersecurity Study,* 2023.
[http://dx.doi.org/10.3233/FAIA230369]

[29]   J. Sivaram, J.M. Narrain, P. Honnavalli, and S. Eswaran, "Adversarial machine learning: the rise in AI-enabled crime", *Comput. Fraud Secur.,* vol. 2023, no. 2, p. S1361-3723(23)70007-9, 2023.
[http://dx.doi.org/10.12968/S1361-3723(23)70007-9]

[30]   C. A. Candra Ahmadi, J.-L. C. Candra Ahmadi, and Y.-T. L. Jiann-Liang Chen, *Securing AI Models Against Backdoor Attacks: A Novel Approach Using Image Steganography,* 2024.
[http://dx.doi.org/10.53106/160792642024052503012]

[31]   J.P. Soon, R.Q. Chan, Q.H. Lee, D.E. Loke, S.L.H. Chun, and P.K. Yuen, "User perceptions of artificial intelligence powered phishing attacks on Facebook's resilient infrastructure", *International Journal of Advances in Applied Sciences,* vol. 13, no. 4, p. 878, 2024.
[http://dx.doi.org/10.11591/ijaas.v13.i4.pp878-886]

[32]   C.S. Eze, and L. Shamir, "Analysis and Prevention of AI-Based Phishing Email Attacks", *Electronics (Basel),* vol. 13, no. 10, p. 1839, 2024.
[http://dx.doi.org/10.3390/electronics13101839]

[33]   E. Altulaihan, M. A. Almaiah, and A. Aljughaiman, *Cybersecurity Threats, Countermeasures and Mitigation Techniques on the IoT: Future Research Directions,* 2022.
[http://dx.doi.org/10.3390/electronics11203330]

[34]   H. Kavak, J.J. Padilla, D. Vernon-Bido, S.Y. Diallo, R. Gore, and S. Shetty, *Simulation for cybersecurity: State of the art and future directions.* Oxford University Press, 2021.
[http://dx.doi.org/10.1093/cybsec/tyab005]

[35] A. Hussain, A. Mohamed, and S. Razali, "A Review on Cybersecurity: Challenges & Emerging Threats", In: *ACM International Conference Proceeding Series* Association for Computing Machinery, 2020.
[http://dx.doi.org/10.1145/3386723.3387847]

[36] H. de Bruijn, and M. Janssen, "Building Cybersecurity Awareness: The need for evidence-based framing strategies", *Gov. Inf. Q.,* vol. 34, no. 1, pp. 1-7, 2017.
[http://dx.doi.org/10.1016/j.giq.2017.02.007]

[37] R. Veeran, and P. Gunasekaran, *Safeguarding the Digital Realm.*, 2024, pp. 81-103.
[http://dx.doi.org/10.4018/979-8-3693-2782-1.ch005]

[38] H.C. Mingo, "The Emerging Cybersecurity Challenges With Artificial Intelligence", *Adv. Med. Technol. Clin. Pract.,* pp. 163-185, 2024.
[http://dx.doi.org/10.4018/979-8-3693-3226-9.ch010]

[39] A. Haleem, M. Javaid, and R.P. Singh, "Encouraging Safety 4.0 to enhance industrial culture: An extensive study of its technologies, roles, and challenges", *Green Technologies and Sustainability,* vol. 3, no. 3, p. 100158, 2025.
[http://dx.doi.org/10.1016/j.grets.2024.100158]

[40] H. Altafi, S. Suresh, and K. Zareinia, "The potential of cloud-based AI-enabled platforms in healthcare education", *Int. J. Intell. Robot. Appl.,* no. Dec, 2024.
[http://dx.doi.org/10.1007/s41315-024-00405-3]

[41] J. Ali, S. Kumar Singh, W. Jiang, A.M. Alenezi, M. Islam, Y. Ibrahim Daradkeh, and A. Mehmood, "A deep dive into cybersecurity solutions for AI-driven IoT-enabled smart cities in advanced communication networks", *Comput. Commun.,* vol. 229, p. 108000, 2025.
[http://dx.doi.org/10.1016/j.comcom.2024.108000]

CHAPTER 5

The Future of Diagnosis, Treatment, and Care with AI-Powered Healthcare

Abstract: AI is radically changing the healthcare industry by providing ground-breaking solutions for surgery, therapy, diagnosis, and patient management. In this chapter, the academic applications of artificial intelligence (AI) in several healthcare disciplines are explored, along with the advantages and difficulties of adopting AI. In order to improve illness identification, lower diagnostic mistakes, and speed up the interpretation of complicated imaging data, machine learning techniques are used in medical imaging and diagnostics. This chapter also discussed AI-driven tools used in robotically assisted operations, showing how these innovations enhance surgical accuracy, shorten recuperation periods, and make difficult treatments more likely to succeed. Predictive analytics and artificial intelligence's role in customized medicine are covered extensively in this chapter.

Keywords: Artificial Intelligence, AI-Diagnosis, Healthcare, Machine Learning.

1. INTRODUCTION TO AI IN HEALTHCARE

Artificial intelligence, broadly transforming industries globally, including healthcare, is an area of interest to researchers. Because AI is known to work with huge volumes of data, recognize patterns and predict outcomes, it is increasingly playing a more vital role in healthcare delivery, clinical decision-making, patient outcomes, and operational efficiencies (Fig. **1**). The emergence of technologies using artificial intelligence (AI) within healthcare holds much promise. AI in healthcare improves patient diagnosis, boosts cost-effectiveness, and helps with prevention and treatment. It also helps ensure that everyone has fair access to healthcare [1].

Artificial Intelligence (AI) is a simulation of human intelligence in machines aimed at programming to think, learn, and solve problems. It incorporates the technologies that enable machines to perform tasks usually requiring human intelligence such as visual perception, speech recognition, decision-making, and language translation.

Researchers have three ideas about how AI may be used in healthcare. According to the first scenario, AI would diagnose every patient, negating the necessity for physicians. This position's main motivation is to save costs while maintaining similar patient outcomes. Another potential is that AI will be able to evaluate more patients while clinicians examine fewer cases, which would result in fewer patients being treated by physicians and lower costs for the healthcare system. Finally, AI may benefit medical professionals by assisting them in making wiser decisions that will enhance patient outcomes and save costs [2, 3].

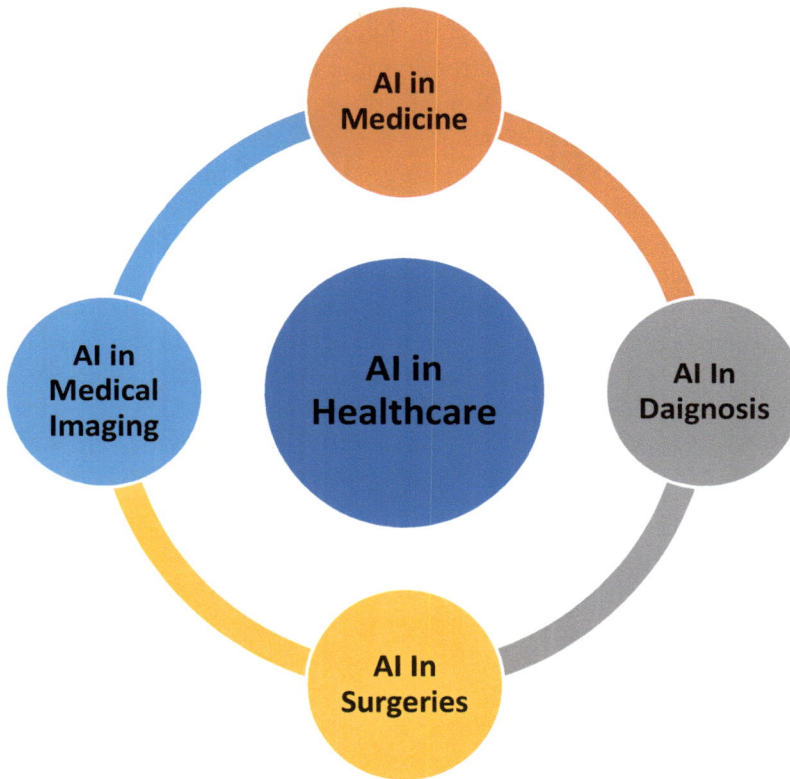

Fig. (1). Role of artificial intelligence in healthcare.

1.1. Significance of AI in Healthcare

Healthcare systems around the world face immense pressure today, either due to increasing pressure from the aging population, chronic diseases, healthcare worker shortages, or increasing costs. AI offers solutions to challenges like these by putting forth tools that can help streamline healthcare processes, better detect diagnoses, and enable personalized treatments. Let's look into why it is indispensable in healthcare:

a. **Data Overload:** Modern healthcare has produced an enormous amount of data such as patient records, imaging data, genomics, and clinical trial results. However, with that size of a dataset, human practitioners cannot analyze and process it efficiently enough to significantly improve the care provided to patients. The reason AI can be an invaluable tool for improving outcomes is its ability to sift quickly through massive datasets accurately.

b. **Accuracy and Precision:** Human fallibility is inevitable in healthcare most often caused by long hours of work, cognitive biases, or even the gaps left in knowledge. AI algorithms make decisions based on data that will always work without getting tired or harboring biases hence allowing more accurate diagnoses and suggestions for treatment. For instance, imaging tools led by artificial intelligence can pick almost imperceptible changes that may define a patient's early diagnosis of cancer.

c. **Personalization:** AI can be more personal and end up being the actual healing for real patients. Most importantly, this is highly crucial because oncology is one of those fields where AI can predict how different patients will respond to specific drugs based on their genetic makeup, medical history, and lifestyle.

d. **Efficiency:** Most healthcare systems are clogged with inefficiencies, from the waste of time trying to schedule appointments to handle records for patients. AI can automate so much of this process that valuable time for healthcare professionals may be left for time spent on patient care. Even a routine administrative task or an initial patient consultation may be replaced by an AI-driven chatbot or virtual assistant as doctors are finally free for the more complex cases.

With rapid growth and changes in AI technologies, the main aim is to research the tools and trends utilized in health care with AI applications by looking at recent trends and algorithms applied to this field. Fig. (2 provides a number of published scientific articles from the years 2005 to 2024 obtained from Scopus using keywords artificial intelligence and healthcare with 4098 research articles. The data states that there are a large number of research articles published in this field.

Artificial intelligence provides a number of techniques that are used efficiently and effectively in the healthcare industry. Some of them are discussed below:

Documents by year

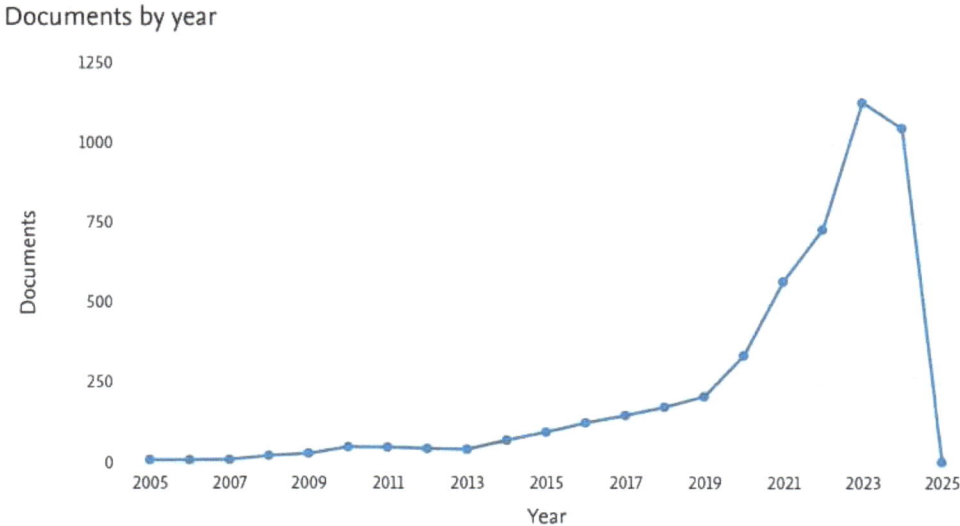

Fig. (2). Graphical representation of research articles obtained from Scopus using keywords artificial intelligence and healthcare.

a. **Machine Learning (ML):** Machine learning is at the heart of most AI applications in healthcare. By analyzing historical data, machine learning algorithms can identify patterns and predict future outcomes. In healthcare, machine learning is being applied in several critical areas:
   i. **Predictive Analytics:** ML can help predict patient outcomes, such as the likelihood of a patient being readmitted to the hospital after discharge, or the progression of chronic diseases like diabetes or heart disease. This allows healthcare providers to intervene earlier and take preventive measures.
   ii. **Diagnosis:** Machine learning algorithms can process large amounts of medical data—such as imaging scans, blood tests, and patient histories—and assist doctors in making more accurate diagnoses. For example, machine learning has shown great promise in diagnosing diseases such as cancer, where early detection is crucial for effective treatment.
   iii. **Drug Discovery:** ML can also be applied to drug discovery, significantly reducing the time it takes to identify potential drug candidates. By analyzing vast amounts of biological and chemical data, machine learning algorithms can predict how certain compounds will interact with the human body, identifying promising candidates for further research.
b. **Natural Language Processing (NLP):** NLP enables AI systems to understand and process human language, which is crucial in a field as complex as healthcare, where much of the valuable data is stored in unstructured text

formats like clinical notes, discharge summaries, and research papers. NLP applications in healthcare include:

    i. **Clinical Documentation:** AI-driven NLP tools can automate the process of converting doctors' notes, which are often handwritten or dictated, into structured, searchable data in electronic health records (EHR). This not only reduces the administrative burden on healthcare providers but also improves data accessibility and accuracy.

    ii. **Sentiment Analysis:** By analysing patient feedback and reviews, NLP can help healthcare providers gauge patient satisfaction and identify areas for improvement. This feedback can be used to improve patient care, streamline services, and enhance overall healthcare experiences.

    iii. **Coding and Billing:** NLP algorithms can assist in coding medical procedures and diagnoses for billing purposes, ensuring that healthcare providers are properly reimbursed for the services they deliver [4, 5].

c. **Computer Vision (CV):** Computer vision is transforming the field of medical imaging, enabling machines to analyze images such as X-rays, MRIs, and CT scans more quickly and accurately than ever before. Some applications include:

    i. **Medical Imaging Analysis:** CV algorithms can detect patterns and abnormalities in imaging data that may be imperceptible to the human eye. For example, AI has been used to identify early-stage lung cancer in CT scans or detect diabetic retinopathy in eye images.

    ii. **Remote Diagnostics:** AI-driven computer vision tools are being integrated into telemedicine platforms, allowing for remote diagnosis and monitoring of patients. This is especially useful in rural or underserved areas where access to specialist care may be limited.

d. **Robotics:** AI is also revolutionizing the field of robotics, particularly in surgical applications. Robots equipped with AI are being used to perform minimally invasive surgeries, leading to faster recovery times and reduced risk of complications [6]. In addition to surgery, AI-powered robots are being used for rehabilitation therapy, medication delivery, and even providing companionship to elderly or isolated patients.

2. APPLICATION OF AI IN THE HEALTHCARE SECTOR

By bringing cutting-edge applications that improve patient care, expedite processes, and increase diagnostic precision, artificial intelligence (AI) is completely changing the healthcare industry. The following cutting-edge AI uses have a big influence on the healthcare industry:

a. **Clinical Environments using Ambient AI:** Ambient AI describes systems that perform seamlessly in the clinical environment without interrupting physician workflow. For example, with ambient AI, it is possible to monitor patients' vital signs, detect abnormalities, and report these to physicians in real-time. With the integration of electronic medical records (EMRs), ambient AI enhances data quality and reduces the administrative burden on clinical staff.

b. **AI in Repurposing and Drug Discovery:** Through a deep analysis of huge datasets and further identification of probable medicinal molecules, artificial intelligence makes the entire process of finding a drug extremely simplified. Even using the new advancement in AI could significantly save the time of introducing new medicines along with significant savings in expenses.

c. **Healthcare with Generative AI:** The synthesis of innovative, artificial medical data through generative AI models, in turn, enables training and research without sacrificing patient privacy. These models can help simulate complex biological processes to create individualized treatment regimens and improve patient outcomes.

d. **AI-Boosted Interoperability of Health Data:** Northwestern Medicine researchers developed a new AI model that improved the conversion of EHR data into standardized health resources better than existing techniques. This development improves coordinated patient care by enhancing health data interoperability and enabling smooth information flow across various healthcare systems.

e. **AI in Diagnostics and Imaging in Medicine:** AI algorithms are being used to scan medical pictures, such as X-rays, CT scans, and MRIs, in order to help make preliminary diagnoses about diseases, such as cancers, fractures, and infections, without relying on human sight and potentially making earlier and more accurate diagnoses.

f. **AI in Remote Surveillance and Virtual Care:** Wearable technology and AI-driven virtual care platforms allow for the continuous monitoring of patients, enabling real-time health assessments and the early identification of possible problems. This technology is particularly helpful when it comes to treating patients in underserved or remote areas and managing chronic illnesses.

These advanced AI applications are transforming the healthcare sector by offering solutions that enhance productivity, reduce costs, and lead to better patient outcomes. With further development in AI technology, its application in healthcare is expected to grow even more, thus leading to ever more creative answers to challenging medical problems.

3. AI IN DIAGNOSTICS

Artificial Intelligence (AI) has emerged as a revolutionary tool in the field of medical diagnostics, offering immense potential to improve diagnostic accuracy, speed, and accessibility. With its ability to analyze large volumes of data, identify patterns, and make predictions, AI is being used to assist healthcare professionals in diagnosing diseases, interpreting medical images, and predicting patient outcomes. This chapter explores the various ways AI is being applied in diagnostics, including its role in early disease detection, medical imaging, predictive analytics, and the development of personalized treatment plans.

3.1. The Importance of Accurate Diagnostics in Healthcare

Accurate and timely diagnosis is the foundation of effective healthcare. The correct identification of diseases and conditions enables healthcare providers to implement appropriate treatment plans, improving patient outcomes and reducing healthcare costs. However, the diagnostic process can be complex, requiring the interpretation of numerous tests, imaging studies, and clinical data. In some cases, human error, cognitive biases, or overwhelming amounts of data can lead to misdiagnosis, delayed treatment, or suboptimal care. This is where AI steps in to assist healthcare professionals by providing tools that enhance diagnostic precision and efficiency.

3.2. AI-Powered Medical Imaging: Revolutionizing Radiology and Pathology

One of the most significant contributions of AI to diagnostics is its impact on medical imaging. AI-powered algorithms, particularly those based on machine learning and deep learning, have shown great promise in analyzing medical images such as X-rays, MRIs, CT scans, and histopathological slides. These algorithms can detect patterns, abnormalities, and subtle changes that might be missed by the human eye, leading to earlier and more accurate diagnoses.

a. **AI in Radiology:** Radiology, the field of medicine that uses imaging to diagnose and treat diseases, has been one of the earliest adopters of AI. AI algorithms are being developed and deployed to analyze radiological images, helping radiologists identify diseases such as cancer, pneumonia, fractures, and neurological disorders with greater accuracy and speed.
   i. **Cancer Detection:** AI has been particularly successful in the early detection of cancers, such as breast cancer, lung cancer, and colorectal cancer. For example, AI systems can analyze mammograms to detect early signs of breast cancer, often identifying tumors that are too small to be noticed by a radiologist. AI's ability to detect minute differences in tissue density or structure helps catch cancers at an earlier stage, when treatment is more likely to be effective.
   ii. **Lung Disease Detection:** In the case of lung diseases such as pneumonia or COVID-19, AI algorithms can analyze chest X-rays or CT scans to

detect early signs of infection. This has been especially useful during the COVID-19 pandemic, where AI tools were used to identify lung abnormalities associated with the virus, aiding in quicker diagnoses and patient isolation to prevent further spread.

iii. **Neurological Imaging:** AI is also making strides in the field of neurological imaging. For instance, deep learning algorithms can analyze brain scans to detect early signs of neurodegenerative diseases like Alzheimer's and Parkinson's. By identifying patterns of brain atrophy or abnormal protein deposits, AI can assist in diagnosing these conditions at an earlier stage, allowing for more proactive management.

b. **AI in Pathology:** Pathology, the study of diseases through the examination of tissue samples, is another area where AI is having a profound impact. Traditionally, pathologists analyze slides of tissue samples under a microscope, looking for abnormalities such as cancerous cells or signs of infection. This process is time-consuming and can be subject to human error. AI-powered digital pathology solutions are now being developed to automate the analysis of histopathological slides, improving both the speed and accuracy of diagnoses.

i. **Histopathology and Cancer Diagnosis:** AI algorithms can analyze digitized pathology slides to identify cancerous cells and classify tumors based on their type, grade, and stage. This has proven particularly effective in diagnosing cancers such as skin cancer (melanoma), breast cancer, and prostate cancer.

ii. **Infectious Disease Diagnosis:** AI is also being applied to the diagnosis of infectious diseases through pathology. AI can be used to identify parasitic infections, bacterial infections, or viral infections by analyzing tissue samples or blood smears. This is especially valuable in resource-limited settings, where access to trained pathologists may be scarce.

c. **AI and Multi-modal Imaging:** AI's ability to integrate data from multiple imaging modalities (*e.g.*, combining CT scans, MRIs, and PET scans) allows for a more comprehensive and holistic view of a patient's condition. This multi-modal approach enables AI to provide a more accurate diagnosis by correlating different types of data, leading to better treatment decisions.

3.3. Predictive Analytics in Diagnostics: Harnessing Big Data for Early Detection

Predictive analytics is another area where AI is transforming diagnostics. By analyzing large datasets of patient information—including medical records, lab results, genetic data, and lifestyle factors—AI can predict the likelihood of a patient developing certain conditions, such as cardiovascular disease, diabetes, or even mental health disorders. This allows healthcare providers to intervene earlier, implement preventive measures, and tailor treatments to individual patients.

a. **Cardiovascular Disease Prediction:** Cardiovascular diseases (CVDs) are the leading cause of death worldwide, and early detection is crucial for reducing mortality. AI-powered predictive models can analyze a patient's clinical history, lifestyle data, and even wearable device data (such as heart rate and activity levels) to predict the risk of developing heart disease or having a heart attack. AI algorithms can identify patterns that indicate early signs of CVD, such as changes in heart rhythm, elevated blood pressure, or abnormal cholesterol levels, allowing doctors to implement preventive interventions such as medication or lifestyle modifications.

b. **Diabetes Prediction and Management:** Diabetes is another condition where AI has shown great promise. By analyzing data such as glucose levels, weight, and diet, AI algorithms can predict a patient's risk of developing type 2 diabetes. For patients who are already diagnosed with diabetes, AI tools can help monitor blood sugar levels and predict complications such as diabetic retinopathy or neuropathy. This real-time analysis enables healthcare providers to adjust treatment plans accordingly, improving patient outcomes and reducing complications [7].

3.4. AI in Genomics and Personalized Diagnostics

AI is playing an increasingly important role in analyzing genomic data to identify genetic mutations, predict disease risk, and develop personalized treatment plans.

a. **Cancer Genomics:** In oncology, AI is being used to analyze genomic data to identify mutations that drive cancer growth. For example, AI can help detect mutations in genes like BRCA1 and BRCA2, which are linked to a higher risk of breast and ovarian cancers. By understanding a patient's genetic profile, doctors can choose targeted therapies that are more likely to be effective based on the specific mutations driving cancer.

b. **Rare Disease Diagnosis:** AI is also helping to diagnose rare diseases, which are often difficult to identify due to their rarity and the complexity of their symptoms. AI algorithms can analyze a patient's genetic data, family history, and clinical presentation to identify patterns that may indicate a rare genetic disorder. This is particularly valuable in cases where patients have undergone years of misdiagnosis or inconclusive tests.

c. **Pharmacogenomics:** Pharmacogenomics is the study of how a person's genes affect their response to drugs. AI-powered tools can analyze a patient's genetic data to predict how they will metabolize certain medications, reducing the risk of adverse drug reactions and improving treatment outcomes. This is particularly useful in fields like psychiatry, where patients often respond differently to antidepressants or antipsychotic medications based on their genetic makeup [8].

3.5. AI-Assisted Diagnostic Decision Support Systems

AI is not only improving diagnostic accuracy but also enhancing the decision-making process for healthcare providers. AI-powered diagnostic decision support systems (DDSS) are being developed to assist doctors in interpreting clinical data, suggesting potential diagnoses, and recommending appropriate tests or treatments. These systems analyze a patient's symptoms, medical history, and diagnostic test results to provide evidence-based suggestions, helping doctors make more informed decisions.

a. **Symptom Checkers and AI Chatbots:** AI-powered symptom checkers and chatbots allow patients to input their symptoms and receive preliminary diagnostic suggestions.
b. **Clinical Decision Support Systems:** AI-driven clinical decision support systems are integrated into electronic health records (EHR) to assist healthcare providers during patient consultations.

4. AI IN PERSONALIZED MEDICINE

Personalized medicine, also known as precision medicine, is an approach to healthcare that tailors medical treatment to the individual characteristics of each patient. This includes their genetic makeup, lifestyle, environment, and personal medical history. The advent of AI has enabled a more nuanced and individualized method, transforming healthcare delivery and significantly improving outcomes for patients. At the core of personalized medicine is the idea that every patient is unique.

4.1. The Role of AI in Personalized Medicine

AI enhances personalized medicine in several key ways. It can help analyze complex datasets, such as genetic information, patient histories, and lifestyle factors, to provide insights that support individualized care. The following sections outline the main ways AI is transforming personalized medicine:

a. AI-Driven Genomic Analysis

One of the most impactful applications of AI in personalized medicine is in the field of genomics, the study of an individual's genes and their functions. Genomic medicine has opened new doors for understanding how genetic variations influence disease susceptibility, drug responses, and health outcomes.

AI algorithms are increasingly being used to analyze large genomic datasets to identify the genetic factors associated with the disease. This approach is particularly valuable in fields like oncology, where identifying specific mutations or genetic markers can guide targeted therapies.

b. AI in Cardiovascular Disease Management

Cardiovascular disease (CVD) is one of the leading causes of death globally, and managing it requires a highly individualized approach. AI-driven predictive models can analyze a patient's risk factors—such as cholesterol levels, blood pressure, genetics, and lifestyle habits (*e.g.*, smoking, physical activity)—to predict their likelihood of experiencing a heart attack or stroke, by providing personalized risk scores [9].

c. AI in Psychiatry and Mental Health

Mental health conditions, such as depression, anxiety, and schizophrenia, are notoriously difficult to treat due to the variability in how patients respond to different medications. For example, antidepressants may work well for some patients but have a little effect on others, and it can take weeks or months to determine whether a medication is effective.

AI can help solve this problem by analyzing genetic data, patient history, and even real-time behavioral data to predict how a patient will respond to psychiatric medications. This is especially important in conditions like treatment-resistant depression, where finding the right medication can be a lengthy process.

d. AI in Pain Management

Chronic pain management is another area where AI is improving personalized care. Pain is a subjective experience, and patients often respond differently to pain medications. AI-driven predictive models can analyze a patient's genetic makeup and pain history to determine which medications or therapies are most likely to provide relief.

4.2. AI in Personalized Vaccines and Immunotherapy

Vaccines and immunotherapy represent cutting-edge areas of personalized medicine where AI is making a significant impact. Immunotherapy, which harnesses the body's immune system to fight diseases like cancer, can be highly effective, but its success varies depending on the individual's immune profile. AI is helping to create more personalized immunotherapies by predicting how a patient's immune system will respond to certain treatments.

a. AI in Cancer Immunotherapy

One of the most promising areas of personalized medicine is cancer immunotherapy, where the patient's immune system is stimulated to attack cancer cells. AI is being used to analyze the genetic and immunological profiles of both the patient and the tumor to design custom immunotherapies that are more likely to be effective.

b. AI in Infectious Disease Vaccination

AI's role in developing personalized vaccines extends beyond just COVID-19. In infectious diseases like HIV and influenza, where the virus mutates rapidly, traditional vaccines can often fall short. AI models, trained on vast viral genetic data, can predict the most likely mutations in the virus and identify which antigens (virus components) are most likely to elicit a strong immune response. By using this information, AI helps researchers design vaccines that are tailored not only to specific strains of the virus but also to individual patients' immune system profiles.

c. AI for Personalized Preventive Healthcare

One of the most promising applications of AI in personalized medicine is its potential to shift the focus of healthcare from treatment to prevention. By analyzing a wide range of data, including genetic information, environmental factors, lifestyle choices, and medical history, AI can predict which patients are at risk for developing certain diseases and recommend tailored preventive measures.

d. AI and Predictive Health Risk Assessment

AI's ability to predict future health risks based on existing data is a game-changer in preventive medicine. For example, AI models can analyze a combination of genetic data and lifestyle factors to predict a person's risk of developing conditions such as heart disease, diabetes, and certain types of cancer. Armed with this information, healthcare providers can design personalized preventive strategies, such as recommending dietary changes, exercise regimens, or medications to mitigate these risks.

5. AI IN SURGERY AND ROBOTICS

Artificial Intelligence (AI) is revolutionizing the field of surgery through its integration into robotic systems and real-time analytics, pushing the boundaries of precision, efficiency, and patient safety. The concept of robotic-assisted surgery has been around for several years, but the inclusion of AI has propelled it into a new era, with applications ranging from improved precision during operations to real-time decision-making support. As healthcare moves into an era of personalized and technology-enhanced care, AI-assisted surgery and autonomous robotic systems are emerging as key drivers of change.

In this chapter, we will delve into the various ways AI is being integrated into surgical robotics, improving precision and reducing recovery times. We will also explore how autonomous surgical robots enhance surgeon capabilities and the role of AI-driven real-time analytics in surgical procedures.

5.1. The Rise of Robotic-Assisted Surgery

Robotic-assisted surgery is one of the most significant technological advancements in modern healthcare. Surgical robots, such as the da Vinci Surgical System, have been widely adopted for minimally invasive procedures, providing surgeons with greater dexterity and control. These robots are operated by highly trained surgeons who manipulate robotic arms to perform complex surgeries through small incisions, resulting in fewer complications, reduced scarring, and shorter recovery times for patients.

While robotic-assisted surgery improves precision, the integration of AI is adding layers of intelligence that take the technology beyond human limitations. AI-powered robotic systems can process large volumes of data, learn from historical surgical cases, and provide real-time insights during procedures, making surgeries more efficient, accurate, and safe.

a. AI in Robotic-Assisted Surgeries: Improving Precision and Reducing Recovery Times

Precision is one of the key advantages of robotic-assisted surgery, and AI is amplifying this benefit. By integrating AI into surgical robots, the accuracy of procedures can be increased substantially. These robots are equipped with machine learning algorithms that help to guide the surgeon's movements, ensuring that delicate procedures are performed with millimeter-level precision.

b. Enhanced Surgical Precision

AI-driven robotic systems can analyze a patient's unique anatomy using preoperative imaging data, such as CT scans or MRIs. Machine learning algorithms process this data to create detailed, 3D models of the patient's internal structures, which the robot uses to guide its movements. During surgery, the AI can track the position of surgical instruments in real-time, adjusting their placement based on the patient's anatomy and any intraoperative changes. This real-time adjustment capability allows surgeons to avoid critical structures like nerves and blood vessels, thereby reducing the risk of complications.

c. Personalized Surgical Approaches

AI is also making robotic-assisted surgeries more personalized. By analyzing preoperative data and patient-specific factors, such as age, weight, genetic markers, and pre-existing conditions, AI systems can tailor surgical plans to each patient. These systems use data from thousands of previous surgeries to recommend optimal techniques and pathways, ensuring that each patient receives a customized approach that improves outcomes and reduces recovery times.

d. Minimally Invasive Techniques and Faster Recovery

Minimally invasive surgeries, such as laparoscopic procedures, have long been favored for their reduced recovery times compared to traditional open surgeries. AI-enhanced robotic systems further reduce recovery times by improving the accuracy of these procedures. By minimizing tissue damage and reducing the need for large incisions, AI-powered robots contribute to faster healing, less postoperative pain, and shorter hospital stays.

5.2. Autonomous Surgical Robots: Enhancing Surgeon Capabilities

While robotic-assisted surgeries currently require the direct input of a human surgeon, the future of surgery may involve autonomous or semi-autonomous surgical robots. These AI-driven systems are designed to perform certain surgical tasks independently or with minimal human intervention, thereby enhancing surgeon capabilities and improving overall surgical efficiency.

a. The Evolution of Autonomous Surgical Robots

Autonomous surgical robots use AI algorithms to interpret imaging data, assess surgical sites, and execute procedures with precision. These robots are not intended to replace human surgeons but rather to assist them by performing repetitive or time-consuming tasks with greater accuracy and speed. By automating certain aspects of surgery, these robots allow surgeons to focus on more complex or delicate aspects of the procedure.

b. AI in Autonomous Endoscopy

Endoscopic procedures, which involve inserting a small camera into the body to examine internal organs, are becoming more sophisticated with the help of AI-driven robots. Autonomous endoscopy robots can navigate through the body, detect abnormalities, and even perform biopsies or remove small lesions without the need for human control. These robots are equipped with advanced AI systems that process real-time imaging data to identify areas of concern, such as polyps or tumors, and take appropriate action.

c. Autonomous Robots in Orthopedic Surgery

In orthopedic surgery, autonomous robots are being developed to assist with tasks such as drilling, cutting, and implant positioning. The Mako Robotic-Arm Assisted Surgery System, for instance, uses AI to plan and execute partial knee replacements with a high degree of precision. The system creates a personalized surgical plan based on the patient's anatomy, and the robot autonomously performs tasks such as bone cutting and implant placement with millimeter-level accuracy.

5.3. AI-Driven Real-Time Analytics During Surgical Procedures

One of the most transformative applications of AI in surgery is real-time analytics. During surgery, AI systems can process data from a variety of sources—such as imaging scans, patient monitors, and surgical instruments—to provide surgeons with real-time insights and recommendations. These insights enhance decision-making, improve patient safety, and increase the likelihood of successful outcomes.

a. AI-Powered Image Recognition and Analysis

AI-driven image recognition systems can analyze medical images in real-time during surgery, helping surgeons identify critical structures and abnormalities that may not be immediately visible to the human eye. For example, during a liver resection surgery, AI can analyze ultrasound or CT images to highlight blood vessels, tumors, or other important structures, allowing the surgeon to plan their incisions with greater precision and avoid damaging healthy tissue.

Real-time image analysis is especially valuable in oncologic surgeries, where the goal is to remove as much of the cancerous tissue as possible while preserving healthy tissue. AI-powered image recognition systems can help surgeons differentiate between healthy and cancerous tissues with greater accuracy, reducing the risk of leaving behind residual cancer cells that could lead to recurrence.

b. Intraoperative Decision Support

AI systems are also being developed to provide real-time decision support during surgery. These systems use machine learning algorithms to analyze data from the patient's medical history, preoperative imaging, and intraoperative metrics (such as blood pressure, oxygen levels, and heart rate) to offer recommendations to the surgeon. For example, AI can suggest adjustments to the surgical plan based on real-time changes in the patient's condition, such as unexpected bleeding or shifts in vital signs.

One area where this technology is being explored is in cardiac surgery. AI-driven systems can monitor the patient's vital signs during surgery, predict potential complications (such as arrhythmias or blood clots), and recommend adjustments to the surgical approach or medication dosages in real time. This level of support enables surgeons to respond more quickly and effectively to unexpected challenges, reducing the risk of complications and improving patient outcomes.

c. AI and Augmented Reality in Surgery

AI-powered augmented reality (AR) systems are another exciting development in the field of real-time surgical analytics. AR systems overlay digital information, such as 3D models or real-time imaging data, onto the surgeon's view of the operating field, providing them with enhanced visual guidance. These systems use AI algorithms to process data from preoperative imaging and intraoperative sensors, ensuring that the digital overlay is perfectly aligned with the patient's anatomy.

6. REMOTE MONITORING AND VIRTUAL HEALTH

The integration of Artificial Intelligence (AI) into healthcare is revolutionizing the way patients are monitored and cared for remotely. Through advancements in wearable devices, telemedicine, and mobile health applications, AI is enabling continuous patient monitoring, early detection of potential health issues, and personalized care. These innovations are particularly crucial in the management of chronic diseases, preventive healthcare, mental health, and even emergency intervention. AI-enhanced technologies are transforming the traditional healthcare model by improving access, reducing costs, and enhancing the quality of care.

This chapter explores the role of AI in remote monitoring and virtual health through three primary avenues: (1) the use of wearable devices and AI for continuous patient monitoring and chronic disease management, (2) AI in telemedicine platforms to facilitate remote consultations and patient follow-ups, and (3) the integration of AI in mobile health applications for wellness, mental health, and preventive care.

7. WEARABLE DEVICES FOR CONTINUOUS PATIENT MONITORING

Wearable devices, such as smartwatches, fitness trackers, and biosensors, have become ubiquitous in today's health-conscious society. These devices monitor a range of physiological data, including heart rate, physical activity, sleep patterns, and even blood oxygen levels. However, when combined with AI, these wearables transcend their role as simple health trackers and become powerful tools for continuous patient monitoring, early intervention, and chronic disease management.

a. AI-Driven Continuous Monitoring

One of the key advantages of AI in wearable devices is the ability to process vast amounts of real-time health data continuously and provide actionable insights. AI algorithms can analyze patterns in the data and detect deviations that may indicate early signs of a health issue. For example, an AI-powered wearable might notice irregular heartbeats or fluctuations in blood pressure that could signal the onset of cardiovascular problems. In such cases, the AI system can alert both the patient and their healthcare provider, enabling early intervention that could prevent more serious complications.

For individuals with chronic diseases like diabetes or hypertension, continuous monitoring is essential to prevent health deterioration. Wearable devices equipped with AI can track blood glucose levels, blood pressure, and other vital signs, alerting patients and doctors to any abnormal trends. For instance, AI can predict when a diabetic patient's blood sugar levels are likely to spike based on historical data, dietary inputs, and physical activity levels. The AI system can then recommend adjustments in medication or lifestyle to prevent a dangerous increase in blood sugar.

b. Early Intervention and Emergency Response

AI in wearable devices also plays a crucial role in early intervention and emergency situations. For example, many smartwatches today come with built-in electrocardiograms (ECGs) that can monitor the heart's electrical activity. AI algorithms analyze this data in real time to detect arrhythmias or other abnormalities. If a severe issue is detected—such as atrial fibrillation, which could lead to stroke—the AI system can prompt the user to seek immediate medical attention or even contact emergency services.

AI systems can also predict potential health crises before they occur. By analyzing historical health data alongside real-time readings, AI can identify trends and patterns that may lead to adverse events. For example, AI can monitor respiratory rates and oxygen saturation in patients with chronic obstructive pulmonary disease (COPD) and predict when an exacerbation is likely to occur. The system can then alert the patient to take preventive medication or seek medical attention before the condition worsens.

c. Chronic Disease Management

Managing chronic diseases such as diabetes, heart disease, and hypertension often requires ongoing monitoring and frequent adjustments to treatment plans. AI in wearable devices helps streamline this process by continuously tracking relevant health metrics and offering personalized recommendations.

For example, AI can assist diabetic patients by analyzing blood glucose data in real time, along with factors such as food intake, physical activity, and insulin levels. The AI system can provide immediate feedback on how to adjust diet, exercise, or medication to keep blood glucose levels within a healthy range. Similarly, for patients with hypertension, AI can analyze daily blood pressure readings and suggest lifestyle changes, medication adjustments, or the need for medical consultation if the readings become dangerously high.

The real-time feedback provided by AI-driven wearables enables patients to take proactive steps in managing their conditions, reducing the need for frequent doctor visits and preventing the progression of disease. In this way, AI empowers patients to take control of their own health, leading to better outcomes and lower healthcare costs.

8. TELEMEDICINE PLATFORMS: REMOTE CONSULTATIONS AND PATIENT FOLLOW-UPS

Telemedicine, the practice of delivering healthcare remotely using telecommunications technology, has experienced explosive growth, especially in the wake of the COVID-19 pandemic. AI is playing an increasingly important role in enhancing the capabilities of telemedicine platforms by facilitating remote consultations, patient follow-ups, and even diagnostics. The combination of AI with telemedicine has the potential to improve access to healthcare, especially in underserved or rural areas, and to provide more efficient, data-driven care [7].

a. AI-Powered Remote Consultations

Telemedicine platforms are leveraging AI to enhance remote consultations by providing doctors with real-time data and decision-support tools. AI algorithms can analyze patient data—such as electronic health records (EHRs), test results, and data from wearable devices—and present the most relevant information to doctors during virtual consultations. This reduces the time doctors spend reviewing patient histories and helps them make more informed decisions during the consultation.

Additionally, AI can assist doctors by offering diagnostic suggestions based on the symptoms and data provided by the patient. For example, during a virtual consultation, an AI-powered system might analyze a patient's reported symptoms, cross-reference them with the patient's medical history, suggest potential diagnoses, or recommend further testing. This not only improves the accuracy of remote consultations but also reduces the risk of missed diagnoses.

For routine check-ups and follow-ups, AI chatbots and virtual assistants are being employed to interact with patients. These AI tools can ask patients about their symptoms, track recovery progress, and even provide medical advice for managing minor conditions. For example, if a patient is recovering from surgery, an AI-powered virtual assistant could check in daily, asking about pain levels, medication adherence, and any signs of infection, and then flag any concerns for a human doctor to review.

b. Remote Diagnostics and AI-Assisted Image Analysis

In telemedicine, one of the challenges is conducting diagnostics without the ability to physically examine the patient. AI is helping to bridge this gap by enabling remote diagnostics through image analysis and other data-driven methods. For example, patients can upload images of skin conditions, and AI algorithms can analyze the images to detect signs of melanoma or other skin disorders. These AI systems are trained on vast datasets of medical images, allowing them to accurately identify and classify skin lesions, rashes, or infections, sometimes more accurately than human dermatologists.

In radiology, AI is being used to interpret medical images remotely. Patients can undergo diagnostic imaging, such as X-rays or MRIs, at local facilities, and the images can then be uploaded to a telemedicine platform for AI analysis. The AI system can detect abnormalities, such as tumors, fractures, or infections, and provide a preliminary report to the patient's doctor. This allows for faster diagnosis and treatment, especially in areas where access to specialists is limited.

c. AI-Enhanced Patient Follow-Ups

Follow-up care is a critical component of healthcare, especially for patients recovering from surgery or managing chronic diseases. However, in traditional healthcare settings, regular follow-up visits can be inconvenient for patients and time-consuming for doctors. AI in telemedicine is transforming follow-up care by automating much of the monitoring and communication between patients and healthcare providers.

For example, after a patient undergoes surgery, an AI-driven telemedicine platform can monitor their recovery by tracking symptoms, medication adherence, and physical activity levels. The AI system can identify signs of complications, such as increased pain, swelling, or fever, and alert the healthcare provider to intervene. This allows for timely follow-ups and reduces the likelihood of readmission to the hospital.

Moreover, AI systems can help manage medication adherence for chronic disease patients by sending reminders and tracking medication usage. If the AI detects that a patient has missed doses or reports side effects, it can notify the healthcare provider to adjust the treatment plan or provide additional support [10, 11].

9. AI IN MOBILE HEALTH APPS

Mobile health (mHealth) apps have become a popular tool for individuals seeking to improve their health and well-being. These apps cover a wide range of functions, from fitness tracking to mental health support, and many are now incorporating AI to offer more personalized and effective care. The integration of AI in mHealth apps is transforming preventive care, wellness management, and mental health support by providing real-time insights, personalized recommendations, and continuous monitoring.

a. AI for Personalized Wellness and Fitness Tracking

AI-enhanced mHealth apps use machine learning algorithms to provide personalized wellness and fitness recommendations based on the user's health data, goals, and preferences. For example, AI can analyze data from wearables—such as daily steps, heart rate, and sleep patterns—and offer tailored fitness plans to help users meet their health goals, whether it's weight loss, improved cardiovascular health, or muscle building.

AI systems in wellness apps can also adjust recommendations based on real-time feedback. For example, if a user has a particularly sedentary day, the app might suggest a more intense workout the next day or remind the user to stand up and move periodically. These personalized recommendations keep users engaged and motivated, helping them achieve better health outcomes over time.

AI-driven wellness apps can also monitor diet and nutrition, analyzing food intake and offering recommendations to improve dietary habits. Some apps use AI-powered image recognition to analyze photos of meals and estimate their nutritional content, making it easier for users to track their food intake accurately.

b. The Role of Data Privacy and Security

As we delve deeper into the potential of AI in remote monitoring and virtual health, it is crucial to address the considerations surrounding data privacy and security. The widespread adoption of wearable devices, telemedicine platforms, and mobile health applications generates vast amounts of personal health data. This data can include sensitive information such as medical histories, biometric data, and lifestyle choices. Thus, safeguarding this information is paramount to ensure trust and compliance with regulations.

i. Ensuring Data Security

Data security involves protecting data from unauthorized access and breaches. AI technologies can enhance security measures by implementing advanced encryption techniques, biometric authentication, and continuous monitoring of suspicious activities. For instance, AI can analyze patterns of data access and detect anomalies that may indicate a potential breach, allowing healthcare organizations to act swiftly to protect patient information.

Telemedicine platforms and mHealth applications must comply with regulations such as the Health Insurance Portability and Accountability Act (HIPAA) in the United States, which sets standards for protecting sensitive patient information. Ensuring compliance not only safeguards patient data but also fosters trust between healthcare providers and patients. AI can aid in compliance monitoring by continuously evaluating systems and practices against regulatory requirements, identifying potential vulnerabilities, and recommending corrective actions.

ii. Patient Consent and Transparency

In addition to data security, patient consent and transparency are critical aspects of AI in healthcare. Patients must be informed about how their data will be collected, used, and shared. AI-driven health applications should provide clear and understandable consent forms, allowing patients to make informed choices about their participation in remote monitoring and virtual health services.

Transparency about AI algorithms and decision-making processes is also essential. Patients should have access to information regarding how AI systems analyze their data and generate recommendations. By fostering transparency, healthcare providers can enhance patient trust in AI-driven solutions and encourage greater engagement in their own health management [12, 13].

iii. Addressing Health Inequities

While AI has the potential to improve healthcare access and outcomes, it is essential to consider the issue of health inequities. Disparities in access to technology, healthcare services, and education can exacerbate existing inequalities in health outcomes. As AI technologies continue to evolve, efforts must be made to ensure that they are accessible to all populations, particularly underserved communities.

c. The Role of Healthcare Providers in AI Integration

While AI technologies offer significant potential in remote monitoring and virtual health, the role of healthcare providers remains critical in ensuring their successful integration into clinical practice. Providers must be equipped with the knowledge and skills to leverage AI tools effectively while maintaining the human touch that is essential in healthcare.

i. Training and Education

Healthcare providers should receive training on the capabilities and limitations of AI technologies. Understanding how to interpret AI-generated insights, integrate them into clinical decision-making, and communicate them effectively to patients is essential for maximizing the benefits of AI in remote monitoring and virtual health.

Moreover, training should also emphasize the importance of empathy and patient-centered care. While AI can provide valuable data and recommendations, the human connection between healthcare providers and patients is irreplaceable. Providers should be encouraged to use AI as a supportive tool that enhances, rather than replaces, their clinical judgment and interpersonal skills.

ii. Collaboration Between AI Developers and Clinicians

Collaboration between AI developers and healthcare providers is vital for creating effective and user-friendly AI solutions. Clinicians can provide valuable insights into the practical challenges they face in patient monitoring and virtual care, helping developers design tools that address real-world needs. By involving clinicians in the development process, AI solutions can be tailored to align with clinical workflows and enhance the overall user experience.

10. OPTIMIZING HOSPITAL WORKFLOWS, PATIENT SCHEDULING, AND RESOURCE MANAGEMENT

AI's application in optimizing hospital workflows and resource management is transformative. Hospitals are complex environments with numerous processes that need to function efficiently for optimal patient care. AI can streamline these processes through automation, data analysis, and predictive modeling.

10.1. AI in Hospital Workflows

Hospital workflows involve multiple tasks, including patient intake, diagnostics, treatment, and discharge. Each of these stages requires coordination among various departments and staff, which can lead to inefficiencies if not managed properly [14]. AI technologies can help optimize these workflows by:

a. **Automating Administrative Tasks**: Many administrative tasks, such as data entry, appointment scheduling, and insurance verification, can be automated using AI-powered tools. By automating these repetitive tasks, healthcare staff can dedicate more time to direct patient care and complex decision-making. For instance, AI systems can automatically extract and input patient information from various sources, reducing the chances of errors and improving the accuracy of data entry.

b. **Enhancing Communication**: AI-driven communication tools can improve inter-departmental communication within a hospital. For example, AI chatbots can assist in coordinating between departments by providing real-time updates on patient status and resource availability. This reduces delays and ensures that the right information reaches the right people at the right time.

c. **Streamlining Patient Flow**: AI can optimize patient flow by analyzing historical data and predicting patient admission rates, wait times, and discharge times. This information helps hospitals allocate staff and resources more effectively, reducing bottlenecks and ensuring that patients receive timely care [15].

10.2. AI in Patient Scheduling

Patient scheduling is a critical component of hospital operations that directly impacts patient satisfaction and care quality. Traditional scheduling methods can be cumbersome and often lead to double bookings or long wait times. AI enhances patient scheduling through:

a. **Predictive Analytics**: AI systems can analyze historical appointment data to predict peak times for patient visits, allowing hospitals to schedule appointments more efficiently. By understanding patient demand patterns, healthcare organizations can optimize their scheduling processes, leading to better resource allocation and reduced patient wait times.

b. **Dynamic Scheduling**: AI can enable dynamic scheduling, where appointment slots are adjusted in real-time based on patient needs and available resources. For example, if a particular provider has a sudden cancellation, AI can automatically offer that slot to patients waiting for an appointment, maximizing the use of available time.

c. **Personalized Scheduling**: AI-powered scheduling systems can take into account individual patient preferences, medical history, and availability to create a personalized scheduling experience. This improves patient satisfaction and adherence to appointments.

10.3. AI in Resource Management

Effective resource management is essential for healthcare organizations to operate efficiently and provide high-quality care. AI can assist in resource management by:

- **Inventory Management**: AI systems can analyze usage patterns of medical supplies and equipment, predicting future needs based on historical data and trends. This helps hospitals maintain optimal inventory levels, reducing waste and ensuring that essential supplies are available when needed.
- **Staffing Optimization**: AI can predict staffing needs based on patient volumes, seasonal trends, and historical data. By ensuring that the right number of staff is scheduled at the right times, hospitals can reduce overtime costs, minimize burnout among employees, and enhance patient care quality.
- **Facility Utilization**: AI can analyze data on room utilization, procedure times, and patient flow to optimize the use of hospital facilities. This ensures that resources are used efficiently and that patients have access to the necessary services without unnecessary delays.

10.4. Reducing Administrative Burdens through AI-Powered Tools

Administrative burdens in healthcare often consume valuable time and resources that could be better spent on patient care. AI-powered tools, such as electronic health records (EHR) management systems and predictive analytics, can significantly reduce these burdens, leading to increased efficiency and improved patient outcomes.

10.4.1. AI-Powered EHR Management

Electronic health records (EHR) have become a standard in healthcare, allowing for the digital storage and sharing of patient information. However, managing EHRs can be time-consuming and prone to errors. AI enhances EHR management through:

a. **Natural Language Processing (NLP)**: AI algorithms using NLP can analyze unstructured data in EHRs, such as clinical notes and patient communications. This enables healthcare providers to extract relevant information quickly, improving clinical decision-making and patient care.

b. **Automated Data Entry**: AI systems can automatically populate EHRs with patient data from various sources, such as lab results and imaging studies. This reduces the need for manual data entry, minimizing errors and freeing up healthcare providers to focus on direct patient interaction.

c. **Interoperability**: AI can facilitate the interoperability of EHR systems across different healthcare providers. By analyzing and standardizing data formats, AI ensures that patient information is easily accessible and shareable among different systems, improving continuity of care [3].

10.4.2. Predictive Analytics for Patient Care Pathways

Predictive analytics powered by AI can significantly enhance patient care pathways, improving patient outcomes and operational efficiency. By analyzing vast amounts of data, AI can identify trends and predict future health events, allowing healthcare providers to intervene proactively.

a. **Risk Stratification**: AI can analyze patient demographics, medical histories, and clinical data to stratify patients based on their risk for certain conditions. For example, predictive models can identify patients at high risk for hospital readmission or complications following surgery. This information allows healthcare providers to tailor interventions and support services to those who need it most.

b. **Personalized Treatment Plans**: By analyzing historical treatment outcomes and patient responses, AI can help develop personalized treatment plans for patients. This ensures that care is tailored to individual needs and increases the likelihood of positive outcomes.

c. **Proactive Care Management**: Predictive analytics can identify patients who may benefit from preventive care measures, such as vaccinations or screenings. By alerting providers to these opportunities, AI promotes proactive care management and improves overall population health.

11. ETHICAL, REGULATORY, AND DATA PRIVACY CONSIDERATIONS

The integration of Artificial Intelligence (AI) in healthcare holds tremendous potential for enhancing patient care, improving operational efficiencies, and facilitating innovative solutions. However, the deployment of AI in healthcare also raises critical ethical, regulatory, and data privacy considerations that must be addressed to ensure that these technologies are used responsibly and effectively. This chapter delves into the ethical challenges associated with AI in healthcare decisions, privacy concerns regarding patient data, the regulatory frameworks governing AI applications, and the potential for bias in AI algorithms, along with strategies to mitigate these risks [4, 15]. AI technologies in healthcare can significantly influence clinical decision-making, impacting patient diagnoses, treatment options, and overall care pathways. As these technologies are adopted, several ethical challenges arise:

11.1. Informed Consent

Informed consent is a foundational principle in healthcare, ensuring that patients understand the risks and benefits of treatments and technologies used in their care. The use of AI introduces complexities in this process. For instance, patients may not fully comprehend how AI algorithms work or how they influence their care decisions. The challenge lies in effectively communicating the role of AI to patients and ensuring they are adequately informed about how their data will be used and the implications of AI-driven decisions.

To address these concerns, healthcare providers must develop clear communication strategies that outline the purpose of AI technologies, the data being utilized, and how decisions are made. Engaging patients in discussions about AI and providing accessible information can help foster trust and enhance understanding.

11.2. Autonomy and Decision-Making

AI systems can assist healthcare providers in making diagnostic and treatment decisions; however, there is a risk of undermining patient autonomy. Over-reliance on AI recommendations may lead healthcare providers to favor algorithmic decisions over individualized patient preferences and values. Patients may feel that their unique circumstances are not being considered, potentially diminishing their involvement in their care.

To ensure patient autonomy is respected, healthcare providers should adopt a collaborative approach to decision-making, integrating AI insights with clinical judgment and patient preferences. This partnership can empower patients to participate actively in their care decisions while ensuring that AI serves as a supportive tool rather than a replacement for human judgment [16].

11.3. Accountability and Liability

As AI technologies become more integrated into healthcare, questions regarding accountability and liability arise. If an AI system makes an erroneous recommendation leading to patient harm, determining who is responsible can be complex. Is it the healthcare provider who relied on the AI's recommendation, the developers of the AI system, or the healthcare institution that implemented the technology?

Establishing clear accountability frameworks is essential to address these challenges. Stakeholders in the healthcare ecosystem must work together to define roles, responsibilities, and liability in cases of adverse outcomes related to AI-driven decisions. This will require collaboration between healthcare providers, AI developers, legal experts, and regulatory bodies to ensure that accountability mechanisms are transparent and effective.

11.4. Privacy Concerns with Patient Data

The use of AI in healthcare involves the collection and analysis of vast amounts of patient data, raising significant privacy concerns. Protecting patient privacy while leveraging data for AI applications is a critical consideration that healthcare organizations must navigate. Data security refers to the measures taken to protect patient information from unauthorized access, breaches, and cyberattacks. The integration of AI increases the complexity of data security, as AI systems often require access to sensitive patient data to function effectively. Protecting this data is paramount to maintaining patient trust and safeguarding their rights.

11.4.1. Ethical Consideration in Patient Data Privacy

The following basic concepts are the basis for ethical concerns with patient data privacy in AI-based healthcare solutions:

a. **Patient Autonomy and Informed Consent:**
   ○ Patients have the right to control what is collected, shared, and used about themselves. Patients should be fully informed of how their data will be dealt with by the AI systems before they can provide their informed consent.
   ○ Only 40% of patients fully understand the terms and conditions of consent forms related to data sharing, according to a study published in JAMA Network, which calls for more transparent communication.

b. **Ownership and Control of Data**
   ◦ The ownership of patient data has been left controversial between patients and healthcare providers. Ethically, patients should remain the owners of their data; they have greater choice on its use while still in the control of the health care provider. For example, some healthcare providers are exploring data stewardship models, where organizations act as custodians but hold themselves back from making decisions on how to use the data themselves.
c. **Impartial Representation in Data Usage**
   ◦ AI needs large datasets often aggregated from different sources. AI models may also suffer from data underutilization by marginalized groups, which might lead to biased AI models. Therefore, a fair representation of data is critical to avoid discrimination.
   ◦ Ethical Challenge: Sharing data among organizations or between nations while resolving privacy issues and the need for different datasets.

11.4.2 Regulatory Challenges with AI in Healthcare

Healthcare firms have to handle complex regulatory regimes to ensure that they stay compliant because patient information is sensitive. The following are the primary regulations and challenges of AI in healthcare:

a. **Health Insurance Portability and Accountability Act (HIPAA):** According to HIPAA regulations, patient data should be protected and disclosed to only those who are allowed. AI systems must adhere to the strict standards of data protection and security implemented by HIPAA, even if they can aid in the proper care of a patient. The challenge is ensuring that AI systems adhere to HIPAA's rules on security and data sharing, especially when using outside AI companies.
b. **General Data Protection Regulation (GDPR):** GDPR imposes strict regulations on the protection of data, such as the right to be forgotten, where patients can request the deletion of personal details. Challenge: Deleting patient-specific data from the generated models, and keeping it non-functional afterward, is particularly challenging, especially in the case where the data has been used to train models.
c. **Data Residency Requirements:** In order to maintain privacy, most countries now insist that medical data be processed and stored within their borders. This complicates the implementation of AI solutions across geographical boundaries. For example, the data localization provisions in India's Personal Data Protection Bill could affect global healthcare AI partnerships.

Healthcare firms have to put in place robust data security procedures to deal with privacy issues and fulfill legal requirements. Privacy-preserving AI techniques such as differential privacy and federated learning should be used to protect sensitive patient data. Federated learning reduces privacy concerns as AI models can be trained directly on decentralized datasets without moving data to a central repository. Differential privacy means that individual data points cannot be identified while leaving the overall useful data intact by including controlled noise with datasets. Another way for enterprises to strengthen their defences is through a zero-trust security approach, which checks each access request before giving permission and greatly lowers the danger of unauthorized access. According to a Gartner analysis, healthcare companies that used zero-trust models saw a 60% decrease in data breaches during the first year of implementation.

12. CHALLENGES AND OPPORTUNITIES IN AI INTEGRATION

While the integration of AI into healthcare presents exciting opportunities, it also comes with significant challenges that must be addressed:

a. **Data Quality and Availability**: One of the primary challenges in leveraging AI in healthcare is ensuring the quality and availability of data. AI algorithms require high-quality, diverse datasets to train effectively. In many cases, healthcare data may be incomplete, inconsistent, or fragmented across different systems. Addressing data quality issues and improving interoperability between healthcare systems is essential for the successful implementation of AI technologies.

b. **Ethical Considerations:**Ethical considerations surrounding AI in healthcare remain a significant concern. Ensuring that AI algorithms are fair, transparent, and accountable is crucial to gaining the trust of patients and healthcare providers.

c. **Workforce Adaptation:**The integration of AI in healthcare will require significant changes to the healthcare workforce. Healthcare professionals must be trained to work alongside AI technologies, understanding how to interpret AI-generated insights and incorporate them into clinical decision-making.

d. **Cost and Accessibility:** While AI has the potential to improve healthcare efficiency and outcomes, the cost of implementing AI technologies can be prohibitive for some healthcare organizations, particularly smaller practices and those in low-resource settings. Efforts must be made to ensure that AI technologies are accessible and affordable for all healthcare providers, regardless of their size or location.

Despite the challenges, the future of AI in healthcare is filled with opportunities for innovation. Advances in AI technologies, such as natural language processing, computer vision, and machine learning, are continually opening new frontiers for improving patient care. Healthcare organizations that embrace AI can enhance their operational efficiencies, improve patient outcomes, and deliver more personalized care [17 - 19].

CONCLUSION

To foster a culture of innovation and adaptability, the healthcare sector can harness the full potential of AI, ultimately leading to a more effective and equitable system for all patients. This collaborative approach will not only address the challenges posed by new technologies but also ensure that advancements in AI are aligned with the core values of patient-centered care. Furthermore, ongoing education and training for healthcare professionals will be essential to navigate this transition effectively, empowering them to utilize AI tools confidently while maintaining the human touch that is vital in patient interactions. Incorporating feedback from both patients and providers will also play a crucial role in refining these technologies, ensuring they meet the real-world needs of those they serve. By fostering an environment of open communication and collaboration, we can create a healthcare landscape that not only embraces innovation but also prioritizes the well-being and dignity of every individual. This holistic approach will ultimately lead to improved health outcomes, as technology and empathy work hand in hand to enhance the patient experience.

REFERENCES

[1]   L.G. Pee, S.L. Pan, and L. Cui, "Artificial intelligence in healthcare robots: A social informatics study of knowledge embodiment", *J. Assoc. Inf. Sci. Technol.,* vol. 70, no. 4, pp. 351-369, 2019.
        [http://dx.doi.org/10.1002/asi.24145]

[2]   M.R. Neves, and D.W.R. Marsh, *Modelling the Impact of AI for Clinical Decision Support.,* 2019, pp. 292-297.
        [http://dx.doi.org/10.1007/978-3-030-21642-9_37]

[3]   A. Sharma, and R. Kumar, "Artificial Intelligence in Health Care Sector and Future Scope", In: *2023 International Conference on Innovative Data Communication Technologies and Application (ICIDCA)* IEEE, 2023, pp. 210-214.
        [http://dx.doi.org/10.1109/ICIDCA56705.2023.10100220]

[4]   Y. Wang, A. Tafti, S. Sohn, and R. Zhang, "Applications of Natural Language Processing in Clinical Research and Practice", In: *Proceedings of the 2019 Conference of the North* Association for Computational Linguistics: Stroudsburg, PA, USA, 2019, pp. 22-25.
        [http://dx.doi.org/10.18653/v1/N19-5006]

[5]   M.N.O. Sadiku, Y. Zhou, and S.M. Musa, "NATURAL LANGUAGE PROCESSING IN HEALTHCARE", *Int. J. Adv. Res. Comput. Sci. Softw. Eng.,* vol. 8, no. 5, p. 39, 2018.
        [http://dx.doi.org/10.23956/ijarcsse.v8i5.626]

[6]   R.P. Dibbs, and L.H. Hollier, "Review of "Artificial Intelligence in Surgery: Promises and Perils" by Hashimoto DA et al in Ann Surg 268:70–76, 2018", *J. Craniofac. Surg.,* vol. 30, no. 3, p. 955, 2019.
        [http://dx.doi.org/10.1097/SCS.0000000000004896]

[7]   A. Chang, *The Role of Artificial Intelligence in Digital Health.,* 2020, pp. 71-81.
        [http://dx.doi.org/10.1007/978-3-030-12719-0_7]

[8]   K. Kister, J. Laskowski, A. Makarewicz, and J. Tarkowski, "Application of artificial intelligence tools

in diagnosis and treatmentof mental disorders", *Current Problems of Psychiatry,* vol. 24, pp. 1-18, 2023.
[http://dx.doi.org/10.12923/2353-8627/2023-0001]

[9]   V. Kalaiselvan, A. Sharma, and S.K. Gupta, ""Feasibility test and application of AI in healthcare"—with special emphasis in clinical, pharmacovigilance, and regulatory practices", *Health Technol. (Berl.),* vol. 11, no. 1, pp. 1-15, 2021.
[http://dx.doi.org/10.1007/s12553-020-00495-6]

[10]   Y. Chen, and M. Wu, "Artificial Intelligence-enabled contactless sensing for medical diagnosis", *Med. Rev. (Berl.),* vol. 3, no. 3, pp. 195-197, 2023.
[http://dx.doi.org/10.1515/mr-2023-0022]

[11]   N.A. Jodhwani, and S.J. Ahir, *AI in Health and Diagnostics.*, 2022, pp. 1-17.
[http://dx.doi.org/10.4018/978-1-7998-8786-7.ch001]

[12]   M.H.B. de Moraes Lopes, D.D. Ferreira, A.C.B.H. Ferreira, G.R. da Silva, A.S. Caetano, and V.N. Braz, "Use of artificial intelligence in precision nutrition and fitness", In: *Artificial Intelligence in Precision Health.* Elsevier, 2020, pp. 465-496.
[http://dx.doi.org/10.1016/B978-0-12-817133-2.00020-3]

[13]   P.J. Cho, K. Singh, and J. Dunn, "Roles of artificial intelligence in wellness, healthy living, and healthy status sensing", In: *Artificial Intelligence in Medicine.* Elsevier, 2021, pp. 151-172.
[http://dx.doi.org/10.1016/B978-0-12-821259-2.00009-0]

[14]   T. Davenport, and R. Kalakota, "The potential for artificial intelligence in healthcare", *Future Healthc. J.,* vol. 6, no. 2, pp. 94-98, 2019.
[http://dx.doi.org/10.7861/futurehosp.6-2-94] [PMID: 31363513]

[15]   T. Le Nguyen, and T.T.H. Do, "Artificial Intelligence in Healthcare: A New Technology Benefit for Both Patients and Doctors", In: *2019 Portland International Conference on Management of Engineering and Technology (PICMET)* IEEE, 2019, pp. 1-15.
[http://dx.doi.org/10.23919/PICMET.2019.8893884]

[16]   D. Khurana, A. Koli, K. Khatter, and S. Singh, "Natural language processing: state of the art, current trends and challenges", *Multimedia Tools Appl.,* vol. 82, no. 3, pp. 3713-3744, 2023.
[http://dx.doi.org/10.1007/s11042-022-13428-4] [PMID: 35855771]

[17]   S. Reddy, J.S. Winter, and S. Padmanabhan, "Artificial intelligence in healthcare-opportunities and challenges", *J. Hosp. Manag. Health Policy,* vol. 5, pp. 23-23, 2021.
[http://dx.doi.org/10.21037/jhmhp-21-31]

[18]   S. El Kafhali, and M. Lazaar, *Artificial Intelligence for Healthcare: Roles.* Challenges, and Applications, 2021, pp. 141-156.
[http://dx.doi.org/10.1007/978-3-030-72588-4_10]

[19]   Zuocheng Wen, and Hua Huang, "The potential for artificial intelligence in healthcare", *J. Commer. Biotechnol.,* vol. 27, no. 4, 2023.
[http://dx.doi.org/10.5912/jcb1327]

CHAPTER 6

Artificial Intelligence in Education: The Future of Learning

Abstract: Artificial intelligence, more commonly known as AI has been integrated into education. The incorporation of AI in education is not without its benefits and as such, brings with it new chances, challenges, and opportunities for teaching and learning. The purpose of artificial intelligence (AI) in education is to enhance the teaching processes by training and relevant and useful experiences and paring out of standard interchangeable modules interfacing, data graphical representation, and probability inference. Giving each student individualized kind of help or advice that may be provided to the learners depending on learning status, learning interests, or learning characteristics is one of the biggest aims of artificial intelligence in learning.

Keywords: Adaptive learning, Classrooms, Class engagement, Educators, Institutions, Predictive learning, Students.

1. INTRODUCTION

There have been a lot of innovative achievements in the field of applying artificial intelligence for education in the last 25 years. Since the advent of computing and information processing technologies, the usage of AI technologies in education is quite widespread and increasingly developing [1, 2]. It takes about two to three years before the new technology is adopted in a given organization. Funding commitments from governments of at least $10 billion and up to $25 billion have already been made. This amount of investment makes sense considering estimates that general-purpose AI technology might provide an extra $13 trillion in short-term economic activity by 2030, or 1.2% greater GDP growth yearly [3]. AI in education aims at using it in supporting instruction whereby teachers have an important role to play respectively; however, the critical role and their acceptance of AI are crucial. Examples of this include availing and facilitating discourse analysis and attaining performance forecasts using education data mining. However, because AI is still a relatively new concept for educators, inexperienced and a large number of educators normally struggle to be able to quickly and appropriately answer to analytics from AI organization applications, which in turn makes them less accepting of and apprehensive about AI.

Madhu Bala & Ritika Sharma

Effective partnerships of academics, educators, policymakers, and professionals should be fostered since addressing new opportunities and challenges emerged with the help of artificial intelligence and big data explosion. They need to ensure that all the students get to be informed on or benefit from efficient completion of their academic work with consumer-led competencies and skills that they require for a job in the twenty-first-century economy. It is only important to note that functions such as automatic grading, adaptation, distant learning, and others are just some of the most basic uses of AI technology in the education sector.

It is accepted that as we live in "technological societies," technology must be used to aid in teaching and learning activities, and curriculum-related instruction on technology use and knowledge must be heavily weighted [4, 5]. This means that, in order to improve education generally, it will become necessary to design programs and technology that fully complement pedagogical endeavours. It is also acknowledged that kids who frequently feel left behind by the conventional educational system would benefit from the technological advancements in education, since access to computers and the internet will enhance their academic performance.

AI-based conversational robots have become new norms of shopping. It also offers advice to people in various situations, such as in finding employment. Artificial neural networks, and speech recognition, have a viable outlook for improving the quality of such feedback [6, 7]. Thus, the automatic grading system is one of the most refined, intelligent computer programs that imitate the teacher's actions to produce the proper learning environment.

AI evaluates and even scrutinizes the students' answers and, at the same time, provides remarks on the responses plus builds training plans that address them exclusively to the intended would be employees. The assessments of learning tests can be explained by the following points in relation to the system: this is followed by the evaluation score of the course and is given to the learner automatically.

1.1. Importance of AI in Technology

Artificial intelligence has brought a significant shift in the field of learning. It offers personalized learning experiences, catering to individual needs and enhancing engagement and retention through gamification, interactive simulations, and virtual reality [8].

• It enables accessible education for all, bridging the gap between remote and traditional classrooms, and understanding how AI affects education as a whole, as a learning ecosystem, can close this research gap.

- AI streamlines the process of grading assignments and tests by automating the process, allowing educators to focus on teaching and providing valuable feedback. It also helps identify and address learning gaps by tracking student progress, pinpointing areas of struggle, and offering additional resources or support. This proactive approach to education can significantly improve student outcomes.
- AI empowers educators by handling routine tasks like grading and data analysis, freeing them to focus on inspiring and guiding students. In essence, AI is not here to replace educators but to empower them, allowing them to focus on their core competencies.

Overall, AI is poised to revolutionize education, making it more accessible, efficient, and effective for all students.

1.2. Impact of AI

AI is only one example of the many ways that technology has changed schooling. As was already said, it is a relatively new field of technical advancement that is gaining attention in academic and teaching circles worldwide [9]. Rapid development is seen in this field due to the inclusion of advanced and high performance computing devices to perform various kind of administrative tasks. This shift has impacted many aspects of education to the point where businesses and government organizations are trying to duplicate the same success in their own industries. Even though the benefits of AI are frequently discussed in the business world, not many people are aware of how it will affect how students and teachers interact.

AI is aiding in the expansion of the education sector by reducing these gaps in knowledge. In particular, it has led to a rise in the quantity of big data intelligence systems-powered online learning platforms. This result has been attained by taking advantage of big data analysis opportunities to improve educational outcomes. All things considered, AI's beneficial effects on the education sector have increased prospects for the industry's expansion and advancement. As a result, instructors stand to gain from the improved learning and development opportunities that arise from the integration of AI into the educational system.

6.2 APPLICATIONS OF AI IN EDUCATION

By developing cutting-edge applications that improve educational opportunities and administrative effectiveness, artificial intelligence (AI) is further transforming the educational landscape. The following are a few recent developments:

a. **AI-Powered Personalized Learning Platforms:** By evaluating individual student data to customize instructional materials, artificial intelligence is making it possible to create individualized learning experiences [10, 11]. AI instructors in the form of platforms like Khanmigo, created by Khan Academy in collaboration with Microsoft, offer instant feedback and encourage self-directed practice. This application provides students with individualized support in an effort to enhance learning results.

b. **AI-Enhanced Special Education Tools:** The use of AI technologies to assist kids with disabilities is growing [12]. Word prediction software and personalized AI-powered chatbots are two examples of tools that help children with dyslexia stay up with their peers. These technologies offer new opportunities for students with various impairments, including visual, speech, language, and hearing difficulties.

c. **AI-Integrated Classroom Management Systems:** AI is being used in classrooms to improve lesson planning and lessen administrative duties for instructors [13]. In order to facilitate the creation of AI-compatible teaching resources, the UK, for example, has established an education "content store," a centralized database. The entire educational system will gain from this initiative's goal of streamlining the production and evaluation of instructional materials.

d. **AI-Driven Adaptive Learning Environments:** AI is being investigated by educational institutions to develop learning environments that are adjustable to the demands of each individual learner [14]. For instance, David Game College in London is testing a program that uses ChatGPT and other AI tools in place of conventional teaching techniques to help students learn more individually. With this method, students can go at their own speed while developing their digital literacy and critical thinking abilities.

e. **AI-Assisted Tutoring Services:** Parents are increasingly considering AI tutors as cost-effective educational choices as a result of the growing cost of living [15]. One-on-one tuition and a range of learning resources are available on platforms such as ChatGPT, Zookal, and Tutor Ocean at a fraction of the price of private tutors. By offering individualized assistance, these AI tutors increase educational accessibility for a larger population.

f. **AI for Emotional Support:** Using language patterns, voice tones, and facial expressions, artificial intelligence (AI) techniques, such as emotion-sensing algorithms, can determine a student's emotional state. AI can provide services or offer assistance by identifying symptoms of stress, anxiety, or disengagement [16]. AI is used by some apps, for instance, to provide coping mechanisms, mindfulness activities, and counsellor connections.

The potential is far more than these AI uses. AI has the potential to significantly improve education as it develops, making it more approachable, interesting, and successful for a range of student demographics.

3. TYPES OF TECHNOLOGIES IN EDUCATION

3.1. Natural Language Processing

In the education system, Natural language processing plays a pivotal role in understanding human language and further processing the language by allowing artificial intelligence to interact with students, and mentors, and provide them with meaningful educational content. The software tools of natural language processing are used to fetch the data from the research articles. Chen *et al.* [17] discussed an NLP technique that is used to transform unstructured data into structured data and includes various text-mining preprocessing techniques for the development of clinical information processing. Based on it, the HEIs in the Philippines collect and store the output of research, which can be further monitored, accessed, and used for submitting reports to the higher authorities for accreditation.

NLP algorithms analyze the structure, content, grammar, and coherence of student essays and assignments. By using techniques such as **text parsing**, **sentiment analysis**, and **semantic analysis**, NLP tools can provide:

a. **Automated grading** based on predefined rubrics or training on a large corpus of graded essays.
b. **Feedback** on writing style, grammar, spelling, and coherence.
c. **Evaluation of content quality**, including argument strength and topic coverage.

In the NLP algorithm, the data is broken down into words, sentences, or phrases. After that, syntax trees are generated to check the grammatical errors. Further, the meaning of sentences is evaluated to ensure coherence and relevance to the topic. In the last, pre-trained models, often using machine learning, assign a score to the essay based on features like argument quality, style, and grammar.

The area of NLP can help the plethora of researchers to understand text data through machine learning and text mining methodologies, which can be further used for better understanding social media trends, enhancing insight into the tourism industry, and for better decision-making.

3.2. Machine learning (ML)

ML has emerged as a transformative technology in education, leveraging data-driven approaches to enhance learning outcomes, personalize educational experiences, and support educators in delivering more effective instruction. Researchers elaborated [18] that ML's application in education is used for the collection and preprocessing of vast amounts of student data, such as performance metrics, engagement levels, and learning behaviors. Through feature selection and engineering, relevant variables are identified, allowing ML models to make accurate predictions about student performance and behavior. Supervised learning models, for instance, are trained on historical data to predict outcomes such as course completion or academic success, while unsupervised learning techniques can identify patterns, such as clustering students based on learning styles. Moreover, ML-driven learning analytics provide educators with actionable insights, enabling data-informed decisions about instruction and curriculum design.

Educators from various organizations are interested in establishing their business to a good level and to achieve this target, they are focused on maximum retention of students. Automated prediction systems that can predict students' retention in an educational organization can be beneficial for this task [19]. A model named RG-DMML has been developed by the researchers by using K-nearest neighbor and k-fold cross-validation techniques. The developed model is based on cross-industry standard procedure for data mining (CRISP-DM) approach. It has shown significant results in terms of precision, recall, and F1-score. Table 1 shows the results achieved by this model.

Table 1. Performance metrics of RG-DMML for retention and graduation of students in the education sector [20].

Parameters	Retention	Graduation
Precision	0.909	0.822
Recall	1.000	0.957
F1-score	0.952	0.885
Accuracy	0.909	0.817

Overall, the integration of machine learning into education holds significant potential for creating adaptive, scalable, and personalized learning environments that improve both student outcomes and the efficiency of educational processes.

3.3. Robotics

Robotics technology in education plays a multifaceted role, enhancing both teaching methodologies and student engagement through interactive, hands-on learning experiences. Robotics introduces learners to interdisciplinary subjects such as computer science, engineering, mathematics, and artificial intelligence by providing a tangible platform for experimentation, problem-solving, and critical thinking.

A study [21] was conducted on over 45 students to check their creative skills using reverse engineering pedagogy (REP). In addition to this, t-tests, ANOVA, and ANCOVA were also used to analyze the data to check whether REP could enhance the students' creativity or not.

Robotics systems are used to engage students in active learning environments where they interact with physical robots. These robots serve as tools for experiential learning, making abstract concepts in STEM subjects (science, technology, engineering, and mathematics) more concrete. Students can build, program, and control robots, offering a hands-on approach to understanding complex theories such as mechanical engineering or algorithms.

3.4. Predictive Analytics

Predictive analytics in education employs statistical algorithms and machine learning techniques to analyze historical data, enabling educators and administrators to forecast future student outcomes and inform instructional strategies. The process begins with the systematic collection of diverse data types, including demographic information, academic performance metrics, attendance records, behavioral data, and engagement levels, which are gathered from learning management systems (LMS), student information systems (SIS), and various educational assessments. Subsequently, the collected data undergoes preprocessing to ensure its quality and reliability, involving data cleaning to address inconsistencies and the handling of missing values. Feature selection is also conducted to identify the most relevant variables that significantly influence student success, such as attendance rates and previous academic performance.

Once the data is prepared, predictive models are developed using various statistical and machine learning techniques, including regression analysis for continuous outcomes and classification algorithms for categorical predictions, such as identifying students at risk of academic failure. The selected models are then trained and validated on historical data, employing metrics such as accuracy, precision, and recall to evaluate their performance and generalizability. Following successful validation, these models can be deployed to make predictions regarding new student data, facilitating the identification of at-risk students and informing intervention strategies.

4. PERSONALIZED LEARNING

AI in education, which is a concept everybody wants to discuss nowadays made individualized learning possible in an effective way. The method of learning adopted by the students has been transformed by its use. Also, the business world has had its working mechanisms transformed by the use of artificial intelligence [22]. AI-enabled systems are capable of analysing a large amount of data related to strengths, weaknesses, learning pace and engagement patterns of students. Based upon this information, such systems can adjust the contents and offer feedback in real time, thereby, providing a great learning experience.

Each student through the use of technology, and personalized learning adjusts the difficulty and type of content based upon his/her progress. It is therefore evident that through the application of machine learning anatomy of algorithms, for analysis of data and making conclusions about trends in students' learning behaviors, preferences, and accomplishments, AI has a vital role in personalized learning. AI may then use this data in developing a person-scores consultancy box.

A few key components are mentioned below:

- **Real-time feedback:** Immediate feedback on assignments, tests, and other tasks is provided that helps the students identify their mistakes and learn effectively. For educators, this feature helps us intervene to enhance the performance of the student.
- **Personalized content delivery:** Content that is customised for a student's preferred method of learning can be selected by AI. For instance, although some students could benefit more from text-based explanations, others might prefer visual aids. In accordance, the system can adjust.
- **Automation of administrative tasks:** Tasks such as grading, scheduling, *etc.* can be made automated by AI. Lesson plans can be made customized which helps in freeing up educators to focus more on teaching and other student-related engagement activities.

Thus, one of the major strengths of personalized learning is that it ensures that every student needs help and direction is needed to achieve their greatest potential. While advanced means that students can be challenged at the level they are in. The poor-performing students can benefit from personalized learning. It is observed that students are more interested and motivated to learn when they get a unique learning whereby the tutors take their time to understand each topic experience, which can improve academic performance and increase retention rates. There are various approaches in which learning is done with the help of artificial intelligence. The modern learning systems can be narrowed to individual learning; for example, it has also been shown that with the application of Carnegie Learning's AI solution for mathematics software, the performance of the students in arithmetic can be enhanced by up to 30%. Similar to this, every learner is given an individual approach with the help of artificial intelligence applied in Duolingo.

Despite all the benefits it has to offer, personalization with the help of AI in learning may be problematic in many cases as with all the advantages, however, there are certain things that need to be addressed in this case. One of the problems is that the AI algorithms need to be fed with accurate and consistent information for it to be informed. Ensuring that the data is accurate and recent is very important since the quality of the data determines the quality of the outcomes. Career development is another important specification that has to be met [23].

The preparation of teachers in order to effectively implement artificial intelligence-based differentiated instructions is another difficulty. It is also imperative that teachers should be trained on the usage of AI tools how concerning the results generated by algorithms, and how such results can be utilized. It is thus imperative to note that AI-driven individualized learning is capable of changing the current face of education. One of them is the condition that exists in which students achieve the highest level of performance. The application of the mode of individualization is known to have the following characteristics: effectiveness, enhanced learning outcomes, attendance, and students' interest through the provision of special attention to each student that is different from others.

5. BENEFITS OF AI IN EDUCATION

The greatest paradigms associated with the development of society would be education, shaping young minds, encouraging innovations, and involving artificial intelligence in the ever-transformation field of learning at a revolutionary speed [24]. Several benefits provided by revolutionary potential of artificial intelligence are mentioned below:

5.1. Benefits to Learners

- **Personalized learning:** The traditional method of learning is in the one-siz--fits-all model which does not always suit any person's needs. The systems of artificial intelligence may detect the learning habits, strengths, and weaknesses of all students and will be able to provide individualized experiences for everyone. This helps change the complexity of lessons, which adaptive learning platforms apply to the learners' progress. The instant feedback system gives insights into action for the improvement of students' mistakes. In this way, it makes sure learners can move at their own pace, thus, there will be less gap in the knowledge, and they understand it in a deeper sense.

- **Enhanced Accessibility:** AI also promotes accessibility as an inclusive form of instruction. Students with diverse needs or requirements can easily interact well with educational material due to certain assistive technologies, a speech-to-text and text-to-speech system can empower a disabled child. Language translation tools reduce these linguistic barriers to provide all forms of content in the language one prefers. In addition, it helps with distance learning through virtual classrooms.

- **Efficient Administrative Processes:** Administrative processes in learning institutions consume much time and sometimes divert attention away from teaching. AI has done away with these problems as they have automated functions such as grading, monitoring attendance, and resource allocation. AI is very accurate in essay grading and multiple-choice testing hence saving many hours spent on grading by the educators. It helps to streamline attendance through facial recognition systems, optimizing classroom space and faculty resource utilization. AI frees the administrative role from the tasks of teachers and allows them to spend more time on what matters, teaching their students [25].

- **Data-Driven Insights:** Another critical strength of AI in learning is data-driven insights. AI systems can flag up learning gaps through ample educational data and point to students, who are at risk of poor performance owing to the curriculum and implementing interventions. This requires the provision of targeted interventions for required support and predictive analytics for those who will need additional help on the curriculum [26].

- **Continuous Learning and Professional Development:** AI provides continuous learning, and professional growth, which enhances the learner's value. Numerous online learning platforms support personalized learning routes according to the learner's goals and interests. The platforms track real-time progress and give the learner feedback and suggestions for additional courses or material. Through automation by AI, certification programs are proven acquired skills that easily allow professionals to prove expertise. AI ensures education extends past traditional classrooms to satisfying modern workforce demands through lifelong learning [27].

AI transforms teaching toward making education more personalized, accessible, and efficient, catering to individual needs, and simplifying processes while connecting the globe. The benefits greatly outweigh concerns over data security, ethical issues, and so much more when it comes to responsible applications of AI in the system of learning for individuals around the globe.

5.2. Benefits to Educators

Artificial intelligence is being utilized by educators in a number of ways and is bringing tremendous changes in the educational sector. In the modern era, the way education is imparted to students is completely changed and has offered benefits to educators. Some of the benefits are mentioned below:

- **Administrative efficiency:** The automated systems have increased administrative efficiency by performing routine tasks of the educators such as scheduling of classes, attendance tracking, and grading.
- **Idea & content generation:** Many powerful AI tools are available nowadays with the help of which innovative content can be generated within a fraction of second. AI-powered virtual labs, simulations, and recommendation systems are helping educators to enrich their teaching material [28].
- **Enhanced engagement:** AI can be used as a personal tutor for both students and teachers. It provides real-time feedback that helps in identifying the areas of improvement and inculcates a competitive mindset among students. Tools such as gamification and chatbots encourage interactive learning and active participation.
- **Scalability of education:** A large number of students can be taught effectively either in offline mode or in online mode by using various AI platforms such as virtual labs, virtual tutors, massive open online courses, *etc*. It helps in keeping track of the submission of assignments, class attendance, evaluating the answers and performance of the students. Teachers can be made free and they can get actively involved in doing some other tasks that are beneficial for the growth of students as well as for their organization.

6. IMPLEMENTATION STRATEGIES

Here's a step-by-step guide on how colleges and universities can integrate AI into their system:

- **Assessment and planning**

Determine the particular niches where the use of AI will be effective, which may include tutoring, clerical work, or course planning.

Define specific instructional objectives and learning outcomes on how AI will be used and incorporated to be on par with the the institution's mission and vision.

- **Gathering stakeholder input**

For this, a survey should be conducted to involve the key stakeholders such as the faculty, staff, and students in the process by identifying their needs, concerns, and expectations with regard to the adoption of this technology.

- **Selecting suitable AI tools and technologies**

Identify and evaluate AI solutions that would be the most suitable for the institution bearing in mind its goals and its financial capabilities. The most frequent use cases are chatbots, learning analytics, and recommender systems based on artificial intelligence.

- **Budget allocation**

Invest wisely – this can be in terms of investment spent on development, time, and effort that will be devoted to finding the right program and considering the long-term implications of the project.

- **Faculty and staff training**

Offer the needed guides and support in the form of training and seminars to the faculty and other staff that would enable them to embrace and incorporate the AI tools in their operations.

- **Student engagement**

Inform the learners about the uses of AI in their training and in the delivery of education in tertiary institutions. Encourage people to be active and express what they feel and what they think. AI integration should be seen as a continuous process that gets refined according to the development of the institution's needs and objectives.

- **Continuous monitoring and evaluation**

Not less important is the necessity to continually evaluate the degree of AI implementation in various aspects of teaching, learning, and administration.

6.7 CHALLENGES WITH AI SOLUTIONS IN EDUCATION

While AI holds great promise in transforming education through personalized learning, AI-based adaptive systems, and smart classrooms, it also poses several challenges that need to be addressed to integrate it effectively [29] such as:

a. **Teacher Training and Skill Development:** The effectiveness of AI tools will depend on the instructors using them. Teachers may have difficulty integrating AI in lesson preparation, assessments, and individualized learning tactics if they are not well-trained [30]. Solution: It is important to provide continuing and easily accessible professional development courses tailored to varying degrees of AI literacy. Such programs should focus on real-world applications of the technology, such as AI analytics and adaptive learning systems, to help instructors use AI effectively.

b. **Bias in AI Algorithms:** Biases in training data can be reflected and amplified by AI models, producing uneven learning results. If the training data is not reflective of varied populations, AI systems used for assessments or tailored learning may create bias in particular socioeconomic groups, learning styles, or demographics [31]. For example, children from under-resourced schools may be unfairly disadvantaged by an AI-powered grading system that was trained on data from students in privileged schools. Solution: Using a variety of datasets and doing routine audits of AI systems can help reduce bias. Furthermore, openness regarding the decision-making process of AI algorithms might promote trust between teachers and pupils.

c. **Data Privacy and Security:** Large volumes of student data are collected by AI-driven educational systems, which raise privacy and security concerns. Private data, including student performance, conduct, and personal information, may be susceptible to illegal access or cyberattacks. Solution: Organizations must implement strong data security methods, like encryption, secure storage, and anonymization of student data, and adhere to data protection laws (such as FERPA and GDPR).

d. **High Cost of AI Implementation:** The cost of setting up AI systems in the classroom can make it challenging for underfunded schools to use these tools. The expenses involve continuing maintenance, improvements to the infrastructure, and the acquisition of AI tools. The answer is that public-private partnerships or subsidies from governments and business groups can lower the cost of AI solutions for educational institutions.

e. **Ethical Concerns:** The use of AI in education raises ethical questions due to worries about an excessive dependence on technology and a decrease in human connection during the learning process. Despite their efficiency, AI systems cannot take the place of human teachers' emotional intelligence and sensitivity. Reduced teacher-student interactions and detrimental effects on student development could result from an over-reliance on AI. Solution: AI should be viewed as an augment to human instructors rather than as a substitute for them. Guidelines and policies must provide a fair approach to the deployment of AI (shown in Fig. **1**).

f. **Resistance to Change:** Due to concerns about losing control, losing their jobs, or doubting AI's efficacy, educators, parents, and students may oppose its use in the classroom. The answer is Reluctance can be decreased by establishing trust *via* open communication, showcasing the advantages of AI, and including all interested parties in the decision-making process. The shift can also be facilitated by testing AI initiatives before implementing them widely.

g. **Digital Divide:** Not every student has an equal opportunity to utilize the technological resources needed for education driven by artificial intelligence. Students may not be able to take advantage of AI-driven learning opportunities in areas with poor internet connectivity or restricted access to digital devices. The answer is investments in digital infrastructure, reasonably priced internet access, and device distribution to disadvantaged students are all necessary to close the digital gap.

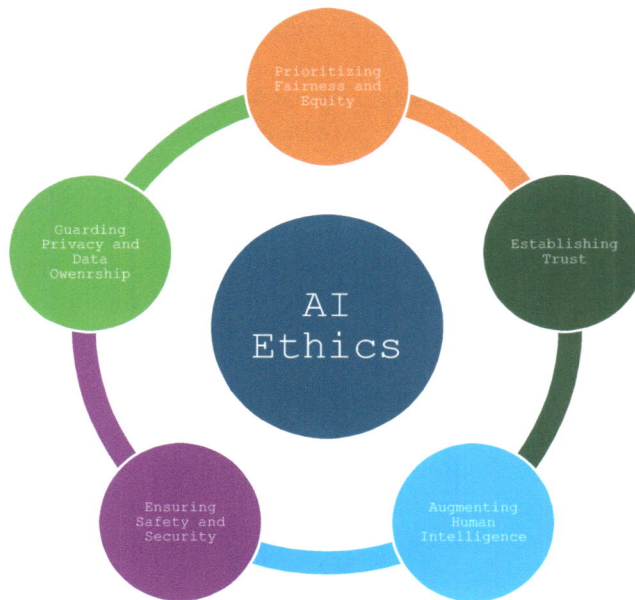

Fig. (1). Ethical Principles of AI.

Even though AI has a lot of potential to change education, these issues must be resolved to guarantee that its use is just, moral, and successful. The obstacles can be addressed and the path for more inclusive and significant AI-driven education systems cleared with the support of solutions like teacher training, frequent audits for bias, strong data protection policies, and improved accessibility [32].

8. FUTURE TRENDS AND INNOVATIONS

There are many AI technologies in use in education that are used widely, and the most prominent technologies are listed below:

a. **An intelligent tutoring system (ITS)**

An intelligent tutoring system (ITS) is a computer program that mimics human tutors with the goal of giving students quick, personalized education or feedback, typically without the need for teacher participation. The common objective of ITSs is to use a range of computing technologies to enable meaningful and effective learning. There are numerous instances of ITS being employed in professional and formal educational contexts, demonstrating both their strengths and weaknesses.

b. **Chatbot**

Chatbots are helpful aids that help educational institutions allocate resources more efficiently. Teachers and staff are able to free up critical time by having these responsibilities handled quickly. Schools can save money by not hiring as many extra support staff members as a result. By ensuring that educational resources are used effectively, this economic strategy eventually helps to make education more accessible and inexpensive for everyone. The future of artificial intelligence in education includes:

- High-quality online lecture videos.
- Employ many online learning websites and applications.
- People will engage in game-based learning and therefore gain experiential learning.
- Artificial intelligence can help improve teaching mechanisms.
- People will offer greater flexibility through increased acceptance in workplaces.
- Online learning can be nearly as effective as the traditional learning style.
- It is not likely to entirely replace the traditional learning experience.

The future of artificial intelligence in education is expected to witness several advancements for sure.

CONCLUSION

Artificial intelligence has brought tremendous changes in the field of education by providing personalised efficient and accessible learning to the users. Educational organizations are using AI in classrooms and virtual learning environments to address the learning needs of individuals, and develop an environment for continuous improvement. Virtual tutors, platforms of adaptive learning, chatbots, and automated assessment systems are some of the potential examples of AI-powered tools that have transformed conventional teaching methods into more dynamic and effective approaches. It is also observed that AI methods penalize a huge amount of educational data to identify valuable insights from it. This extracted information can be used in better decision-making to improve the outcomes of the students. However, the use of AI technologies in the education sector also raises concerns about data privacy and security as sensitive information of the organization can be misused, and overdependence on AI tools is responsible for lacking creativity and interpersonal interactions. Though AI tools are really doing good in this sector, at the same time, careful planning strategies are required to address these challenges.

REFERENCES

[1]   D. Schiff, "Education for AI, not AI for Education: The Role of Education and Ethics in National AI Policy Strategies", *Int. J. Artif. Intell. Educ.,* vol. 32, no. 3, pp. 527-563, 2022.
        [http://dx.doi.org/10.1007/s40593-021-00270-2]

[2]   A. Haleem, M. Javaid, M. Asim Qadri, R. Pratap Singh, and R. Suman, *Artificial intelligence (AI) applications for marketing: A literature-based study,* 2022.
        [http://dx.doi.org/10.1016/j.ijin.2022.08.005]

[3]   "Emerging Digital Technologies for Kenya EXPLORATION & ANALYSIS," 2019.

[4]   C. Conati, K. Porayska-Pomsta, and M. Mavrikis, "AI in Education needs interpretable machine learning: Lessons from Open Learner Modelling", http://arxiv.org/abs/1807.00154 2018. Available from:

[5]   A. Guilherme, "AI and education: the importance of teacher and student relations", *AI Soc.,* vol. 34, no. 1, pp. 47-54, 2019.
        [http://dx.doi.org/10.1007/s00146-017-0693-8]

[6]   W. Holmes, K. Porayska-Pomsta, K. Holstein, E. Sutherland, T. Baker, S.B. Shum, O.C. Santos, M.T. Rodrigo, M. Cukurova, I.I. Bittencourt, and K.R. Koedinger, "Ethics of AI in Education: Towards a Community-Wide Framework", *Int. J. Artif. Intell. Educ.,* vol. 32, no. 3, pp. 504-526, 2022.
        [http://dx.doi.org/10.1007/s40593-021-00239-1]

[7]   T.N. Fitria, *Siri (Apple), and Cortana (Microsoft). 3) Smart Content, 4) Presentation Translator. 5) Global Courses, for example.*https://www.blackboard.com/teaching-learning/learning-

[8]   H.C. Davies, R. Eynon, and C. Salveson, "The Mobilisation of AI in Education: A Bourdieusean Field Analysis", *Sociology,* vol. 55, no. 3, pp. 539-560, 2021.
        [http://dx.doi.org/10.1177/0038038520967888]

[9]   F. Ouyang, and P. Jiao, "Artificial intelligence in education: The three paradigms", *Computers and Education: Artificial Intelligence,* vol. 2, p. 100020, 2021.
        [http://dx.doi.org/10.1016/j.caeai.2021.100020]

[10]   J. Ali, S. Kumar Singh, W. Jiang, A.M. Alenezi, M. Islam, Y. Ibrahim Daradkeh, and A. Mehmood, "A deep dive into cybersecurity solutions for AI-driven IoT-enabled smart cities in advanced communication networks", *Comput. Commun.,* vol. 229, p. 108000, 2025.
        [http://dx.doi.org/10.1016/j.comcom.2024.108000]

[11]   F.Z. Tan, J.Y. Lim, W.H. Chan, and M.I.T. Idris, "Computational intelligence in learning analytics: A mini review", *ASEAN Engineering Journal,* vol. 14, no. 4, pp. 135-151, 2024.
        [http://dx.doi.org/10.11113/aej.v14.21375]

[12]   Y. Yang, L. Chen, W. He, D. Sun, and S.Z. Salas-Pilco, "Artificial Intelligence for Enhancing Special Education for K-12: A Decade of Trends, Themes, and Global Insights (2013–2023)", *Int. J. Artif. Intell. Educ.,* no. Aug, 2024.
[http://dx.doi.org/10.1007/s40593-024-00422-0]

[13]   A.M. Elsayed, A. Kholikov, I. Abdullayeva, M. Al-Farouni, and M.R. Wodajo, "Teacher support in AI-assisted exams: an experimental study to inspect the effects on demotivation, anxiety management in exams, L2 learning experience, and academic success", *Lang. Test. in Asia,* vol. 14, no. 1, p. 53, 2024.
[http://dx.doi.org/10.1186/s40468-024-00328-7]

[14]   L. Liu, "Impact of AI gamification on EFL learning outcomes and nonlinear dynamic motivation: Comparing adaptive learning paths, conversational agents, and storytelling", *Educ. Inf. Technol.,* no. Dec, 2024.
[http://dx.doi.org/10.1007/s10639-024-13296-5]

[15]   J. Jose, and B. Jayaron Jose, *Educators' Academic Insights on Artificial Intelligence: Challenges and Opportunities,* 2024.
[http://dx.doi.org/10.34190/ejel.21.5.3272]

[16]   A. Przegalinska, T. Triantoro, A. Kovbasiuk, L. Ciechanowski, R.B. Freeman, and K. Sowa, "Collaborative AI in the workplace: Enhancing organizational performance through resource-based and task-technology fit perspectives", *Int. J. Inf. Manage.,* vol. 81, p. 102853, 2025.
[http://dx.doi.org/10.1016/j.ijinfomgt.2024.102853]

[17]   L. Chen, P. Chen, and Z. Lin, "Artificial Intelligence in Education: A Review", *IEEE Access,* vol. 8, pp. 75264-75278, 2020.
[http://dx.doi.org/10.1109/ACCESS.2020.2988510]

[18]   K. Okoye, J.T. Nganji, J. Escamilla, and S. Hosseini, "Machine learning model (RG-DMML) and ensemble algorithm for prediction of students' retention and graduation in education", *Computers and Education: Artificial Intelligence,* vol. 6, no. January, p. 100205, 2024.
[http://dx.doi.org/10.1016/j.caeai.2024.100205]

[19]   A. I. Regla, and M. A. Ballera, "An Enhanced Research Productivity Monitoring System for Higher Education Institutions (HEI's) with Natural Language Processing (NLP)", In: *Procedia Computer Science* Elsevier B.V., 2023, pp. 316-325.
[http://dx.doi.org/10.1016/j.procs.2023.12.087]

[20]   K. Okoye, J.T. Nganji, J. Escamilla, and S. Hosseini, "Machine learning model (RG-DMML) and ensemble algorithm for prediction of students' retention and graduation in education", *Computers and Education: Artificial Intelligence,* vol. 6, p. 100205, 2024.
[http://dx.doi.org/10.1016/j.caeai.2024.100205]

[21]   X. Liu, J. Gu, and L. Zhao, "Promoting primary school students' creativity via reverse engineering pedagogy in robotics education", *Think. Skills Creativity,* vol. 49, no. June, p. 101339, 2023.
[http://dx.doi.org/10.1016/j.tsc.2023.101339]

[22]   J. Borenstein, and A. Howard, "Emerging challenges in AI and the need for AI ethics education", *AI Ethics,* vol. 1, no. 1, pp. 61-65, 2021.
[http://dx.doi.org/10.1007/s43681-020-00002-7] [PMID: 38624388]

[23]   B. Berendt, A. Littlejohn, and M. Blakemore, "AI in education: learner choice and fundamental rights", *Learn. Media Technol.,* vol. 45, no. 3, pp. 312-324, 2020.
[http://dx.doi.org/10.1080/17439884.2020.1786399]

[24]   C. Perrotta, and N. Selwyn, "Deep learning goes to school: toward a relational understanding of AI in education", *Learn. Media Technol.,* vol. 45, no. 3, pp. 251-269, 2020.
[http://dx.doi.org/10.1080/17439884.2020.1686017]

[25]   F. Kamalov, D.S. Calong, and I. Gurrib, "New Era of Artificial Intelligence in Education: Towards a

Sustainable Multifaceted Revolution", 2023. Available from: http://arxiv.org/abs/2305.18303

[26]   R.E.R. Kurian, and Y. Al-Assaf, "Impact of high school curriculum on student performance at university", In: *2020 IEEE Global Humanitarian Technology Conference, GHTC 2020* Institute of Electrical and Electronics Engineers Inc., 2020.
[http://dx.doi.org/10.1109/GHTC46280.2020.9342924]

[27]   S. Ahmad, S. Umirzakova, G. Mujtaba, M.S. Amin, and T. Whangbo, "Education 5.0: Requirements, Enabling Technologies, and Future Directions", 2023. Available from: http://arxiv.org/abs/2307.15846

[28]   J. Kim, H. Lee, and Y.H. Cho, "Learning design to support student-AI collaboration: perspectives of leading teachers for AI in education", *Educ. Inf. Technol.*, vol. 27, no. 5, pp. 6069-6104, 2022.
[http://dx.doi.org/10.1007/s10639-021-10831-6]

[29]   M.J. Gómez, J. Dabbah, and L. Benotti, "A workshop on artificial intelligence biases and its effect on high school students' perceptions", *Int. J. Child Comput. Interact.*, vol. 43, p. 100710, 2025.
[http://dx.doi.org/10.1016/j.ijcci.2024.100710]

[30]   M.M. Asad, S. Shahzad, S.H.A. Shah, F. Sherwani, and N.M. Almusharraf, "ChatGPT as artificial intelligence-based generative multimedia for English writing pedagogy: challenges and opportunities from an educator's perspective", *International Journal of Information and Learning Technology,* vol. 41, no. 5, pp. 490-506, 2024.
[http://dx.doi.org/10.1108/IJILT-02-2024-0021]

[31]   A. D. Samala, and S. Rawas, *Bias in artificial intelligence: smart solutions for detection, mitigation, and ethical strategies in real-world applications,* vol. 14, no. 1, p. 32, 2025.
[http://dx.doi.org/10.11591/ijai.v14.i1.pp32-43]

[32]   R. Veeran, and P. Gunasekaran, *Safeguarding the Digital Realm.*, 2024, pp. 81-103.
[http://dx.doi.org/10.4018/979-8-3693-2782-1.ch005]

SUBJECT INDEX

A

Abiotic agents 65
Abnormal protein deposits 107
Abnormalities 65, 86, 107
  identifying plant 65
  lung 107
  spot 86
Activity 63, 87, 116
  electrical 116
  microbial 63
Agricultural 60, 62, 72
  operations 60, 72
  production processes 60
  products 62
Agriculture 25, 55, 60, 61, 62, 69, 70, 72, 73, 74, 75, 76
  industry 62
  revolutionise 73
  sector 75
  urban 74
AI 23, 112, 116, 118, 134
  -compatible teaching resources 134
  -driven continuous monitoring 116
  -empowered predictive maintenance systems 23
  image analysis 118
  surgery 112
  tutoring services 134
AI-based 64, 65
  plant disease detection techniques 64
  techniques 65
AI-enabled 62, 69, 75, 138
  drones 75
  monitoring systems 62
  systems 138
  wind power forecasting system 69
AI-enhanced 113, 115, 134
  robotic systems 113
  special education tools 134
  technologies 115

AI-powered 60, 63, 95, 106, 112, 114, 118, 124
  cybersecurity platform 95
  EHR management 124
  image recognition systems 114
  imaging systems 60
  medical imaging 106
  remote consultations 118
  robotic systems 112
  soil health monitoring 63
Algorithms 10, 11, 13, 14, 33, 61, 63, 67, 74, 86, 87, 88, 92, 102, 106, 108, 116, 118, 128, 139, 143
  machine-learning 61
  supervised learning 14
  supervised machine learning 10, 13, 88
  unsupervised machine learning 92
Amazon web services (AWS) 94, 95
American association of artificial intelligence (AAAI) 3
Antivirus systems 82
Artificial neural networks 32, 33, 34, 38, 39, 40, 41, 42, 44, 132
Attribute selection measure (ASM) 13
Augmented 48, 72, 115, 136, 146
  reality (AR) 115
  architectural search techniques 48
  assessment systems 146
  farming 72
  prediction systems 136
Automatic grading system 132

B

Binary cross-entropy loss 43
Biotic agents 64
Blood 108, 115, 117
  clots 115
  glucose data 117
  pressure, elevated 108
Brain 2, 38, 40, 41, 44, 107
  artificial 2

atrophy 107
scans 107
visual 44
Branches, mechanical engineering 9

C

Cameras, high-resolution 74
Cancer(s) 5, 35, 102, 103, 105, 106, 107, 108,
    110, 111
  breast 106, 107
  colorectal 106
  detection 106
  genomics 108
  immunotherapy 111
  ovarian 108
  prostate 107
  skin 107
Cardiac valves 22
Cardiovascular 108, 110, 116
    disease management 110
    disease prediction 108
    problems 116
Cars, autonomous 52, 62
Chemical signaling 41
Chronic 110, 117
    obstructive pulmonary disease (COPD) 117
    pain management 110
Chronic diseases 101, 103, 115, 116, 117, 119
  managing 119
Clustering algorithms 24
CNN 45, 46, 48
    architectures 46
    designs 45, 46, 48
Computational framework 88
Computer 36, 145
    -aided design (CAD) 36
    program 145
Computer vision (CV) 8, 9, 24, 31, 34, 35, 38,
    48, 60, 65, 68, 72, 74, 104
    technologies 48, 68
    tools 104
Convolutional neural networks (CNNs) 22,
    30, 34, 39, 44, 45, 46, 47, 48, 52, 67
COVID-19 pandemic 107, 117
Crop 55, 60, 61, 69, 70, 72, 73, 74, 75
    conditions 75
    health monitoring 55, 72, 74
    management 60
    monitoring 60, 61, 73

resilience 70
rotation 69
Cross-validation techniques 136
CT 22, 35, 104, 105, 106, 107, 112, 114
    images 114
    scans 22, 35, 104, 105, 106, 107, 112
Cyberattacks 126, 143
Cybercrimes 82
Cybersecurity 81, 82, 83, 84, 88, 89, 90, 91,
    92, 94, 95, 96
    hygiene 91
    landscape 94
    platform 95

D

Damage 69, 113
  minimizing tissue 113
Data 10, 30, 33, 36, 43, 52, 70, 93, 94, 127,
    133, 136, 143
    aggregation 93, 94
    analytics 30, 33, 70
    augmentation 36, 52
    density 43
    intelligence 133
    localization provisions 127
    mining 10, 136
    protection laws 143
Datasets 10, 11, 12, 14, 15, 19, 20, 21, 33, 34,
    54, 67, 87, 88, 89, 102, 127, 128
  massive 54, 102
  plant disease 67
Deep 34, 37, 44
    learning and conventional machine learning
    34
    neural networks (DNNs) 37, 44
Density 20, 106
    -based spatial clustering 20
    tissue 106
Depression, treatment-resistant 110
Detection 20, 22, 23, 25, 66, 74, 81, 82, 85,
    86, 87, 88, 89, 90, 94, 96
    automating weed 74
    breast cancer 22
    cloud 94
    incident 94
    nutrient deficiency 25
Device(s) 38, 47, 48, 55, 72, 74, 108, 115,
    116, 117, 118, 120, 144
    computational 38

data, wearable 108
digital 144
dispersed 55
monitor 116
wearable 115, 116, 117, 118, 120
Diabetic retinopathy 104, 108
Diagnostic decision support systems (DDSS)
    109
Disease(s) 35, 60, 61, 64, 65, 66, 67, 105, 106,
    107, 108, 110, 111, 117
abiotic 65
chronic obstructive pulmonary 117
detection 66
diagnosis 35
infectious 65, 107, 111
lung 106
neurodegenerative 107
predicting 67
rare 108
transmit 65
DNS system 86

E

Education 131, 133, 142
data mining 131
revolutionize 133
transforming 142
EHRs, managing 124
Electronic 104, 105, 109, 118, 123, 124
    health records, (EHRs) 104, 109, 118, 123,
    124
    medical records (EMRs) 105
Emergency 115, 116
    intervention 115
    response 116
Emerging cybersecurity ethical dilemmas 94
Endoscopic procedures 113
Environment 4, 9, 32, 36, 37, 61, 67, 68, 69,
    70, 75, 87, 88, 94
cloud 94
operation 70
real-time IDS 87
Environmental 63, 64, 65, 67, 71, 111
    conditions 63, 65, 71
    data 67
    factors 64, 65, 111
Erosion-prone locations 63
Ethical principles 144

F

Facial 48, 140
    features 48
    recognition systems 140
Farmers, small-scale 76
Farming 25, 62, 75
    methods 62, 75
    techniques 25
Farming practices 73, 74, 75, 76
    sustainable 75, 76
Fertiliser, applying 70
Food 62, 117, 120
    intake 117, 120
    quality 62
    spoilage 62

G

Gated recurrent units (GRUs) 49
GDP growth 131
General data protection regulation (GDPR)
    127, 143
Generative adversarial networks (GANs) 30,
    36, 50, 51
Genetic 107, 108, 110, 111, 113
    data 107, 108, 110, 111
    factors 110
    markers 110, 113
    profile 108
Glucose levels, blood 117
Google 8, 53
    search engine 53
    translators 8, 53
GoogLeNet 47
Google's 4, 39
    DeepMind 39
    Gemini 4
    PaLM 4
Growth, drive cancer 108

H

Harnessing big data 107
Health 63, 65, 74, 93, 102, 110, 115, 116, 117,
    119, 120, 121, 124
care 102
crises, potential 117
deterioration 116
mental 110, 115, 116

mobile 119
population 124
virtual 115, 120, 121
Healthcare 22, 54, 100, 102, 104, 105, 126, 129
  ecosystem 126
  industry 22, 54, 100, 102, 104
  sector 22, 104, 105, 129
Heart 103, 108, 111, 117
  disease 103, 111, 117
  rhythm 108
Hospital facilities 123

I

Image(s) 47, 56, 65, 106
  digital 65
  processing, digital 56
  radiological 106
  recognition tasks 47
Image analysis 35, 67, 118
  medical 35
ImageNet large scale visual recognition challenge (ILSVRC) 46
Imaging 100, 104, 105, 106, 107
  medical 100, 106
  neurological 107
Imaging data 102, 104, 113, 114, 115
  real-time 114, 115
Immune system 92, 110, 111
Immunotherapy 110
Industries 26, 31, 36, 37, 44, 54, 55, 56, 60, 133, 135
  agricultural 60
  financial 54
  tourism 135
  transform 31
Infectious disease vaccination 111
Infestations 61, 65, 74
  insect 61
  pest 74
Information 82, 131
  processing technologies 131
  technology 82
Intrusion detection systems (IDS) 87, 88, 90
IoT 64, 66, 71
  -based smart irrigation system 71
  sensors 64, 66
Irrigation systems 70, 71, 72, 75

J

Java virtual machine (JVM) 54

L

Language translation 8, 34, 37, 39, 100, 140
  real-time 39
  tools 140
Learning algorithms 8, 33, 35, 37, 76, 107
  applying machine 8
Learning management systems (LMS) 137
LISP machines 3
Long short-term memory (LSTM) 49

M

Machine learning 5, 6, 7, 18, 25, 30, 31, 32, 33, 34, 35, 55, 75, 81, 83, 85, 91, 100, 103, 112, 135, 136, 137, 138
  algorithms process 112
  anatomy 138
  techniques 18, 25, 33, 81, 83, 100, 137
  tools 75, 85
Machine 50, 51, 74
  translation 50, 51
  vision 74
Machinery 36, 60, 75
  autonomous 60
  industrial 36
Medical imaging analysis 104
Melanoma 107, 118
Mental health 1, 107, 110
  conditions 1, 110
  disorders 107
Metabolic processes 40
Mobile 53, 76, 93, 115, 116, 120
  apps 76
  devices 53, 93
  health applications 115, 116, 120
MobileNet designs 47
MXNet's support 54

N

Naive Bayes algorithm 11, 12
Natural language processing (NLP) 8, 34, 35, 38, 39, 40, 49, 51, 54, 55, 67, 103, 104, 124, 135

Nervous system 40
Network(s) 38, 39, 41, 42, 45, 46, 47, 48, 49,
    52, 84, 85, 86, 87, 88, 92, 94, 95
  activity 87
  anomalies 86
  computer 87
  topologies 48
  traffic 84, 86, 87, 88, 95
Neural 48
   architecture search (NAS) 48
Neural network(s) 1, 3, 4, 30, 32, 33, 34, 37,
   39, 40, 43, 44, 46, 49, 50, 54
  architecture 39
  construction 54
Neurological disorders 106
Neurons 1, 34, 38, 39, 40, 41, 42, 44, 45
  artificial 38, 39, 41, 42
  biological 41
  motor 41
NLP technique 135
Nutrient deficiencies 25, 65, 74

P

PET scans 107
Plant(s) 60, 62, 64, 65, 66, 67, 69, 70, 71, 74,
   75
  density 69
  disease detection 64, 66
  diseased 67
  diseases 60, 64, 65, 66, 67, 74
  food-producing 62
  injury 65
  pathology 64
  stress 65
Planting, seed 70, 72
Pollination 73
Polynomial regression methods 24
Populations 60, 73, 101, 121, 134, 143
  aging 101
  bee 73
  varied 143
Psychology, cognitive 2

R

Random forest (RF) 10, 14, 15, 23, 25, 67, 85,
   87, 88, 89, 90
Rare disease diagnosis 108
Real-time 48, 89, 114
  application 48, 89
  image analysis 114
Real-time network 86
  monitoring 86
  traffic monitoring 86
Recurrent neural networks (RNNs) 30, 34, 39,
   49, 50, 67
Reinforcement learning (RL) 6, 8, 36, 52
Resources, financial 76
Revolutionizing radiology 106
Risk 35, 54, 94
  assessment 35, 94
  management 54
Robotic(s) 9, 31, 36, 49, 60, 62, 72, 73, 75,
   104, 111, 112, 137
  farming 60, 72, 73
  harvesters 72
  surgical 112
  swarm 73

S

Security 55, 64, 82, 87, 91, 94, 96, 120, 127,
   143, 146
  cyber 87
  devices 87
  electronic information 82
  flaws 91
  food 64
  problem 87
  teams, cyber 96
Sensor(s) 9, 25, 35, 61, 63, 66, 67, 70, 71, 72,
   74, 75
  advanced 74
  -based procedures 66
  ground-based 61
  soil moisture 71
Sensory neurons 41
Software tools 135
Soil 25, 60, 61, 62, 63, 65, 68, 69, 71, 74
  analysis 60
  conditions 60, 61, 65
  dense 62
  health monitoring 25, 62, 63
  management techniques 69
  moisture 63
  moisture data, real-time 71
  quality 62, 63
  sensors 63, 68, 74
Storage 60, 62, 124, 143

digital 124
  facilities 62
Supply chain 62, 95
  attacks 95
  management 62
Support vector machines (SVM) 7, 10, 15, 16, 25, 43, 67, 88
Surgery 8, 22, 100, 104, 111, 112, 113, 114, 115, 118, 119, 124
  cardiac 115
  gynaecologic 22
  liver resection 114
  orthopedic 114
  real-time 8
Sustainability 37, 55, 60, 67, 74, 75
  environmental 37
Sustainable agricultural practices 63, 64

T

Therapies, rehabilitation 104
Threat(s) 93, 94, 87, 95
  cyber 87, 95
  intelligence 93, 94
Traditional machine learning 30, 34
  methods 34
  techniques 30
Training 10, 13, 15, 16, 39, 42, 43, 47, 49, 51, 87, 88, 121, 129, 131, 142
  data augmentation 51
  dataset 10
Transformative 60, 61, 122
  effects 60
  force 61

V

Variational autoencoders (VAEs) 36, 52
Vinci surgical system 22, 112
Virtual health services 120

W

Wearable technology 105
Weather monitoring 70

www.ingramcontent.com/pod-product-compliance
Lightning Source LLC
Chambersburg PA
CBHW041708210326
41598CB00007B/571